The W

"In these pages, you will discover clear, lucid instructions for contacting the dead, as well as explanations for why you might want to do so. While simultaneously emphasizing the sacred nature of his subject, Christian has written a fun, easy-to-read and easy-to-access instructional manual for interaction with the ever-present souls of the dead."

—Judika Illes, author of *The Encyclopedia of Spirits*,
The Encyclopedia of 5000 Spells, *The Element Encyclopedia of Witchcraft*,
and *The Weiser Field Guide to Witches*

"Jam-packed with practical advice, easy-to-follow instructions, and covering everything from exorcism to necromancy, *The Witches' Book of the Dead* truly is the quintessential guide to working with the spirit world. A must have for every magical practitioner's bookshelf!"

—Dorothy Morrison, author of *Utterly Wicked*

"A powerful modern manual for practitioners seeking to add necromancy to their repertoire, rooted deeply in history and tradition."

—Christopher Penczak, co-founder of the Temple of Witchcraft
and author of *The Plant Spirit Familiar*

"This book is an invaluable text that can open pathways to subjects otherwise deemed unapproachable in a way that makes necromancy understandable to all."

—Leilah Wendell, author of *The Necromantic Ritual Book*,
Encounters with Death, and *Our Name Is Melancholy*

"Christian Day presents every aspect of necromancy clearly, practically, and matter-of-factly. From start to finish, this is a fascinating compendium of necromantic lore, and I recommend it highly!"

—Oberon Zell-Ravenheart, headmaster of The Grey School of Wizardry
and author of *Grimoire for the Apprentice Wizard*

"This book is fresh, exciting, and like nothing you have ever read before!"
—Rosemary Ellen Guiley, author of *The Encyclopedia of Ghosts and Spirits*

"A shocking, witty, and scholarly thesis offers the historian, the sorcerer, and the curiosity seeker something to ponder and something to remember—we do not walk alone."
—Bloody Mary, Voodoo Queen of New Orleans, occult historian, psychopomp, and owner of Bloody Mary's Tours

"This book delivers a call back to an often-neglected source of power, wisdom, and guidance: necromancy and communion with the unseen side of humanity. It is a fascinating compendium and a useful tool but definitely a controversial challenge. Read and enjoy, *but apply the techniques with care and caution!*"
—Orion Foxwood, co-founder of the House of Brigh Faery Seership Institute and author of *The Tree of Enchantment*

"Filled with mystery and magick, *The Witches' Book of the Dead* is deliciously dark, edgy, thought provoking, and beautifully crafted."
—Ellen Dugan, author of *Practical Protection Magick*

"Christian Day is an amazing resource when it comes to magic and Witchy legend and lore. Day breaks down Witchcraft history, humanizes the folks who have always stood casting and conjuring at the outskirts of society, and then celebrates them like one would cheer a rock star. A great book and mystical look into connecting with the other side and transforming the universe around us."
—Jeff Belanger, founder of *Ghostvillage.com*, author of *The World's Most Haunted Places*, and host of *30 Odd Minutes*

"Christian writes with wisdom and authority, and makes the reader feel safe and secure, knowing they are being lead through advanced ritual practices by someone who knows his stuff A-Z."

—Edain McCoy, author of
Advanced Witchcraft: Go Deeper, Reach Further, Fly Higher

"Without a doubt this is the most useful and unambiguous book available to the modern practitioner."

—Peter Paddon, author of *The Book of the Veil*, *Through the Veil*,
and *A Grimoire for Modern Cunningfolk*

"You may not agree with all that Day proposes—and you get the sense he'd probably welcome a good intellectual brawl—but you can't deny that this passionate, personal take on the meaning and practice of magic is thoughtful, bravely-drawn, and fascinating."

—Lesley Bannatyne, author of *Halloween Nation:
Behind the Scenes of America's Fright Night*

"Christian Day has outdone himself with this rare, beautifully written, brilliant work. If you are tired of reading regurgitated, watered-down 101 books or have found yourself in a place where you wish to delve deeper into the core of the occult, then this is a must read."

—Starrfire Price, founder and webmistress, *PaganSpace.net*

"If you're one of those of the living who subscribes to the notion that magick is exclusively about love, light, and life, and death is a subject to be avoided, put this book down. It is neither for the faint of heart, weak of mind or the fear enslaved soul."

—Mulysa Mayhem, priestess of Hekate, Magickal Tattoo Artist,
and Owner of Good Mojo Tattoos, Beverly, MA

"*The Witches' Book of the Dead* offers contemplative, genuine methods, while written in a gratifying narrative style. Read it for the information other manuscripts have lacked."

–Sabrina The Ink Witch, artist and founder of *www.theinkwitch.com*

"From Altars to Yew wands, no (grave) stone was left unturned in this well researched and beautifully written compendium of necromancy."

–Marla Brooks, author of *Workplace Spells, Animal Spells and Magick,* and host of *Stirring the Cauldron Radio*

"A rare gem on the proverbial bookshelf of any working Witch!"

–Rev. Jonathan Sousa, Southern Italian Traditionalist and author of *WitchHeart: Essays in Traditional Craft Philosophy*

"*The Witches' Book of the Dead* is without a doubt one of the most in depth works on darker magic I have ever had the pleasure to read."

–Corvis Nocturnum, author of *Cemetery Gates: Death and Mourning through the Ages*

"Destined to be a classic in occult literature."

–Denise Alvarado, author of *The Voodoo Hoodoo Spellbook*

"This beautiful tome piercingly reaches to the psyche of genuine magickal practitioners, reminding us that we have always, and shall continue to, work with forces beyond our immediate consciousness. For those exploring the serenity of shadow and the deeper levels of Craft, this book is most definitely for you."

—Raven Digitalis, author of *Shadow Magick Compendium* and *Goth Craft*

The Witches'
Book of the Dead

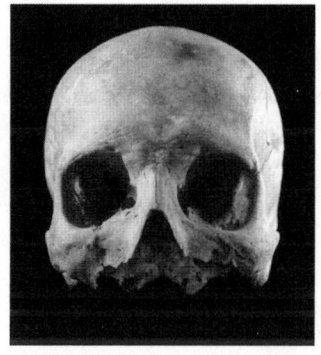

CHRISTIAN DAY

Foreword by Raven Grimassi

⊕ WEISERBOOKS
San Francisco, CA / Newburyport, MA

First published in 2011 by
Red Wheel/Weiser, LLC
665 Third Street, Suite 400
San Francisco, CA 94107
www.redwheelweiser.com

ISBN: 978-1-57863-506-1

Library of Congress Cataloging-in-Publication Data is available on request.

Cover design by Jim Warner
Skull image on cover © Christian Day
Candles on cover © Shutterstock/ dragasanu
Interior by Kathryn Sky-Peck
Typeset in Garamond BE

Printed in the United States
QG
10 9 8 7 6 5 4 3
The paper used in this publication meets the minimum requirements of the
American National Standard for Information Sciences–Permanence of Paper
for Printed Library Materials Z39.48-1992 (R1997).

Dedications

This is a book of the dead and so only the dead shall be honored here:

Mary Elaine Taeger, 1950–2008
Mom, you always encouraged me to be strong, to stand up for what is
right and true, and to believe that I could do anything.

John Day, 1947–2000
Uncle Johnny, you were a father to me throughout my childhood.
You were Santa, the Easter Bunny, and the very embodiment
of compassion and generosity.

Shawn Poirier, 1966–2007
Shawn, you were my first true mentor and the best friend I've ever had.
You taught me to believe in magic and that the spirit world
is real indeed.

Rebecca Larivee, 1969–2011
Becci, you were my cousin, my soul sister, my friend, and coven-sister.
Your kindness, laughter, love, and ferocity will be with us always.

Patricia Ann Tadiello, 1963–2008
Cousin Patty, your warmth, humor, and your ability to see the good in
others continues to inspire those whose lives you touched.

Catherine Larivee, 1950–1986

Auntie Cathy, you were an adventurer and
one of the strongest people I've known.
Thank you for helping my mother find strength to survive.

Roscoe F. Day, 1920–1993

Grampy, your entrepreneurial spirit lives on in me.
Witches were the original pharmacists, so, in a way,
I'm still keeping it in the family.

Dr. Leo Louis Martello, 1931–2000

Leo, we've never met, but your courage to say what must be said
inspires me. I wield your ritual sword with great honor and reverence!

Contents

Foreword

The earliest mentions of Witches in Christian times depict them as people who communicate, or claim to communicate, with the dead. This theme appears even in ancient writings of the pre-Christian era. It is noteworthy that the association of Witches with the dead predates the insertion of Satan or the Devil into Witchcraft. This association was primarily concocted by Catholic theologians and became the basis for so-called historical Witchcraft. However, the data used by scholars that now constitutes "historical Witchcraft" is not an ethnographic study of a people known as Witches. It is instead a record of beliefs held by non-Witches *about* supposed Witches, mixed together with theological agenda.

I have long held to the "Old Magic" of Witchcraft, the ways that are rooted in pre-Christian beliefs and practices. This type of magic is not watered down or repackaged to suit political correctness issues in the ways that modern practices have come to present Witchcraft. It is for this reason that I was particularly interested in writing the foreword to Christian Day's book on Witches and spirits of the dead. With this work, Christian adds significantly to this rarely explored subject.

I have known Christian Day for several years, and it is no secret that he is a controversial figure, particularly in Salem, Massachusetts. Therefore it will come as no surprise that this book is controversial as well. But controversy can help break up complacency and dismantle worn-out concepts, and I believe this is part of the destiny of this book.

Among the most controversial elements in this book is the author's self-identification as a Warlock. The term has long been regarded in modern Wiccan and Witchcraft circles to define an "oath-breaker" or a renegade male Witch who violates the ethics of the Craft. In earlier periods it was used to denote a male practitioner of Witchcraft as distinguished from a female Witch.

In the 1960s the term "Witch" was regarded as a negative term in mainstream culture; it bore the stigma of devil worship and diabolical practices. During this decade, modern practitioners envisioned the Witch as a misunderstood and wrongfully maligned figure. These people openly claimed the word as an empowering term, and argued for the Witch as a practitioner of Old Magic (with a spiritual lineage to ancient fertility practices rooted in pre-Christian European beliefs).

I first entered the Craft community in the summer of 1969. It was not uncommon for male Witches of the period to refer to themselves as Warlocks. In time, modern Witches (while holding to the term "Witch" despite its negative connotations) rejected the name Warlock, dismissing it as a defamed term like the name "Witch" had previously been regarded.

During the 1960s and early 1970s, the women's movement included female Witches who felt empowered by the authoritative nature of the Witch figure. It gave them a dynamic identity and helped them better understand and define themselves. Christian Day has embraced the term "Warlock" in the same spirit, and feels that it is an empowering and distinctive identity for male Witches. But he has been met with anger and scorn from many within the Craft community. His battle to redeem the name "Warlock" is reminiscent of the battle of women in the '60s and '70s to claim the term "Witch" despite its previously negative associations.

The Witches' Book of the Dead is presented in the serious and sobering manner that is its topic's due. It deals with powerful and timeless issues that possess a sacred nature. Over the decades of my practice of Witchcraft

I have met few modern Witches who appear to be formally trained in the skills of working with the dead, although some Witches do possess a natural talent for communication. Through the material in this book, the reader can reclaim the ability that has traditionally been an integral part of Witchcraft.

Ideas surrounding spirits of the dead have evolved into a confusing, and at times contradictory, conglomeration. The same is true of Witchcraft beliefs and practices in general. Do souls remain on Earth after the body dies? How does this fit with the concept of reincarnation? Do sentient ghosts haunt places and sites? Or are such phenomena merely residual energies of some type? Until now this topic has not been fully addressed by a practitioner of Witchcraft.

Among the interesting remnants of ancient beliefs about the dead there is the original Italian version of Cinderella. Folklorist Christine Messina writes that in the early tale of Cinderella, the now popular Fairy Godmother was actually the spirit of her dead mother come to aid her.[1] Other tales retain similar themes in which the dead aid the living. However, we equally find beliefs and stories in which the dead can harm the living, and offerings are required to ensure peace.

Our ancestors understood the world to be both light and darkness. It formed their magic as it formed their worldview. Witchcraft is a system that balances light and darkness, and its practitioners know the ways that heal and the ways that harm. The Witch stands between the worlds and acts to restore balance whenever it is disrupted. We need to understand that there was good reason why the Witch was both feared and respected—but this is true of any powerful creature of Nature.

In ancient literature, the Witch is depicted as a commanding figure. She summons the aid of deities in the manner of colleagues, and she holds power over spirits. We do not find the modern sentiment of "Stay if you will, leave if you must" when she releases spirits or bids farewell to a goddess or a god. The Witch in "days of old" was an authoritative presence, and it was her demeanor and reputation that kept her magic vital and effective. Christian Day keeps true to this ancient view in his book.

The use of a human skull in Witchcraft is a very ancient concept, but it is one that some modern Witches no longer approve of even as a symbol. But for our ancestors the skull represented the ancestral spirit as well as an oracle device intimately linked to the Other World. The dead were not relegated to the graveyard and remembered with an occasional visit and the placing of flowers. Witches believed that the dead were still part of life. Through the presence of a skull, the dead could speak and receive messages from the living.

In the ancient tales of the Greek writer Homer, a Witch directs a band of heroes to the Underworld and reveals how to communicate with the dead. This involves offering a drink of blood; it was an ancient belief that when the dead taste blood they remember life and are able to speak. While this can be a squeamish thought for people today, Witchcraft has always involved the vital essences of body fluids. Unfortunately, this aspect of Witchcraft became misunderstood, which led to the distortion of sacred foundational beliefs and practices. In time the ignorant came to view the arts of Witchcraft as evil and the intent of its magic as always harmful in nature.

Christian Day masterfully handles the old art of Witchcraft. It is a refreshing change to find serious scholarship and the absence of sugarcoating in a book of this popular genre. Day went to painstaking measures in his research, and references from both obscure and dominant sources were collected and expertly integrated for the reader. Political correctness is not an issue for the author, and his focus is upon the tried and true. Through this book, I feel that the spirits of the dead have found a voice for all to hear.

—Raven Grimassi

1

A Covenant with the Dead

"Witchcraft"—the word evokes images of strange rituals held in forgotten corners of gnarled forests lit only by the moon and perhaps a candle or two. Within a bramble-lined clearing is a stone altar, upon which is spread a gathering of roots, charms, daggers, and other tools of the magical arts. At the center of the altar, the stark presence of a leering human skull presides over the ceremony as a venerated representative of the mighty dead. A lone sorceress, draped in tattered black robes, pricks her finger to draw three drops of her blood as an offering to the spirits as she whispers her dark oaths and secret desires on the wind. As the Witch waits, the dead hearken to her call, rising from their shadowy resting places to serve their mistress's bidding.

This foreboding image of the Witch as necromantic sorceress, working under the guise of moonlight and conjuring spirits, continues to lurk in the unconscious depths of peoples throughout the world despite the hopes of the well-intentioned to turn the ancient arts of Witchcraft into just another mainstream religion, lush with spiritual devotion but nearly devoid of magic.

Something within each of us knows that Witches are creatures of magic; Witches cast spells, heal, and foretell the future; Witches commune with spirits of the dead and otherworldly entities and employ those powers to weave their intentions into the world around them. This book explores the enduring relationship between Witches and the dead, and shares rituals and incantations to help you open doorways to the spirit world.

The Witch in Myth and History

Dig into the past and you will find that Witches have nearly always lived on the fringes of society, casting their spells by candlelight, mixing potions for love and elixirs for healing, and calling on spirits, fairies, and other strange denizens of the unseen worlds to bring about change and to teach the wisdom of arcane secrets. Ordinary people sought out Witches in the dead of night, hoping to divine the future and procure all manner of spells for love, health, and prosperity—or to deal justice to those who deserved it. The Witches were proficient at all of these things.

It is not certain when Witches first walked the Earth, but the arts of magic have been practiced since humans first endeavored to understand the hidden workings of the world around them and to solve the great mystery of death. It is difficult to outline in great detail all of the practices of ancient magical peoples because, aside from the occasionally unearthed curse tablet, amulet, or sacred inscription, early sorcerers rarely wrote down what they did. They passed their knowledge only to family or long-prepared apprentices, and often took their greatest secrets with them to the grave. We discover the Witch among the dusty bones and relics of archeology, in the whispers of folklore, and through direct communication with the spirits of those who lived long ago.

Among early tribal cultures, those individuals who could do magic were often separated out and given roles of recognition and honor. In this way, the earliest shamans and medicine people came to be. These tribal magicians were not that far removed from Witches, with one important exception:

their practices were revered by the people around them, whereas Witches were typically outsiders who did magic according to their own rules.

As humans settled down and civilizations were born, priesthoods evolved from those early shamanic cultures. Priests served an important function in the emerging warrior-based states because they provided spiritual nourishment for the masses—a role they still play today. Magic itself was gradually assimilated into the state as an officially sanctioned practice, but also began to be restricted to those who were authorized to use it. Others, especially those for whom magic was their birthright, refused to bow to these emerging authorities, preferring to practice magic in the ways they understood it. From these early rebels, the idea of the Witch was born.

Those who chose the path of priesthood often had magical and necromantic talents, but their practices grew more and more liturgical and political as time went on, gradually losing the power of spirit and magic. Thus, their people were left with oracles proclaiming the will of the state as "divine prophecy."

In classical Roman times, Witches often caused much fear; their craft was sometimes even outlawed, but still these magical people carried on in secret. The literature and commentary of the era paints the Witch as a dark and formidable enemy. Roman emperors of the pre-Christian era, for example, welcomed the practice of virtually hundreds of faiths, but not Witchcraft. The reason for this is simple: Witches had the power to affect the tides of reality around them. The Roman leaders of the time feared this power, knowing that, just as they could be stripped of their rule as the result of a few drops of poison in their wine goblets, the Witch's curse, a far more undetectable danger, could bring their reign crashing down around them if they proved to be unjust rulers who abused their people.

Witches were feared in ancient Greece as well. There, they were believed to practice necromancy, summon dark forces, and consult with daemons—spirits good or evil (that would later evolve into the Christian concept of the entirely evil demon) that the Witch employed to perform all manner of tasks. It was this use of spirits that caused the Greeks to associate Witches with the powers of darkness and the underworld. They were looked upon as strangers in their native land, sometimes to be consulted, always to be feared.

In the fourth century, a new spiritual behemoth arose in the form of the Christian church. It began as a small cult that honored its founder's principles of peace and love, but through the seduction of political power, this young faith merged with the Roman Empire to become one of history's most cruel scourges on humanity. Before long, the Church, one of many competing faiths of the time, could suffer no rival and began persecuting what it deemed to be "heresy" as a means of suppressing any threat to its political might. In doing so, the Christian authorities began to designate other supernatural forces, such as spirits, faeries, and deities, as demons, devils, and evil spirits. In doing so the Church not only set the stage for later persecution of Witches, but of all non-Christian faiths.

Among the deities that the Church of Rome recast as evil were the horned nature gods, such as Herne, who led the wild hunt, a metaphor for the spirits of the dead who maraud the land by night; Kernunnos, lord of animals and the underworld; and Pan, the classic goat-footed god of indulgence and carnality. Because the emerging Church held a fundamental worldview that nature was sinful, the horned gods were considered formidable enemies and were the primary targets of ecclesiastical wrath. The Church created the concept of the Devil from a composite of the Satan, or adversary, in Judaism (who was not originally considered the personification of evil but rather a tester of faith), and the horned gods and spirits throughout the known world, reaching as far as Celtic and Persian lands for inspiration.

The persecution of Witches came to full force during the thirteenth through the seventeenth centuries, when authorities thoroughly associated Witchcraft with the worship of Satan. According to trial records, the spirits of the dead that Witches worked with were seen as demonic familiars, and sometimes even the Devil himself. The familiar spirit was described as more of an evil assistant—a watchdog from the depths of hell, rather than the spirit of the Witch's beloved grandmother or an old friend.

Much of what we know about the practices of European Witches is gleaned from the records of the countless Witch trials that took place over several hundred years. Most of the records dealt with men in black (and no, not the kind who hunt aliens), queens of the underworld, and, of course, the Devil himself. But recent translations of Hungarian Witch trials records by Hungarian Professor Éva Pócs show possible links to ancient cults of the dead as well as connections to both Nordic and Celtic shamanism hidden within the testimony of the accused. The word *wicca* (pronounced "Witcha"), which is the root of Witch, is a Germanic term, and an increasing number of scholars are looking to the Germanic Norse for the roots of European Witchcraft.[2] While the word "Witch" is specifically Germanic, I personally take the route of using the word more broadly, to apply to similar magical peoples throughout the known world.

Ever rebellious, Witches continued to practice their ways in secret, keeping the knowledge underground and passing it only to members of the family. Some hid in Christianity, becoming priests, nuns, and other religious functionaries while continuing to work the arts of magic in the quiet of darkened rooms, midnight chapels, lonely woods, and decrepit tombs.

Witches were magical mercenaries—an elite breed of supernatural power brokers. While they often served the communities they lived in from the edges of the village, the Witch's first loyalty was to herself and her family. For many, Witchcraft was the path of the lone practitioner, seeking wisdom in hidden places.

Witches appear in the myths and legends of almost every culture in history, and are often portrayed as enemies of cultural authorities that disapprove of them, labeling them as potentially dangerous outcasts and heretics. These magic-makers came shrouded in many guises, and did not always use the word "Witch" to describe themselves. Rather, they used the words of sorcery within their own languages. You can recognize Witches by their talent for controlling natural and supernatural forces, their ability to see into the past and future, and their skill at summoning the dead.

The Witch as Necromancer

Many of the great Witches of history, folklore, legend, and literature worked with the dead. These fearsome figures have become part of cultural traditions worldwide, inspiring both honor and fear many centuries after passing into the realm of spirit. Modern Witches aspire to emulate these illustrious enchanters and often call them to be part of present-day magic.

Perhaps no conjurer of spirits is more famous than the Witch of Endor, a woman who practiced her arts in spite of the condemnation of her ways by the authorities of her time. The Witch of Endor makes her first appearance in the Old Testament book of Samuel. The Prophet Samuel has died and King Saul, an insecure and bitter ruler, has begun to harshly impose the scriptural ban on sorcery and necromancy. But when his priests are unable to bring him the truth he seeks, Saul realizes that it's the Witch who is able to conjure truth when all else fails. He goes to the Witch of Endor (disguised and in the dead of night, of course) and beseeches her to raise the spirit of Samuel, who promptly foretells his impending death on the following day. It turns out that the spirit of Samuel was correct in his prediction. Perhaps such bans on Witchcraft by authorities were brought about by their understanding that the Witches could get results, and that these results were not always what the authorities wanted to hear. Because of her mastery of the necromantic arts, this skilled sorceress of Endor is still remembered and called upon by Witches in the present day.

The greatest Witch of classical Greek times is the legendary Circe, who appears in Homer's *Odyssey* as both benevolent helper of the hero, Odysseus, and feared wielder of justice to those whose hearts are untrue. Circe lived on a desolate island near to the entrance of the underworld and worked with the goddess Hecate, guardian of the crossroads and patroness of the dead. Circe tells Odysseus to travel beyond the Western horizon to the edge of Hades, land of the dead. She teaches Odysseus the process by which he can conjure up the shades of the dead through blood sacrifice, and so the hero makes his journey to the underworld, performing the rituals where the rivers Acheron and Cocytus meet, into which the waters of the river Styx flow—waters that separate the lands of the living and the dead.

In the saga of Erik the Red we find one of the most dramatic examples of the Seidr—the Norse form of Witchcraft. The Witch Thorbjorg was a seeress who was often invited to winter feasts so that she might share her visions of the future with guests. Thorkell, a chief farmer in a region of Greenland where famine had struck, called Thorbjorg to one of his feasts to hear her foresight of just when that famine might end. She arrived in a strapped blue cloak bedecked with stones, calfskin shoes, and catskin gloves, and carried a staff bound with brass and also adorned with stones. Around her waist hung a pouch in which her many magics were stored. Thorbjorg stayed the night and the next day; as she prepared to perform her Witchcrafts to answer the questions asked, she asked for a woman to perform a song of spirit-summoning called the varðlokur, also known as the Warlock song or warding song. A Christian woman who was not a Witch, but who knew the song from the teachings of her foster mother, came forth and sang the varðlokur so beautifully that the spirits of the dead emerged. Thorbjorg divined the future from these spirits, among them several that the Witch said would normally stay away. She imparted to the guests that the famine would end by the springtime and all would be well with the crops. This story not only shows a significant tie between Witches and the dead, but has provided a strong but much-debated possible source for the word "Warlock," and is why I use it today to describe myself.

Each of these Witches of old, as well as others we will meet later on, worked with the spirits in daily life. The power and wisdom they received from supernatural beings infused their ability to better understand the inner workings of magic. These great sages of Witchcraft now inhabit the twilight world of the dead, yet they continue to inspire Witches today, and are often conjured to bring their magical legacy into modern times.

Modern Wicca: Witchcraft Renewed

In the early 1950s, a new image of the Witch emerged in the form of modern Wicca, which portrays Witchcraft as an ancient fertility cult that worships a god and a goddess. Blended together from bits of pre-Christian religions, Freemasonry, and nineteenth-century ceremonial magic, Wicca incorporates magic into its practices, but it is often secondary to worship. While it is true that some historical Witches have been associated with this deity or that, religious devotion did not *define* those individuals as Witches, and was certainly not the reason why they were both vilified and deified–their power was.

Real Witches were distinguished by their magic, their cunning powers of manipulation, their connection to the spirits, and, most importantly, their willingness to exploit these powers for their own ends and to meddle in the affairs of others. I sometimes wonder if the gods and goddesses we call on today might once have walked the Earth as Witches themselves, having been so magical in life that they were deified in death. Consider the story of Jesus, who performed miracles and magic, preached from the fringes of society, and was later referred to as a god. While these facts do not necessarily mean that Jesus was a Witch, he certainly fits some of the criteria that I use to distinguish one. The Buddha also began as an actual person, Siddhartha Gautama, and is now revered by traditions throughout the world. So if it's safe to say that if this is true of other magical people, then it just may be that our very dieties are the departed Witches of long ago.

Contrary to the Earth mother goddesses and jovial gods of modern Wicca, when Witches were associated with gods or goddesses, these deities were usually even darker and more feared than the Witches themselves. The spiritual intelligences employed by the Witch were typically not the officially sanctioned deities of the culture he resided in.

Modern Wicca has two ironclad, dogmatic rules that adherents follow. The first, "Do what you will and harm none," is a concept likely adapted from the teachings of Aleister Crowley. The second, the "threefold law," is a precept stating that everything the Wiccan does will return to her three times. Neither of these axioms appears in history prior to the twentieth century. In real Witchcraft, there are no rules. Morality and ethics are situational and dependent upon the culture, upbringing, and personal philosophy of the Witch. There are times, such as when danger is imminent, that the Witch must take defensive action. It is not evil to protect yourself, your family, and your community. The competent Witch learns to work within the balance of nature and the tides of magic.

While modern Wicca has contributed much to the old traditions of Witchcraft, these paths have also encouraged a culture of Witches who do not have to have any occult talent to participate in the latest religious fad—Witches without magic, if you will. In this new form where everyone is welcome, Witches can be just like everyone else—mainstream, scrubbed up, and acceptable. While inclusiveness is a foundation of our modern society, applying this principle in Witchcraft distorts the simple truth that Witches have never been representative of the masses—they were gifted seers who dwelt on the edges of society. Not everyone can do magic and talk to the dead. Those with real magical talent have always earned a healthy balance of fear and admiration.

Because real Witches and their powers can be rare, modern Wiccans often seek them out when their own magic fails to bring them their desired results. In this, they are like the masses of ordinary people who have always come to the Witch in times of need—and usually only in the dead of night. Some things never change.

Spirits in the Modern Age: Today's Witches

The tides of ancient magic still flow in the world and the spirits of the dead await those brave enough to call them up and seek their wisdom. Modern Witches, while rare, dance upon the edges of a society caught between the obsessed extremes of religious fervor and soulless science. But we have not been idle. Still weaving wonders and spinning miracles, the Witch remains both feared and respected, shunned in the bright light of day, sought under the secrecy of night.

It's time to sweep the dust off the old spell books, merging ancient wisdom with modern science to give Witches a place in today's bustling society. Witches see between the concrete cracks of reality, ever seeking to pick the hidden bones of truth that can take us deeper into the foundations of magic. Today's Witches still listen for the whispers of the dead, as they always have. They are not afraid of facing death's embrace or of studying the necromantic wisdom that resides in old graveyards, crumbling churches, and the sepulchers of yesteryear.

In Salem, Massachusetts, you will find a strange brew of Witchcraft and occultism that brings the world of the supernatural to a city infamous for once having accused its residents of being Witches and sending them to the gallows. In a strange, ironic twist, Salem has become a Mecca of modern Witchcraft, with tourists visiting from around the world to learn about our practices, have spells cast, and have readings performed.

These visitors often come to us seeking psychic consultations about the important events in their lives and hoping to make contact with souls and loved ones who have crossed over. Law enforcement agencies near and far contact us in hopes that we may help them crack tough cases. As Witches, we are able to go within the spirit realms to ask the dead directly for the information we need.

At Halloween, the ancient holiday of the dead, the Witches of Salem host an annual Festival of the Dead to celebrate the spirits and to invite them to join our city's guests in exploring death's macabre customs, heretical histories, and strange rituals. The Festival draws the curious from around the globe, seeking to confront their own mortality and embrace the dance of the dead.

In my work as a modern Witch, I am not far removed from the Witch of Endor in my daily life, though thousands of years have passed since she conjured up the spirit of Samuel. I live the arts of Witchcraft in my every thought and deed, and conjure the dead to assist me in virtually all that I do

2

Opening the Doorway

Those who fear the study and use of supernatural powers often warn that exploring this path will open doorways to worlds best not explored. This fear-mongering has especially been used by authorities seeking to keep the masses from increasing their own personal power. While this view of danger lurking behind every closet door and under every bed is naïve to the true nature of the hidden realms of existence, the metaphor of the doorway is quite accurate. To work with the shades of the dead, the student must approach the spirit world with an open mind and be ready to experience levels of awareness that can unlock the hidden doorways of the soul.

Trafficking with the spirits of the dead offers us the ability to extend our intuitive senses and increase our magical power. When we welcome the dead to play a part in our supernatural workings, our visions become their aspirations and our wishes become their goals. The dead can be summoned to perform such tasks as helping you to seduce the object of your affection, influencing the minds of others, reaching into the dreams of the unwary, and spying on people. According to some legends, the dead knew where lost treasures where buried. Not much has changed. The spirits can still discover hidden opportunities and unearth profitable secrets. They can still convey magical talents, fame, love, and wealth to those brave enough to summon them.

But to begin working with the dead, you must be willing to surrender yourself to the arts of Witchery, immersing yourself in magic and knowing that part of you will die in order to be filled with the powers of the spirit world.

The Shroud and the Veil: Living Witchcraft

Establishing a pact between yourself and the spirits is only the beginning of living a spirit-filled life. You must also be willing to face your fears of the unknown and transform the fabric of your life itself. It is not necessary that you creep up and down the streets each night in tattered black robes and ghoulish makeup. The spirits recognize those who are different. Learning to distinguish yourself as a creature of wonder and mystery will show the spirits that you are one of their own.

Working your magic in both the worlds of the living and the dead can be challenging. The mundane fear what they do not understand, and thus the Witch has often become the object of that fear. Yet the reward for conquering your fear of death and creating a primal shift in your own reality is to obtain the passport to the realms of the dead.

The Body, Mind, Spirit Connection

To conjure the dead, you must tend to your living earthly temple, which is made up of the body, mind, and spirit. Spirits are drawn to those built on strong foundations, not crumbling ruins of weakness and poor health. Maintain a healthy body, mind, and spirit and you can forge links to other planes of existence, becoming a beacon to the Other Side, a candle flame from which the dead can draw comfort and inspiration.

Your body is the living altar of your temple. Getting enough nourishment, exercise, and sleep helps to transform you into the proper vessel for the dead. Each time you summon the spirits, they take a bit of your life force; thus a well-maintained body becomes a battery for them to draw on. This process surely gave birth to the myth of the Witch's teat, from which it was believed that demons would suck upon the sorcerer's soul.

Conjuring spiritual forces stresses the body and can tire you out; the better health your body is in, the more prepared it is for working with the dead. Some psychics have told me that increasing their B12 actually helps them to perform spiritual work, so be sure to fortify your body with nutrients as well.

Having a sharp, stable mind, strong in will and imagination yet free of delusion and fear, is essential. Conjuring the dead is not a crutch for the desperate and lonely. You are dealing with forces that are often old and crafty, and your will must be as cunning as theirs if you wish for them to heed your call. The most important aspect of this is confronting your fear. Fear can usually be found at the root of most problems; fear of death, in particular, can be a major hindrance to your travels between worlds. Allow your fears to rise to the surface, confront your own mortality, and slay the inner demons that blind you from the truth. It is important to keep one's emotions in check, not allowing the stresses and strains of everyday life to consume you. A mind that is free of fear and sharp of thought is ready to understand the secret and silent language of the dead.

Discovering the power of your undying spirit, the most crucial of the three, will connect you to the very essence of the dead, who are creatures of spirit themselves. We are kith and kin to the denizens of the underworld. The key to this spirit connection is magic. Every time a Witch performs an act of magic, he becomes more godlike and less human. As the Witch evolves, he becomes more attuned to the guiding presence of the spirit forces around him. Our spirits yearn to fly across time and space and to travel as dignitaries to the kingdoms of the dead. For this to happen, we must set our souls free from the obsolete restrictions of antiquated religious dogma. A Witch's spirit bows to no one.

Letting Your Inner Witch Out

Witchcraft is both a practice and a way of life. As in any lifestyle, we immerse ourselves in its elements and embody its truths. In the case of the Witch, this immersion dares us to be different, to be unique, and to live our lives in both this world and the world of spirit. Witches have a fascination with the dark and mysterious; we dance with the dead every day. We honor them by draping ourselves in the black of night, wearing spidery veils and such adornments as the silver of Hecate's moon, mourning jewelry, charms, and bones. Enveloping ourselves in shadow, we dress to impress the dead!

Spirits hate boring people and would rather avoid them. If you want the spirit world to take notice, celebrate your nonconformity! The competent Witch weaves herself between the worlds in exciting and sometimes shocking ways. When you allow your own unique soul to come through, you will discover your inner Witch, an archetype of great magical power and wisdom.

Keeping One Foot in the Real World

While it is important for the Witch to keep one foot in the grave, so to speak, don't let the powers of death consume you. The Witch must learn to balance the worlds of matter and spirit. While this is a book about how Witches can work with the dead, Witchcraft is also devoted to life, and no book on the subject would be complete without urging readers to savor the living world of earthly senses. The simple pleasures of the flesh are important aspects of the magical experience. Spirits are attracted to your life force, so enjoy life! Get out there! Feel the passion and vitality of every second of your existence!

Tools, Places, and Times of Power

In the chapters to come, you will find the mysterious trappings of the magical arts employed to enhance your personal power or aid in contact with spirit forces. Whether the task at hand entails lighting a black candle, acquiring a human skull, or visiting a graveyard at midnight in the dark of the moon, you will find that the proper tools and the right ambience are vital elements of magic.

Witches know how to accessorize. Iron keys, graveyard dust, human bones, powders, daggers, and makeshift dolls stuck with pins are just some of the tools of the trade. The strange paraphernalia the Witch uses in magic are powerful mental keys that unleash her will upon the worlds. The more powerful the symbol, the stronger the connection. Finding just the right elements for our rituals and incantations is often challenging, but always rewarding. We scour graveyards, antique shops, flea markets, and even the Internet searching for unique items to increase our powers.

The appropriate surroundings help the Witch to attain a mood conducive to magic. A candlelit room drenched in shadow, a desolate crossroads at midnight, a decaying cemetery overrun with weeds, or a deathbed chamber filled with the sweet smell of mourning are settings that create the perfect atmosphere and invite the spirits to participate.

The clever Witch understands the spirit and power of place and knows that certain otherworldly intelligences and energies become associated with particular locales, holding dominion over the land. These spirits may be the shades of those who once lived in the area and remain attached to it, or more ancient beings of unknown origin that have chosen to become mighty sentinels. In both cases they have bonded with the very energies of the land itself, creating vortexes of immeasurable power. On an even larger scale, we recognize the sacred geometry of ley lines: places where the spirit world intersects with our own. You will often find pyramids, temples, stone circles, and other sacred markers at these power spots. Such magical sites radiate metaphysical energy through which the spirits manifest most strongly.

Time is a key ingredient in magical conjurations. Who hasn't heard tell of the enchantments of the Witching Hour? When bringing to mind the Witch of legend, we see her standing on the precipice of a lonely cliff while a thunderstorm rages, or moving stealthily under the pale glow of a full moon at midnight. Certain magical times may be fixed and determined in advance, such as astrological aspects or moon phases, helping the Witch to plan her work ahead. At other times, such as the arrival of a sudden gust of wind to fan the flames of magic, the Witch will act swiftly to tap into the power of the moment.

When the Witch combines her steely determination with the shadowy accoutrements of the art, the spirit of place, and the times of magic, the greatest works of Witchcraft can be spun. Using these methods in your work with the Other Side will serve to usher the spirits to cross the inky black waters of death.

The Death Current

Virtually every exercise, tool, or ritual that deals with accessing the wisdom and power of the dead involves tapping into the cosmic force known as the Death Current, an energy that pervades the universe, passing through all of us and guiding us toward our own physical finality. It is similar to the Yin element of the Tao, the destructive chaos from which all life springs and to which all life must return; and to the Akashic records, the psychic storehouses of all knowledge, wisdom, and even emotion. It is through this vibrational current that the spirits of the dead swim, waiting to be reached through the gifted seership of the Witch. Every second that the dead lived, everything they learned, every tear they shed, every joy they experienced, and all that they have been resides in the celestial tides of the Death Current. It is within this current that you will find the Witch, channeling her life force to balance and connect with the forces of death.

The Dangers of Spirit Work

You may be curious to know if there are dangers and pitfalls to interacting with the dead. The forces you will learn to conjure in this book are not to be trifled with, nor are these pages to be skimmed over; you must be willing to learn and absorb the teachings before you attempt any form of conjuration or contact. In fact, I recommend that you read this book in its entirety to make absolutely sure that this path is for you, and only then begin to practice the exercises herein.

The dangers are legion. If you enter into this intricate dance of life and death with the mind of a mere dabbler, you open yourself up to a host of possible complications ranging from fatigue, melancholy, and minor poltergeist disturbances to mental and physical illnesses, malevolent hauntings, and even possession by malefic forces! It is of grave importance that you engage in this work with care.

Be of sound mind and body, nurture your spirit, and approach the work with both caution and determination, and you will succeed in opening doorways through which the dead can penetrate this world. Your inner strength will serve to protect you, and your understanding will be a light to guide the way.

With these warnings prowling about your mind, you may wonder why I would consider doing this sort of thing at all, never mind teaching it in a book. You may also question whether there are any tangible benefits to such work.

The rewards and gifts of the spirits are limitless. Court the dead and they will help you to achieve love, wealth, and knowledge, and enable you to strike fear into the hearts of those who would commit injustice—all while leading you into realms of consciousness where death as we know it does not exist. It is through these altered states of awareness that the Witch discovers her greatest reservoirs of power.

The Visionary State

What you are about to learn is perhaps the most fundamental component of the magical arts, one we will refer to throughout the remainder of the book. It is the mental key that unlocks the treasure chests of universal wisdom. I refer to this as the visionary state—an altered state of consciousness through which we connect with unseen forces and our spells take form and flight. It is also the method the Witch uses to walk between the worlds of the living and the dead.

Exercise: Entering the Visionary State

*Whenever a ritual or spell you encounter in this book instructs you
to enter the visionary state, the following exercise is the one
you will use.*

Step One

Find a comfortable chair where you can relax and connect to
the spiritual forces around you.

Step Two

When you are comfortably seated, close your eyes and focus
on your breathing. Allow your breath to become slow, deep,
and deliberate. In your mind's eye, see your breath as a living
force of energy, inhaling the powers of the spirit world and
exhaling your own thoughts and dreams so that the spirits
may experience them. Realize that the air you exhale becomes sustenance to the dead as they absorb your essence
through your breath. With each inhale, the dead align with
your life force. Your breath should continue this way over the
course of the visionary state.

Step Three

Feel the flesh of your body tingle as the Death Current begins to flow through you. Notice the changes that take place:
your breathing may become shallow, your limbs may become

numb or tingly, and your heart rate may drop. Trust the process—it is like falling into a deep, dreamlike sleep, yet one in which you are still aware. Let your spirit release itself from the heaviness of flesh and bone. Breath after breath, slower, heavier, and deeper, descend into the depths of the underworld. To define the state, you will now count to yourself from ten to one. When you reach one, say in your mind, "I am now in a visionary state. I am at one with the spirits. They flow through me as I flow through them."

Swim in the dark waters of the Death Current, feeling those currents within your very blood. You are now able to communicate with the spirits at the core of your body and soul, able to share in their memories and experiences.

When you are ready to come back, count from one to ten and open your eyes. It is important to count back up whenever you can so that you do not have the feeling of suddenly being jarred awake. Do this exercise daily or whenever possible and you will have the key to reaching the spirit realms whenever you desire.

The visionary state is an active form of meditation. Rather than quieting thoughts, we are pushing our mental ability to its most creative, allowing spirit vision to dance across the screen of the mind.

As with all meditation, the foundation of its success is in proper breathing. Deliberate breath, slow and relaxed, in through the nose and out through the mouth, is the first step to achieving the state of awareness required. Practicing this style of breathing daily not only increases your ability to enter into the visionary state, but it also helps to bring your physical body into balance by oxygenating the blood and thus giving the brain more power.

Once you have connected with the correct form of breathing, it is necessary to clear the mind of mental flotsam and jetsam. Here we inherit the wisdom of the Yogis, masters of "passive" meditation—the quieting of the mind—who are able to hold mental states of emptiness for days at a time. Before we can paint the canvas of our mind's eye with information from the spirit world, we must clear it of the stresses and worries of everyday life.

Once the mind is cleared, focus on your desired target. This could be as simple a task as finding a lost object, or as complex as a necromantic graveyard ritual. In both cases, it is important that you remain centered and focused on the work at hand. Do not allow the thoughts of the mundane world to creep into your consciousness. In this way, you will learn to discern between real psychic information and mere imagination.

Those who practice the visionary state regularly tell of hours flying by in what seem to be only moments. Others tell of time stopping completely. Thus, you may want to limit your exercise to an hour when you're first starting out, using an alarm clock if necessary. Since alarms can be uncomfortably jarring, it is important that you use them as a backup, coming back to an alert state of consciousness on your own. As you progress in skill, you will be able to gauge your surroundings more clearly, becoming more attuned to the seen and unseen phenomena that surround you. Once you have truly mastered the visionary state, your mind and spirit will know when to return from the veil and reenter normal waking consciousness.

Making Pacts with the Spirits

In order to open the doorways to the spirit world, your will must be strong, your determination unwavering, and your commitment to a mutual relationship with the dead resolute. There is no room in your mind for doubt, skepticism, or fear. The spirits can see through all of that. You must know in your heart and in your soul that you want to walk the path of the Witch, and this path includes the deepest understanding of the realms of the dead.

This symbiotic bond between the living and the dead is at the root of what became known in the Middle Ages as the pact between Witches and their "familiar spirits." While the term conjures images of your soul being carried off by Furies and devils, the reality is much simpler.

In a sense, you do sell your soul, but you sell it to yourself! From the moment you were born, others have been exerting control over you. As a Witch, you claim your own power to do what you choose, serving no master but your own will. In fully embracing the source emanating from within you, the spirits will recognize you as one of their own: a being of supernatural might and intelligence. It is only when they see you as a master of the magical arts that they will deign to consider working with you.

The dead sometimes long for the pleasures of the material world and fear being forgotten. Spirits become lost souls when no one takes time to remember them. A lost soul is a spirit whose life and legacy have been forgotten. Often adrift in obscurity, buried beneath the dust of time, the souls of the dead call out to be remembered. When a Witch summons forth a denizen of the spirit world, he shares with that soul the spark of life once lived, often making offerings of food, drink, and other indulgences of the physical plane. In turn, the spirit serves the Witch.

RITUAL: MAKING THE PACT

Gather together the following items:
- A page of parchment paper.
- Two black candles.
- A black table covering.
- An iron pot or cauldron.

- A ceramic tile to place the pot on.
- A garnet ring.
- A black pen.
- A medical lancet.
- Photographs and mementos of deceased loved ones, friends, and those you admire.

Set a small table with the black table covering. Place the candles in candlesticks on either end of the table. Lay the ceramic tile in the center of the table (to protect from heat) and place the iron pot on the tile. Assemble the photos and mementos around the pot on the table. Place the parchment, pen, garnet ring, and lancet on the table in front of you.

Enter into the visionary state (see above). Light the candles. Upon the parchment, write the conditions of the pact:

"I, [your name], son (or daughter) of [father's name] and [mother's name], renounce all religious dogma, guilt, shame, and all thoughts and feelings that would limit my powers. On this night, I reclaim my soul that I may embrace the full and unlimited might and cunning of the Witch. Both the worlds of the living and the dead will now hear my commands and work with me as an equal among them! I offer my blood as a living sacrifice and a symbol of my ancestry to seal this pact. My breath and my free will are the only things to which I am subject by seal of my holy offering. Through this sacrifice of blood and fire, I receive my Witches' mark and consecrate my life anew as a creature of magic!"

Sign your name at the bottom of the parchment, realizing that once you make this decision, there is no turning back. Now, prick the fore-finger of your left hand with the lancet. Take your blood and seal the pact with a red "X" smeared across your signature. Take another three deep breaths, inhaling the forces of spirit that are present in the photos and mementos. Hold the parchment before you and read it aloud in a strong, determined voice, giving life to your words.

Once you have spoken the spell, hold the parchment to each candle flame to light it; then, holding it above the pot, allow the flames to envelop the parchment and drop it in, thus fixing the pact. Once the spell burns down, take the forefinger you pricked and dip it into the ashes. Take that finger and make the sign of an "X" on your forehead. You have baptized yourself with the Witches' mark and now walk in a world of magic. Take the garnet ring and mix it into the ashes of the spell. Leave it there for three days and three nights so it may be infused with all the power of your will. Wear it as a reminder of your pact and to summon extra courage and skill when needed.

· · ·

3

The Altar of the Dead

If you walk into HEX, my Witchcraft shop in Salem, Massachusetts, one of the first things you'll see is the large altar looming imposingly against the wall and completely bedecked with all manner of curious bric-a-brac. This is our altar of the dead. Every square inch is covered with photos, statues, candles, jars of strange powders, and dozens of scribbled notes on parchment. Featured most prominently is Robert, an actual human skull leering out at our customers, most of whom are wondering why there's a skull in the middle of a shop at all. Few of the Witch shops in Salem even have an altar, and those that do eschew the dead in favor of standard images of the Wiccan god and goddess; even by Salem standards, the altar at HEX is considered quite unusual!

For all of us who work at HEX, the altar of the dead is the heart of the shop. It is where we build a powerful relationship with the spirits who bless us with prosperity, love, healing, and protection. It is also where visitors to Salem from all over the globe leave written notes, photographs, and other mementos in honor of their beloved dead. By October's end, we have thousands of notes and dozens of mementos left by those who sought to remember loved ones who had passed over during the year.

On November 16th, Hecate's night, the Witches of HEX gather before a fireplace in my home—fireplaces were considered places to communicate with spirits in the Old World—to read the notes and burn them in honor of all those who have touched our lives and those of our shop's many guests. While a retail consultant might insist that we rid ourselves of the altar in favor of more product, I could never imagine taking it away because it would diminish the very soul of the shop and the reason I opened the store at all—to help people come back to knowing those spirits who have helped to shape who we are.

I once gave a class in Witchcraft and Necromancy at which a student came up to me after the class and asked why she was having such a hard time communicating with a particular spirit that had been visiting her home. She was an accomplished medium and accustomed to speaking with the dead, but this particular spirit just didn't want to make conversation. I asked her if she had left the spirit offerings or had an altar of the dead in her home. She said no.

For any of you who are trying to establish a psychic connection with your loved ones who have passed on, an altar of the dead is one of the most powerful ways to do so. The altars at my home and shop are filled with symbols of the dead from around the world, powders, candles, dried flowers, and, as mentioned, even a human skull, used as one of the most ancient, sacred, and powerful methods of connecting to the world of spirit.

Yours doesn't have to be so complex. It can be as simple as an end table with some pictures of your loved ones, a vase of flowers, and a candle or two. Every so often, you might leave a small plate of your mother's favorite food, your grandma's favorite tobacco, your best friend's favorite rum, or the occasional lottery ticket your uncle loved to play. Doing these things shows respect for our dead, and if you respect the dead, they will respect you and will be more likely to aid you in your pursuits.

Finding an Altar

If you're hoping to build an ongoing relationship with the spirits, the most important place to begin is by creating an altar of the dead. This is where most of the spiritual work you do to connect with the dead happens. It's mission control for the spirit world. As we at HEX often tell our visitors, this doesn't have to be anything weird that makes your oh-so-normal neighbors think you've gone crazy when they visit your home. As mentioned, it can be as simple as a photo of your grandmother on your bedroom dresser with a bowl of her favorite candy and a bottle of her favorite perfume as offerings—a place where you go each day to spend a moment to remember and honor her.

But this book is about taking it to the next level and building a serious working partnership with the dead, and so I recommend going all out—bringing those you want to remember into a true place of honor in your home!

The first step is to find the right piece of furniture for your altar. Those old, tall sideboards with the multitiered shelves and mirrors at the top are the type that I use at HEX because they give various spirit images their proper and unique places. You may consider obtaining a nice sheet of glass to cover your altar so that the wax from the many candles you're going to burn here does not damage the wood. Flea markets, antique stores, thrift shops, and auctions are among the best places to find the perfect old piece to set the mood—and remember, mood is paramount to the shift in consciousness required for magic. Sure, a particleboard table from Walmart will work in a pinch, but it definitely doesn't carry the same power as something that has been once owned by others, especially those now in spirit. If you can get the heirloom piece of an honored relative who has passed on, that's even better! The altar at HEX once belonged to the late Shawn Poirier, my dear friend and a well-known Warlock of Salem.

Where to Put the Altar

Once you have an actual altar, you've got to find a place in your home to put it. The spirits of the dead are known to enter from the "west gate" so most altars to the dead are placed in the west. This likely originated because the sun sets in the west each night, which is why the Egyptians preferred to place tombs along the west bank of the river Nile; why the Greeks saw Elysium in the west; and the Irish believed their Blessed Isles of the dead to be west across the ocean. The Norse believed the souls of heroes passed west beyond the sea. J.R.R. Tolkien drew on these myths for his concept of the Blessed Lands of the West for his popular trilogy, *The Lord of the Rings*, and this same theme was carried into the 2003 adaptation of the third novel in the trilogy, *Return of the King,* with the Academy Award-winning song "Into the West" sung by Annie Lennox. Evidence of the west as the land of the dead can also be seen in the Pre-Columbian Americas, in the beliefs of cultures as far apart as the Aztecs of Mexico and the Yosemite Indians of California.

An altar of the dead must be handled with the utmost respect and so it should not be accessible to just anyone who enters your home. Perhaps you'll keep yours in a hidden closet or dark corner of the basement. We've been lucky with the altar at HEX because most visitors read the signage not to touch unless they're writing a note for their dead, and the staff quickly stops those who ignore the warning. My home altar is kept from prying eyes in a private temple space. Remember, a truly developed altar is going to attract attention, and you won't want it desecrated by those who do not have the utmost respect for the arts.

Ritual: Blessing the Altar

Before you put anything on the altar, it's important to cleanse it. The best way to do this is with a mixture of spring water and kosher salt; if it's wood, add a little bit of extra-virgin olive oil. All three of these ingredients are sacred to the dead. It's important not to use sea salt for this process. Kosher salt comes from the Earth where the dead are buried, and it is sanctified, so it is very important to use that instead. Rub the altar down with the liquid counterclockwise—the direction of the dead—as you repeat the charm,

> *Beloved spirits, hear my call*
> *Bless this altar that it be*
> *A crossroads between the living and dead*
> *From now until eternity!*

It is important to note that this is the **only** time that salt of any kind should ever be on your altar of the dead or used in any rituals regarding the spirits. While salt is often used in magical rituals, it is anathema to many spirits and shouldn't be used when working with them.

• • •

Personalizing Your Altar

Now that your altar is in place and ready to be adorned, you must choose the spirits with whom you wish to make a connection. This can be done with photos, mementos, and possessions of the dead, funerary prayer cards, and even their ashes, arranged upon the altar in ways that honor and respect each of them. These choices should not be made lightly. While some advocate placing every departed soul you ever knew on an altar, there may be some you don't want to make connections with. The uncle that tried to swindle your father out of his house or the great aunt who poisoned her husband may not be the energies you want to partake in on a daily basis. Since dealing with the dead will become an important part of your daily spiritual practices, it is crucial that you choose those that you actually can connect to. Once you create these bonds, you must nurture them. While the dead can be benevolent advocates for your causes, they can also get quite angry when you ignore them. The ancient Romans believed this so strongly that they feared that any mistake in honoring the dead would incur their wrath. The Babylonians believed that their eldest child must honor them in death in order to prevent them from becoming wrathful towards the living, and so they adopted a child if they didn't already have one! Ponder this before you choose whose faces you want to adorn that altar.

The most obvious choices are those who cared the most for you in life. I often say that the Virgin Mary is busy and Isis has better things to do, but your grandmother will care about your problems. Our personal dead often stick around to help us. Bonds made in life often live on in death.

This brings us to an interesting and age-old question. Don't all the good souls reincarnate, ascend to heaven, or end up grazing in some Elysian paradise? As Witchcraft and necromancy became demonized over time, the spirits of the dead were recast as sinister creatures of a lower vibration, leeching the life force from those who call upon them. While there are certainly shades of the dead that you don't want to traffic with, they aren't all automatically bad. The ancient Romans, in particular, saw the dead as good (Lares), bad (Lemures), and as yet undetermined (Manes). Their understanding of nature of spirits was pretty accurate even if they did shy away from using them in sorcery. Many good spirits stay behind to help those they love. It doesn't mean they aren't evolved. On the contrary, reincarnating into a new form can be a burden to the spirit that feels she can be of greater service in the spirit world. But you do need to know who is going to actually lift up your life through the relationship, so choose your associations wisely.

Not all of the spirits you put on your altar have to be blood relatives, either. Some, like those who have been adopted, will honor members of their adopted family. We often choose our family from among our cherished friends, so placing photos of those who have touched your life, now that they are in spirit, is a powerful way of keeping that connection alive. I have both a photo and a vial of ashes of my "Auntie" Kathy—in truth my mother's best friend when she was alive—on the altar at HEX because she was a strong person in life and I call on that strength when I need it. You might also consider including photos of those you revere as heroes—great leaders, spiritual mentors, compassionate charity workers, successful businesspeople, even celebrities whose talent inspires you. Some even include bone relics of the Catholic saints or other important spiritual people, though competition for their interest can sometimes be great.

Witches do not discriminate against other faiths, but rather honor the paths by which we all advance our spirituality. By connecting with those people and honoring them, you allow their gifts to come and flow through you—one of the most important benefits to working with the dead. If you're having trouble securing a job, call on the grandfather who was a master of industry. If you're unlucky in love, call on someone whose strong marriage you admire. The dead thrill in the joys of life once lived and will jump at the chance to be part of your life.

The images on an altar need only be comprised of the dead to be considered an "altar of the dead," but some also like to put other images of death, including deities of the dead. For deities, you might include a statue of Anubis, the Egyptian god who guides the spirits to the land of the dead; Persephone, the queen of the underworld; or even the Mexican image of Santisima Muerte, the popular saint of death in that country. I give prominence on my altar to Marie Laveau, the famed Voodoo Queen of mid-1800s New Orleans. While not a goddess, per se, she was a powerful and compassionate sorceress who has since become the very spirit of the Crescent City—

a place I feel very connected to. She is considered a Loa—or intermediary spirit—of the city. By having her on the altar, I keep my connection to both Marie's spirit and a city so close to my heart. Deity statues should be blessed and consecrated to the deities they represent according to their own preference. A list of deities and their preferred offerings is featured in appendix B.

Other ways of connection include animal skulls and bones, including artwork carved from bone such as statuary, beads, and jewelry made from animal bone; Katrina dolls from Mexico (skeletal ladies dressed in Victorian finery); photos of graveyards; and more. As you learn to make offerings to the dead, your altar will become quite full!

The Skull

If someone were to ask me what I would choose if I could only keep one of my many magical tools, my answer would be Robert, the human skull that resides on the altar of the dead in my shop. I inherited Robert from my departed best friend and business partner, Shawn Poirier, who passed into spirit in the year 2007. Shawn was one of the most magical people that I have ever known, and he taught me the ways of necromancy and spirit work. Shawn ordered his two skulls, which are named Robert and Claudia, from *BoneRoom.com,* a website and retail shop based in Albany, California, that specializes in bones both human and animal. When Shawn died, my coven-sister, Leanne Marrama, received Claudia. I became the caretaker for Robert, an honor I cherish deeply, as I know the power inherent in this most ancient tool of magic.

Among the greatest tools a Witch can possess is a human skull—if "possess" is the right word, for we are caretakers and the dead are equal partners in our magic. If you truly seek to walk the ways of Witchcraft, you should consider obtaining a skull, for it is, quite literally, a doorway to the spirit world. To fully become a Witch, you must be able to walk in the worlds of the living and of the spirits. Bones of all different creatures can connect us to the Other Side. The bone of a wolf, for example, will connect us more fully to the spirit vibration of the Wolf. Thus, the human skull connects us to the legacy of our own humanity, the great river of DNA that reaches into the deepest places of the long history of our species. Through the skull, we are able to draw upon the entire spectrum of the spirit realms, calling on information and sending out our will upon the spectral winds.

The skull you choose and how you choose it is important. The spirit and legacy of the person whose skull it was will absolutely influence the magic you do with it. You can't always know to whom the skull once belonged, but you should be able to use your psychic ability in a visionary state to tap into the skull before you purchase it. This can be done in person, or even with a skull you only have an online picture of, since psychic ability works across great distances. You will want to get a skull that does not have much negativity associated with it!

The condition of the skull can also be crucial depending on what you're using it for. According to lore, a skull that has a mandible or lower jaw is able to communicate the voices of the spirits in the ancient tradition of the Oracular Head—what the Tibetans refer to as Yama and the early Hebrews called the Oboth. The Witch of Endor probably would have had an Oboth. These were often adorned with jewels, carvings, sacred metals, and other embellishments. A skull without a lower jaw, however, is considered to be silent and so is used primarily for calling the dead in magic—soliciting the spirits to perform tasks for you, which you'll learn about later. Robert, the skull that I work with, does not have a lower jaw and thus I use it for magic.

Where you obtain the skull is also important. Just as you don't want the skull of a serial killer, you should avoid the skull of someone who has been treated in a disrespectful way. We definitely don't recommend digging up grandma to get her skull. This would be considered a desecration not only of her grave, but probably of her wishes as well. In ancient times, people would bequeath their skulls to family members to carry on traditions of magic, but this practice is very rare today, and we must honor the wishes of our dead. It is wiser to choose skulls that belong to people who donated themselves to science for the advancement of medicine and other noble causes. This shows selflessness on the part of the donor. Robert was once just such a man.

Another good choice is a skull that was prepared in a spiritual way. *BoneRoom.com* offers several examples of the Tibetan Yama, a skull that has been ritually prepared in a sacred manner and lovingly carved with Buddhist symbols. I gave my mentor, Lori Bruno, a Yama carved with a pair of Buddhist Dorje–symbols of lightning–forming an equilateral cross, which is a very old symbol of protection and power.

Finally, it is most important to obtain the skull in a legal manner. This is, of course, the other reason you shouldn't dig up grandma. It certainly wouldn't look good to the rest of the family if they had to bail you out of jail for desecrating her corpse. So again, please use a reputable source for such purchases. It is perfectly legal under federal law to purchase and possess a human skull. Certain states and municipalities may have their own rules, so check first.

If, in the worst-case scenario, you cannot obtain a true human skull, that will not render your altar useless. You will simply want to obtain a representation of it, perhaps of ceramic, resin, bronze, or my preferred substitution: quartz crystal. While these materials will not contain the full power of a real skull, when combined with your magical intent, they can be an effective doorway to spirit.

Ritual: Blessing Your Skull

A ritual of consecration is very important after obtaining a skull. The following is a simple method to connect yourself to your most powerful spiritual tool.

What you will need:

- An anointing oil. (See appendix A.)
- A black candle to draw in the energy of the spirits. The color black draws in light and creates a psychic battery, which is also, by the way, why Witches wear so much black!
- A white candle to honor the dead and send energy out. White has often been worn as a way of respecting those who have passed.
- Necromantic incense (see appendix A) with a pot and charcoal to burn it. Stick incense is fine if it has the right ingredients. Myrrh, copal, wormwood, and dittany are safe bets for conjuring spirits.

Place the skull upon your altar; place the white candle to the right of the skull and the black candle to the left. The incense burner should be in front of the skull but not impede your ability to access it. The oil should be accessible on the altar as well. Prepare by going into a visionary state (see chapter 1) and continue to breathe deeply. Anoint the forehead of the skull with the oil in the form of an "X." Lift the skull with both hands until the eyes of the skull are facing your own eyes. Stare into the eye sockets for several minutes or more, until you feel a strong connection with the skull. When you can feel the energy of it boring into your soul, speak aloud the words:

> *I gaze into the eyes of my own mortality*
> *For I shall be as you one day*
> *Be now my guide to the realms of spirit*
> *My intermediary between the living and the dead!*
> *May our bond be in perfect love and perfect trust*
> *And may I serve you as you serve me*
> *As my will, so mote it be!*

Continue to gaze into the eyes of the skull until you feel that the connection has been made. Then, place it reverently back upon the altar. Your skull is now blessed and ready to become your portal between the worlds. The very first task you should now ask the skull to perform is to give you its name. To name something is to be able to understand and know its power. Thus it is important to know the name of your new guide in the spirit realms. It is rare that you will already know the name of the skull you are working with, so take a few moments while in your visionary state and ask the skull for its name. Wait a few moments and it will come to you. From that moment forth, you should always refer to the skull by that name, just as I refer to Robert.

• • •

Sacred Offerings and Daily Devotions

Your altar is now a true crossroads between the worlds of the living and the dead. You have those you have chosen to honor and, hopefully, you also have your skull—though that can sometimes take time to acquire, so I hope that you at least have a worthy substitute. Now we come to the real, everyday work of the altar—the regular offerings that build the relationship!

As I mentioned earlier, the spirits remember the joy of life once lived, and so leaving offerings of things they enjoyed in life is an effective way of drawing their energy. The spirit of your departed grandmother is not likely to literally consume the chocolate chip cookie you leave on the altar, but everything, including that cookie, has a spiritual energy signature, and the dead, who are also made up of energy, will be drawn to patterns of energy they understand. Occasionally, the spirits actually will consume the food you leave for them. In 2007, Leanne Marrama left a dirty martini for Shawn Poirier on the back windowsill in the ballroom of the Hawthorne Hotel where she hosts Salem's annual séance. No one went near that martini all night, as it sat behind the podium where Leanne spoke. When Leanne turned to retrieve it, the glass was empty! If anyone could have pulled off this trick from the spirit world, it was Shawn.

To decide what offerings you should leave, think about what your loved ones liked. Was your mother partial to Opium perfume? Did your grandfather like cigars? Was your nephew an avid reader of comic books? Did your great-aunt have a penchant for expensive champagne? There are certainly more general offerings you can leave, but the most powerful are those that directly connect to the spirits you are trying to work with!

More common offerings through history include honey, wine, olive oil, flowers, a mixture of milk and honey (a fantastic libation of the dead!), honey wine (mead), sprinkled barley, fava beans (popular in Sicilian Catholic areas for Saint Joseph's day—he is the patron saint of a happy death), blood (pricked from your own finger with a sterile medical lancet, available at any drug store), jewelry, your own hair, and resins of myrrh, copal, and other funerary incenses. Sicilian Strega Lori Bruno shared with me her ancient family recipe for the food for the dead, which you can find in appendix A.

Whether you do this daily, weekly, or (at least!) monthly, try to keep the connection flowing by leaving both the more common, universal offerings and those items that speak personally to the spirits you are trying to attract.

4

The Witches' Tools of Spirit Work

In the previous chapter you learned about the altar of the dead and its offerings. But Witchcraft is also about magic and rituals of power. Tapping into that power can be accomplished by the use of the Witches' tools—sacred implements used by magical practitioners to conduct their magic and channel spirit powers. The skull is certainly the most important implement to have on your altar. However, if you want to elevate it even further from merely a place of reverence to a fully working magical power center, there are other tools you will want to acquire as well.

The truest magic of the Witch lies within the heart, the spiritual center of being where we are most connected to the wondrous energies that flow through all of creation. Even the aforementioned skull is but a doorway through which your own power manifests. Tools are not the source of the Witch's power, but rather an extension of it, a means by which she can amplify her inner reservoirs of magic.

Magic allows us to send out spiritual energy from the body while psychic ability allows us to draw it in. Each process requires a different kind of tool. Tools for sending energy include the wand, the ritual dagger, and other points of focus, while tools for drawing energy include the chalice, the pentacle, and other objects of receptive nature. Jewelry and other adornments can often be used for either purpose, such as a labradorite ring worn on the left hand to bring in spirit power or a pentagram ring worn on the right index finger to direct the will of the Witch.

Working with the dead can be as simple as psychic interaction with them, but it is also important to note that certain items can help fuel the process by increasing the level of spiritual energy necessary to draw the spirits to participate in your magic. The tools of spirit work vary from tradition to tradition. The ones shared here are those that I find to work the best. These tools will also be employed in the rituals found in later chapters, so it is important to try to obtain as many of them as you can. You will likely add to this list over time, but this is an important foundation for beginning your magical practices.

The Bronze Dagger

As old as the tale of Homer's *Odyssey*, the bronze blade was used to shed the blood of those animal sacrifices meant to raise the spirits. Some may find this barbaric, and it is not a practice I personally prefer. However, the bronze blade is also a powerful symbol of protection and commanding. While steel or iron may repel spirits altogether, a bronze dagger is a softer energy, welcoming in the spirits with the warning that they not run afoul of the sorcerer lest that blade be taken up in defense. The bronze dagger is also used where a magic circle of protection is to be cast. My own dagger is a solid piece of bronze with a hilt formed of two dragon talons, and the blade itself textured with dragon scales. The dragon is an ancient symbol of wisdom and protection. The dagger is also a symbol of the element of Air—one of the great four elements that should be represented on any working Witch's altar.

The Yew Wand

Shawn Poirier first taught me to conjure the spirits with a wand of the poisonous yew tree, which represents the powers of death and rebirth. The wand is an extension of the Witch's will and is used to channel her energy into the universe. The yew is sacred to the Witch goddess Hecate in her guise as queen of the underworld and helps the Witch to direct the spirits of the dead to go and do her bidding.

According to lore, the wand must be measured from your elbow to the tip of your middle finger to represent an extension of your power. However, I am flexible about this rule. Whatever size your yew wand, be sure that you feel a connection to it, for it will be among your most frequently used magical tools. Not incidentally, J.K. Rowling, the author of the popular *Harry Potter* novels, chose yew for the wand of the Dark Wizard Voldemort, whose army of "death-eaters" were competent necromancers. The wand represents the element of Fire.

The Pentacle of Protection

Often found on the Witches' altar, the pentacle, or five-pointed star, is typically carved or etched upon a flat platter known as a paten. The pentacle is one of the earliest symbols that humans learned to draw. Within the star are formed the extensions of the human body: head, arms, and legs surrounded by the sacred circle, a symbol of divinity and protection in many cultures. Placing charms and spells upon the pentacle will help to energize them with the power you call up in your rituals; you can also place your offerings to the dead upon it. You should always try to keep the pentacle present during any ritual involving the dead, in case any harmful spirits show up. The pentacle represents the element of Earth.

The Chalice of Libation

Traditionally, the chalice is used by Witches to draw down the powers of the gods to be shared among those participating in the ritual. The chalice represents the deepest feminine mysteries of the goddesses of old. In the case of the altar of the dead, however, the chalice is used for offerings of libation for the dead and for the deities who represent them. It can be used to pour small amounts into the cauldron (see below). You must only drink from *this* chalice when you wish to share in the communion of the dead. Such drink is often accompanied by spirit visions and intense dreams. The chalice represents the element of Water.

The Spirit Rattle or Bell

Sound is often used to help call the spirits. In my own practice, I use a papier-mâché rattle that was made by an artist into the head of Anubis, the Egyptian guide and guardian of the dead. In the Voodoo still practiced today in Haiti, the Houngans (priests) and Mambos (priestesses) use the sacred Asson rattle, much like magicians might use a wand, to raise spiritual energy and to invite the spirits to participate in the ritual. In traditional European magic, a bell was the tool of choice for using sound to invoke the spirits. It was also used to banish them in rituals of exorcism, though I prefer a rattle for this as well. Sometimes, Witches will use a drum to raise the spirits. Whatever your preference, it's important to have some ritual sound tool to work with the dead.

The Cauldron

In ancient rituals of the dead, a fire pit was often used to make offerings to the spirits. For the altar of the dead, we will use the cast iron cauldron, preferably with three legs. The cauldron is a symbol of the great womb of creation, hearkening back to the days when mother goddesses were worshipped for their creative powers. The cauldron contains the mighty powers of death and rebirth. Your cauldron will be used to burn spells written on parchment asking for the dead to grant your wishes. You will also put some of the offerings to the dead into the cauldron, particularly offerings of your own blood (only a few drops are needed!), honey milk, wine, olive oil, and other offerings, some of which may be poured from the chalice or a libation bottle. You may also create a fire in the cauldron to see visions of the dead in rites of necromancy, which you'll learn about in chapter 9. Just be careful not to allow too much fire, and be sure to place the cauldron on a ceramic tile so as not to damage your altar. As with any fire, whether candle or cauldron, never leave it unattended. The cauldron itself is a symbol of Water, but when we add the element of Fire, we combine the powers of divine masculine and feminine to ignite the spark of life—attracting the dead like moths to a flame.

Spirit Incense and Burner

It is good to keep powdered spirit incense to burn over charcoal in an incense burner. I recommend my Necromancy Incense, which is listed in appendix A. Incense further carries your will and intention into the realms of spirit. I prefer granular incense that is sprinkled onto a disk of charcoal within a small pot or cauldron. Stick incense is acceptable as well, as long as it contains ingredients of spirit such as wormwood, copal, dittany, and myrrh. If you're using a burner with powdered incense, add a bit of sand to the bowl and place a ceramic tile underneath it so the heat from the charcoal doesn't damage the bowl or the altar.

Spirit Powder

Spirit powder is used to create a boundary of sacred space. You sprinkle it much like some traditions of magic would sprinkle salt, in an area—preferably circular—around where you're going to be doing your magic. There is a powerful recipe for this in appendix A. As you'll learn in the chapter on necromancy, it's important to create boundaries through which only benevolent spirits may pass. There are energies out there that are not conducive to your work, and using a barrier of spirit powder creates both a physical and spiritual boundary through which only that which is true and pure shall enter!

A Jar of Honey

Honey is one of the best ways to sweeten your relationship to the spirits. It is one of the oldest ways in history to honor and make offerings to the dead—so much so that it should always be on your altar.

Skeleton Keys

Skeleton keys, especially those once used by people who have passed over, can also open doors to other worlds. In New Orleans Voodoo, Papa Lebas (who corresponds to the Haitian Legba) is the keeper of the crossroads, often represented by Saint Peter with his equilateral cross of keys. Having them on the altar symbolizes the opening of doors.

Anointing Oil

Use anointing oil to bless ritual tools, statues, the skull, and your person in the ritual space. See appendix A for a recipe for anointing oil.

Candles

Some Witchcraft traditions observe strict guidelines on what candles should be where on an altar, but the ancestral altar is flexible. Typically, the candles on the altar at HEX are seven-day candles in glass, decorated with imagery of various ancestors, deities, or magical intentions. If you don't have such candles, simple white and black candles will do. A white candle on the right of the altar sends out energy and honors the dead, while a black candle on the left draws in universal light and wisdom.

There are many more tools that you can incorporate into your magic that are beyond the scope of this book, but I urge you to personalize your magic by seeking those items that speak to you, draw upon your own ethnic bloodlines and traditions, or are essential symbols of those spirits you are hoping to build relationships with. Just as you get to know your friends in this world, get to know your new friends in spirit and discover what they relate best to!

5

Banishing and Exorcism

Working with the dead opens doorways to other worlds. It rings a bell that lets the spirits know that you're here and ready to work with them. Unfortunately, you aren't just alerting spirits that you may actually want to work with; you're also getting the attention of some that might not be so friendly. Those kinds of spirits love to cause trouble. Some may already be lying dormant around you, silently creeping about your home, waiting to be awakened by your magical dabbling. This is why it is so important to understand how to rid your home of spirits when they begin to cause problems.

The best offense, as they say, is a good defense, and so you need to know how to keep yourself safe from supernatural dangers. One of the best ways you can do this is to enter into your visionary state and visualize an energy shield of protection around your body that strengthens your own aura—the psychic energy field that surrounds all living things. Another is to carry protective jewelry, charms, and other accoutrements of magic that harmful spirits have learned to recognize and fear, much like the vampires in movies recoil from the cross.

The skills of psychic protection, banishing, and exorcism are crucial to magic, so if you're looking to study them more in depth, I recommend Dion Fortune's 1930 classic *Psychic Self-Defense*. In the meantime, this chapter should provide you with the basic information you need to keep yourself safe and sound as you make your exploration into the worlds of the dead. To begin, it's important to figure out what you're dealing with.

Unwelcome Spirits

While the work you do will draw many good spirits to your altar, you might not want some of them around. Such unwanted visitors can be very hard to dismiss. Angry spirits can often be strong and take more effort to usher off. Other spirits, regardless of their intentions, may be energized by peculiar energies of place. This is one reason why certain places become haunted—the dead are able to use place and land as an anchor in the physical world, especially in those places to which they had a personal connection. It is important to close the doorway to the spirit realms after the dead have been summoned and business is concluded lest an entity that you don't want to contend with comes wandering through.

The restless and unquiet dead can cause a host of unpleasant phenomena, such as apparitions, cold spots, unexplained sounds, shadowy figures, movement and misplacement of objects, breaking and throwing of objects, mental disturbances, nightmares, and interferences with anything electrical.

The ancients respected and feared the dead, recognized the dangers of working with them, and had ways of heading trouble off at the pass. Some cultures even performed entire festivals to exorcise the dead, such as the Roman Lemuria or the Anthesteria of Greece (see chapter 13). If you maintain your boundaries and keep your psychic shields up, you are not likely to have many difficulties. However, exceptions may arise; let's look at ways both supernatural and scientific to send unwanted spirits packing.

Eliminating Natural Causes

Sometimes what you think is a spirit presence is not one at all. When your attention is focused on the unseen, it is tempting to interpret every creaking floorboard and chill breeze as paranormal. If you are experiencing phenomena, first eliminate all possible natural causes. Changes in climate can make a house creak, especially during certain times of the year as ground contracts and swells, and humidity levels change. Poorly fitting doors and windows can cause strange breezes and abrupt closings. Odd smells can sometimes seep into a house from outside sources. What might seem like the fetid stench of malevolent spirits could just be a dead rat in your central heating system.

You also must honestly ask yourself if your own imagination is involved. It's easy to unwittingly fill in blanks when it comes to the supernatural world. We all want to believe. And sometimes it's just plain tempting to dine out on embellished, creepy ghost stories and be the center of attention; but, as I mentioned in chapter 2, the occult should not become a crutch for the needy. You impede your own development if you mire yourself in delusion.

Spirit of Place Residue versus Hauntings

Not all supernatural phenomena that you might experience are the products of an active spirit. In fact, most of what we call hauntings are actually the residual energy called "spirit of place." That is, they are the psychic "vibes," both good and bad, left behind by the living, much like the photos, videos, and audio recordings of ourselves that we leave behind after we are gone. Witches believe strongly in the spirit of place, and the energy of all those who have been in a place, whether they are dead or still living. Psychic residues cling to places, seeping into the very fabric of the land, homes, and objects in the area. They are neither conscious nor intelligent, and they can often fade away over time, though this might take centuries.

Sometimes, psychic residues lie below our threshold of awareness until we begin our psychic or magical workings, both of which increase our subtle senses. Trafficking with the dead may increase your sensitivity to spirit of place residues already in existence. However, if your home was free of supernatural activity until you started working with the dead, then you are probably not dealing with residues, but rather with active presences that have entered through the spiritual doorway you opened. Active presences react to you and your thoughts and actions, and can impose themselves on you and your environment when their intentions are impure.

A number of years ago, the *Boston Herald* asked me to perform an exorcism at the site of the infamous Danvers State Mental Hospital, which had at that time recently been converted to apartments. Apparently fires were breaking out in the new construction and some were saying that this was the result of ghosts. Having investigated the location in the past, I did not believe that it was haunted. In fact, I told the reporters that the energies present at the former asylum were in fact the residual energies of the spirit of place. I believe that the ghosts there have largely moved on but that the suffering is still contained in every particle of the building. The cure, I told them, was for the people living there to live the best lives they could and create good energy where it once was bad. For all of you who get "bad vibes" in your home or another place, remember that you have the power to make those energies transform. We are shapeshifters. We bend and turn energies to our advantage.

Spirit Attachments to Objects

Occasionally, spirits can attach themselves to physical objects. No matter how emphatically you tell the spirits to go, they won't budge as long as they have their "house." This is similar to the residual energy in objects that the practice of psychometry helps us to detect, but in this case, it's actually a spirit. As part of a paranormal investigation hosted by The Biography Channel's *Dead Famous,* Shawn and I encountered a haunted chair in one of the rooms of the old Salem Witch House, the only existing home with ties to the trials of 1692, as it was the home of Witch Trials Judge Jonathan Corwin. Psychic medium

Chris Fleming, cohost of the show, picked up a lot of spirit energy around this chair, and it became clear to all of us that this was just such an attachment.

Spirits can attach to literally anything. Spirits sometimes ride in on objects, especially those that are acquired secondhand. Something you buy for your altar of the dead—including the furniture itself—may have some invisible residents that come in through the back door, so to speak. In particular, spirits may be able to attach to objects on your altar, especially if they have a strong personal connection to an item. It is not necessarily a terrible thing that spirits want to be attached to objects, but if the spirits are harmful or bear ill will, this can cause problems. Such attached objects require cleansings (see below) or, in severe cases, proper disposal.

In some cases, spirit-attached objects can assist us in our magical work. You will sometimes want a bit of a soul's energy in a ring or other spiritually energized object that once belonged to a powerful Witch or someone you loved and respected. Sometimes, objects can become portals of communication to the spirit world. My friend Ken Glover has a puppet named Myrna, formed from clay over three days to look like a skeletal reaper. He made it with a friend who later died of complications from AIDS, and the now-deceased friend's old t-shirt went to make Myrna's clothes. Over the years, Ken has used this puppet to communicate to people when and how they are to die or if serious illnesses are on the way. Myrna's accuracy has been rather astounding. When my late friend Shawn Poirier asked Myrna when he would die, the puppet predicted a near-fatal carbon monoxide leak that, while it didn't kill Shawn, preceded his actual death by only three days. Personally, I don't speak to Myrna. I don't want to know.

Spirit Attachments to People

The most dangerous unwanted spirits are those that attach to people. Once they have invaded your energy field, they can psychically infect your entire being, wreaking havoc on your thoughts, mood, behavior, and even health. The level of intrusion can range from mischievous tricks as it follows you around;

to oppression, in which your thoughts and mental stability are constantly affected; to full-blown physical possession. We usually associate possession with nonhuman spirits, but the dead can take possession as well. You are unlikely to find your head spinning or spitting up pea soup like Linda Blair in *The Exorcist*, but you can become "not you." If you have reason to think that a spirit has latched on to you or anyone you know, take immediate action (see below).

Simple Solutions for Ridding Yourself of Unwanted Spirits

The following simple remedies are all effective ways of taking control of the situation, but not necessarily against all spirits, or in all cases. You may have to try more than one before you succeed, and if the simple solutions don't work, a full-blown exorcism may be necessary.

Assert Yourself

Turn up the attitude. This may sound simple, but asking or telling an unwanted spirit to leave works in most cases. Be polite yet firm, and let invasive spirits know that you are the master of your space. The physical world belongs to the living, and you have the upper hand.

Put 'Em to Work!

When I have unwanted spirits around, I give them tasks to do. While you should always prefer to work with spirits you have an amicable relationship with, if you've got annoying ghosts around, find something for them to do. Go to your altar of the dead, give these meddlesome spirits some offerings, and build a relationship with them so that they, too, can exercise your will.

Cleanse and Purify Your Space

Changing the psychic vibration in a space can make it difficult for unwanted spirits to remain. There are a number of simple rituals you can do to cleanse and purify a space.

Ritual: Cleansing

The following are rituals you can use to purify your space of unwanted spirits.

- Take a lighted white candle and go from room to room, walking the perimeter of each. Then crisscross each room from corner to corner, forming the equilateral cross in the form of an "X." Command all unwanted presences to immediately depart. Seal each room by visualizing white light around it in a visionary state. Give a blessing of protection, asking that only the invited may enter: *Spirits of an impure heart, I now command you to depart!*

- Place a bowl of water near your front door with four camphor cubes in the bowl. Change the water daily and the cubes as needed. Clean-smelling and repugnant to harmful energies, camphor cubes can be found at most botanicas.

- Using red thread, hang iron scissors or a cross of iron coffin nails near every entrance to your home.

- Place crystals in rooms. Hematite and obsidian are considered protective stones, so those are fantastic to use. Avoid black onyx entirely, as it absorbs and amplifies malefic energies. Clear quartz helps to keep spiritual energies clean.

• • •

Cleanse Objects

In a visionary state, sense the energy of objects that may be causing trouble—including furniture and the tools of your altar—and cleanse them, if necessary, with a mixture of spring water and kosher salt (adding a small amount of extra-virgin olive oil if it's wood). You can leave an item buried in kosher salt during a waning moon. After this, place the item outside in the sunlight to energize it anew. Objects that are truly "cursed," or that are at least beyond your ability to manage, may require more serious help, or even disposal of the object. Before disposing, bury in kosher salt for three days during a waning moon and then bury it at a desolate place where it can do no more harm.

Keep Yourself Clean!

Far too many people these days don't shower as much as they should. Remember, your body is a temple, not a garbage scow. For the sake of everyone around you, including the spirits, bathe regularly! And, for the record, patchouli does not equal soap. To add a magical element to your daily rites of hygiene, take a palm full of kosher salt and add it to your bath. Or, sprinkle it in the bottom of the shower and swish your feet in it. It's also a good idea to bathe at night before you go to bed. This can help rid yourself of any psychic ooze that has affixed itself to you during the day.

Invoke Spiritual Help

Ask the gods, angels, spiritual teachers, or those spirits you have good relationships with to intercede on your behalf. Your faith can be a powerful way to rid yourself of bad spirits.

Ritual: The Roman Ritual of the Beans

This spell was done on the final night of the seven-day festival of Lemuria, on May 15th, by the head of the household so that he might exorcise unwanted spirits. We invite you to try this ritual when the unquiet dead are simply not leaving you or your family alone.

In the middle of the night, wash your hands three times and place three black beans—an important food of the dead—in your mouth. Walk barefoot through your house, tossing more black beans over your shoulder and calling out: *With these beans I do redeem me and mine.*

Repeat this incantation nine times, and never look back. While you are doing this, keep one hand closed in the sign of the horns—the thumb crossed over the two middle fingers and the index finger, and the little finger extended—which wards off both the evil eye and evil spirits. Your final stop should be through your front door, where you should spit the three beans in your mouth outside the house. The spirits will follow your trail of beans and depart the house with you. Now, turn and go inside. To conclude, wash your hands again three times and then bang a brass cymbal (you can also use your ritual bell or rattle for this) and command all unwanted presences to depart! Later, pick up the beans and deposit them at a local graveyard.

• • •

Exorcism

When things get really tough, there is one final technique used to rid a space of unwanted spirits. The rites of exorcism are far older than those of the Church and are powerful ways of ridding your life of nasty ghosts and harmful energies once and for all.

In early 2011, Sicilian hereditary Strega Lori Bruno and I were asked by the *Wall Street Journal* to perform a house blessing on a recent foreclosure property that the new owner felt had a bad vibe. Lori and I brought the implements of exorcism and first went through the house to get a sense of where the problem areas were. We discovered that this was a classic case of the psychic pollution of the spirit of place. There weren't any ghosts there; just the residual muck of emotional suffering that had seeped into the very structure of the building. This did not comfort us, though—sometimes that form of energy is even harder to get rid of than spirits, because it lacks a definitive consciousness and cannot be reasoned with or frightened. It must be rooted out by the sheer will of the sorcerers involved. Lori wielded a large, loud bell and the sheer strength of her powerful voice as she conjured the powers of the four elements and the archangel Michael, while I brandished the ritual sword of the late Strega, Dr. Leo Louis Martello, which Lori has passed to me that I might use it for justice. With much effort and strength, we wrested control of the house back from the malefic powers that had held dominion over it. The owner was quite grateful and Lori and I were featured on the cover of the *Wall Street Journal*.

The power we call on for this ritual is Saint Michael. Before you stop and say, "Well, isn't this one of the archangels of the Catholic Church," remember that the Church layered many of its practices on older religious and magical customs and even built its churches over the sites of temples of old. The veneration of Saint Michael—who is properly an archangel rather than a saint, since the latter is the venerated dead—is no exception to this. Michael, whose name means "who is like God," is often seen with a spear or sword, standing over a demon he's about to slay. This represents Michael's power over the forces of evil. Michael is also often seen with a sword and scales, symbolizing his role as the enforcer of truth, fairness, and justice.

A number of scholars have argued that Michael's roots are pre-Christian, though they don't always agree on what those roots are. Michael has been traced back to Mithra, the Persian god of war.[3] He's been compared to Marduk, "Babylonian deity of the springtime sun," who, like Christ, was said to rise again from death and, like Michael, was associated with slaying a great devil—in this case, the dragon Tiamat.[4] Connections have been drawn between Saint Michael and the Sumerian Mukhla, invincible warrior and archangel of the Sun god, and to Miok, son of the Norse god Thor. He also appears as the solar angel Mikalu on the coins of the European Phoenicians of Cicilia as early as 500 BCE.[5] Finally, much of Michael's imagery, especially the scales and the spear, have tied him to the great Egyptian Anubis, guide of the dead.[6] So it all comes full circle. By having dominion over the dark spirits, Michael also becomes a guide to those dead who lived nobler lives. From a scholarly perspective, all of these competing origins for Michael may seem confusing. From a spiritual perspective, it merely lends evidence that this being does in fact exist and that he has been called by many faiths and by many names.

Ritual: The Ritual of Exorcism

Strega Lori Bruno taught this rite of exorcism to me and I pass it to you. You will need:

- A red candle for Saint Michael, preferably a seven-day candle with his image on it.
- A bowl of water small enough for you to carry around.
- A bowl of kosher salt, also small enough for you to carry around.

- Incense and burner, preferably a swinging censer. The incense should be a basic purification blend of one part frankincense, one part myrrh, and one part benzoin. Spirit conjuring incense *should not* be used here.
- A sword or dagger made of iron or steel. The bronze dagger would be too soft for this purpose. Be sure to tie a red thread to the handle with nine knots. The red thread has long been a powerful ward against dark powers, so much so that it has been popularized anew by modern students of Kabbalah.
- Your ritual bell or spirit rattle. The bell is more traditional and Lori prefers that, but I prefer the rattle.

Prepare the ritual by going into a visionary state (see chapter 2). Now, start by blessing the water. Add a small palm full of kosher salt to the water and mix it with your right hand. Then, draw a pentagram (five-pointed star) over the surface of the water, beginning at the top point and moving down to the lower left, ending at the top point again. Now, make the sign of the equilateral cross, and draw a circle around both, clockwise, saying, *I bless this water by the power of my will and the might of Michael the Archangel that it rid this space of all evil!* You must say this with the strongest feeling and determination you have ever felt. The most powerful ingredient in this ritual is you!

Draw another invoking pentagram and cross onto the surface of the bowl of salt, saying, *I bless this salt by the power of my will and the might of Michael the Archangel that it rid this space of all evil!* Draw yet another invoking pentagram over the incense, saying, *I bless this incense by the power of my will and the might of Michael the Archangel that it rid this space of all evil!* Draw a final invoking pentagram over the candle, saying, *I bless this candle by the power of my will and the might of Michael the Archangel that it rid this space of all evil!* This may seem repetitive, but it is in the repetition that your mind is reinforcing the mental will and power necessary for the work at hand.

To begin the ritual, walk through each room of the house with the bowl of kosher salt. Sprinkle the salt into all four corners of the room and say, *By the element of Earth, the power of my will, and the might of Michael the Archangel, I banish all evil and harm from here!*

Walk through each room again, this time with the incense. Swing the censer into each corner of the room (or raise up a censer that you're holding) and say, *By the element of Air, the power of my will, and the might of Michael the Archangel, I banish all evil and harm from here!*

Now, light the candle and say, *By this sacred flame, so shall the element of fire cleanse and purify this space!* Walk through each room with the candle. Raise it to each corner of the room and say, *By the element of Fire, the power of my will, and the might of Michael the Archangel, I banish all evil and harm from here!*

Walk through each room again, this time with the bowl of water. Sprinkle the water into each corner of the room with your right hand and say, *By the element of Water, the power of my will, and the might of Michael the Archangel, I banish all evil and harm from here!*

Now, go into each room with the bell or rattle and loudly ring or shake it, saying, *Let all things evil that hear this sound depart from this space at once! At my command and by the might of Michael the Archangel, I banish all evil and harm from here!*

Go into each room a final time with the sword or dagger, and at each window and each door that leads outside the home, draw an equilateral cross in the air before the window and say, *With this sword and the power of my will, I call upon the great might of Michael the Archangel, that he may forever protect this home from all evil and harm! Let all who would dare bring evil here fall upon the blade of this sword!*

Finally, go to all doors that lead outside the home and sprinkle kosher salt along the threshold and say, *By this salt of Earth, the power of my will, and the might of Michael the Archangel, I consecrate this threshold, that it serve as a shield against all evil and harm. Let no evil dare enter here! So mote it be . . . from now until eternity!*

The ritual is now complete. As Lori and I do, a team of people can perform this ritual, with a person assigned to each element, the bell, and the sword. Consult some of the simpler methods of protection discussed earlier in this chapter to keep your home or other space free from malefic energy. After you are done with this ceremony, take a ritual bath with kosher salt or a shower with kosher salt sprinkled about your feet. This will cleanse you of any residual psychic filth.

. . .

Get Help from Others

There are times when even the most experienced Witches have to consult others. It can sometimes be difficult to be objective when you're under spiritual attack. If several attempts at banishment or exorcism do not succeed, do not hesitate to consult other Witches, mediums, exorcists, and similar experts. They may have favored methods and tools that will work better in your specific situation. If you think a spirit has attached itself to you and you haven't been able to rid yourself of it, get outside help *immediately*.

6

Methods of Spirit Contact

Now that your altar of the dead is set up and you're beginning to use it, you're probably wondering how to find out what the dead have to say to you. Throughout this book, you will learn ways of interacting with the dead, but the following methods are considered among the easiest ways to understand what the spirits of the departed are trying to tell you. Remember, it's probably good that you've familiarized yourself with the methods of banishing and exorcism in the previous chapter. Before you open a door, know how to close it!

Automatic Writing and Automatisms

Visit any Spiritualist church fair and you will often find psychics who are able to create spirit drawings and other such physical records of supernatural phenomena, including written messages and symbols. Such communications are referred to as automatisms. The most popular of these is automatic writing, where a spirit is said to move through the body of the writer in order to spell out what the departed soul is trying to say.

Automatisms are a variety of unconscious muscular movement often attributed to supernatural guidance. They include virtually any physical activity, but usually refer to creative activities such as writing, drawing, painting, speaking, playing musical instruments, composing, dancing, and singing. Some psychologists see automatisms as an expression of a person's own subconscious—often referred to as an ideomotor response. However, it is hard to explain away some of the more extraordinary cases, especially those where a person provides information or exhibits a talent beyond his training, reach, and knowledge.

Automatisms can be stimulated through ritual as a deliberate and direct way of channeling the spirits. Either the anonymous dead or a specific dead personality can be invited to use a person's body through a unique form of temporary possession. (This form of automatism is called mediumship, explored in the next chapter.)

Automatisms sometimes start spontaneously, and if allowed to continue, can become increasingly more inspired and sophisticated. For example, in 1924 a seven-year-old English girl named Rosemary Brown was visited in a dream by the ghost of composer Franz Liszt—who had died in 1886. The composer told Rosemary that when she grew up, he would come back and bring her music. At age seven, she had no idea who Liszt even was.

Brown later married, had children, and led quite an ordinary life. Her husband died in 1961. In 1964, she was in an automobile accident during which several ribs were broken. While recuperating, she spent time playing her piano—something she had not done for twelve years.

Suddenly the spirit of Liszt sat beside her and guided her hands to play flawless music entirely unfamiliar to her. Brown soon found herself in an automatism of channeling music, including new compositions, from other dead musical greats: Bach, Berlioz, Brahms, Chopin, Debussy, Grief, Mozart, Monteverdi, Rachmaninoff, Schubert, and Schumann.

Brown's talent expanded. She took dictation in automatic writing, recording the words of famous persons such as playwright George Bernard

Shaw, psychiatrist Carl G. Jung, and physicist Albert Einstein. Artists drew and painted through her as well.

Brown baffled the experts, even though some tried to say she was just imitating styles she knew. She died in 2001, her legacy still a mystery.

EXERCISE: AUTOMATIC WRITING

Automatic writing is one of the easiest methods of automatism and can often bring astounding results. To begin, gather a pen and a piece of paper. I prefer those rollerball style pens that are easy to grip and yet glide smoothly across the page. You should probably bless with anointing oil any pen that you use, and make sure that there is nothing written on the pen that could interfere with its energy. Find a comfortable chair and sit in a straight upright position at a desk or table; then hold the pen over the paper as you normally would hold it.

Close your eyes and descend into a visionary state (see chapter 2). Embrace the energies of the Death Current as you begin to feel the spirit forces moving in the space around you. Let their energies come into you and flow through your entire body. You will begin to feel as though other forces are layering themselves over your consciousness. If spirits are present, the pen will likely begin to move, writing out messages. Do not attempt to force the movement, for you shall prevent the spirits from coming through. Your consciousness must take a back seat for this process to work.

When the writing stops, come back up from the visionary state. Look over the paper. Is there anything written that makes sense to you? Look for drawings and symbols. Did the spirit draw an actual face? If so, it could be the face of the spirit itself or someone he wants you to know about. Save all such writings in a binder or scrapbook so that you can look back to see if patterns emerge.

. . .

The Pendulum

One of the oldest and simplest forms of divination and spirit communication, the pendulum remains popular. At HEX and OMEN we sell many pendulums of copper, brass, and a myriad of styles made of different kinds of crystals and stones. I personally prefer the simple copper coil for its powers as an energy conductor, while you might prefer one made of quartz crystal, moonstone, rose quartz, or amethyst.

To use a pendulum, you simply hold it in your hand or over a pendulum board in a visionary state and wait for it to move. Typically, the answers are said to come from your inner, spiritual self or from your subconscious. To use it as a necromantic tool, you simply need to affirm at the beginning of the session that you are using the pendulum to contact the dead.

To begin, find a pendulum that works for you. It also helps to get a board; you can program the pendulum to answer you according to the layout on the board. Typically, a pendulum board will designate "Yes," "No," "Maybe," and "Ask Again." Without a board, you could simply affirm that a clockwise circle means yes while a counterclockwise circle means no, though there is no hard and fast rule on how the pendulum will work for you—and the spirits may have their own ideas.

Descend into a visionary state and, once there, open your eyes and hold the pendulum in whichever hand you write with. Hold it as still as you can by the top of its chain. Ask the spirits your question; if you have a specific person you wish to contact, ask for him by name. Wait patiently, and the pendulum should start to move in the direction that corresponds to your answer.

The Ouija Board

Of all the necromantic tools, none is more maligned, misunderstood, and misused than the infamous Ouija board. Thanks largely to the sensational fictions of Hollywood and the media—as well as misinformed "experts"—the Ouija board has come to be regarded as a problematic device that can open a doorway to demonic entities eager to torment and possess the living. The late demonologist Ed Warren once called the Ouija board a proven "notorious passkey to terror." From my perspective, however, the negativity has been blown *way* out of proportion.

While it's true that using the Ouija can result in the kinds of problems we discussed in the previous chapter, those warnings apply to *any* method for conjuring spirits. I do not believe that the Ouija board is uniquely hazardous. That being said, if you have a hard time getting past your personal fears about the board, it's best to skip it as a tool of spirit contact in favor of a method you feel more comfortable with. For the bold and fearless, the Ouija can serve a useful purpose. Just remember, any spirit work will open doors, so be ready to handle the results!

"Ouija" is a trademarked name for a mystical parlor game and mediumship device created in late nineteenth-century Baltimore. It was also known as the William Fuld Talking Board, named for the man who would bring the game to people worldwide and later referred to as the "Father of the Ouija Board."[7] In 1927, Fuld died in a freak accident at work. He fell off the roof of his three-story company building, and died from his injuries. The company remained in the Fuld family until 1966, when it was sold to Parker Brothers and produced right here in Salem! In 1967, the Ouija Board was the best-selling board game in America, outselling even Monopoly. Hasbro bought Parker Brothers in 1991, and today the Ouija is marketed as purely entertainment.

The generic terms for Ouija are "talking board" or "spirit board." The board employs a person's body, so using one can be considered a method of automatism. Its operation is simple: a board printed with letters of the alphabet; numbers; the words "yes," "no," "hello," and "good-bye"; and a pointer—called a planchette—on three legs that sits atop the board. Typically, two or more people place their fingertips lightly on the planchette, ask questions of the board, and hope that the spirits will answer by moving the planchette and spelling out words. Skeptics contend that eager users subconsciously push the planchette themselves, but those who have gotten results know that "something" other than the living is facilitating the process.

The origin of the name "Ouija" is not clear. According to one story, one of the people who helped bring the Ouija to popularity, Charles Kennard, was given the name by a spirit while he was using the board with a lady friend. Original Ouija patent lawyer, Elijah Bond, referred to the Ouija as "The Egyptian Luck Board," and some claimed that "Ouija" was Egyptian for good luck. Fuld later claimed it was the combination of the French Oui and German Ja—a "yes yes" board that would always answer you.

The Ouija is the modern answer to the ancient pointing and spelling devices used for divination. In the past, such devices were used by specially trained diviners or priests, who served as mediums between worlds. Today, anyone who visits a local toy store can be the medium in the sanctuary of her own living room.

Fears of the Ouija Board

Mediums were initially afraid to see the Ouija placed in the hands of the public—not because of any "demonic" threat, but because it took business out of their spirit parlors. Who would come and pay for readings when anyone could contact the dead at home? After World War I, the Ouija was especially in demand by those who were grieving their war dead. It was also marketed as home entertainment: advertisements showed happy families or romantic settings with participants cozily playing with the board in front of the hearth fire. In particular, the board's use as a tool of love divination was promoted, since the age-old questions of "does he/she love me" and "who will I marry" have been among the goals of divination tools throughout history.

On the flip side, occasional newspaper articles did tell of obsessions with the Ouija factoring into personal tragedies and crimes. People blamed the board when they went insane or committed theft and even murder. Ministers denounced the Ouija board as evil.

An example of one murder case was the sensational "Ouija Board Killing," which took place in Biggs, California, in 1923. A woman became obsessed with the board, claiming it told her that her husband was having an affair. Apparently, the entities communicating through the board informed her that her husband was planning to murder her with an axe. Petrified, she shot him to death. She testified at her trial that she shot him first before he could kill her. She was convicted and sentenced to ten years in prison. In all likelihood, there was no affair or plans for an axe murder–just a paranoid, unstable wife who probably suspected her husband of cheating, and found "corroboration" through her reckless dabbling. This is a perfect example of why you must keep your mind free from delusion when working with spirits!

Nonetheless, many thousands of people quietly used boards without problems. Some found it to be a springboard to creativity, channeling "voices" that turned into literary works. In 1913, Pearl Curran, a St Louis housewife, began receiving communications from "Patience Worth," a sixteenth-century English spinster, via the Ouija. Worth, speaking in an old English dialect, dictated an astounding volume of poetry and novels. In 1919, Betty and Stewart Edward White were using the Ouija as a lark with friends, when suddenly Betty was instructed to "get a pencil" and take dictation. The entities coming through identified themselves as the "Invisibles," higher beings who dispensed metaphysical wisdom. Stewart compiled it into *The Betty Book*. In 1963, Jane Roberts was using the Ouija when she met Seth, who purported to be a highly evolved entity who later dictated very popular books on metaphysics. Pulitzer Prize-winning poet James Merrill composed his epic *The Changing Light at Sandover* from two decades of spirit communications via the Ouija. And author Ruth Montgomery began her channeling with the Ouija, then moved to automatic typing for her books on ETs, walk-ins, and New Age phenomena.

By the 1960s, Hollywood began to see the Ouija as a convenient and eye-catching device to feature bad spirits as the villains. Movies such as *Thirteen Ghosts* cast the board in sinister roles, manipulated by evil-minded entities. But the film that did the most to forever alter public perception of the board was *The Exorcist* (1973), based on the novel by William Peter Blatty. Blatty's tale of a demonically possessed girl was in turn based on the documented case of the possession of a young boy, who may have used a Ouija board with his aunt prior to her death. In the film, the Ouija makes a brief but impacting appearance as the device that opens the doorway to the demonic world.

The Exorcist terrified audiences when it opened on a Christmas day. Some moviegoers fainted, and ministers once again denounced the Ouija as a device of the Devil. Going even further, claims were made that merely using the board once could invite legions of demons to plague and torment the user or even his entire household.

Once *The Exorcist* cemented the idea of the Ouija as a portal to evil, Hollywood continued to reinforce the perception that using a board brings nothing but trouble. I stress once again that this is *mis*perception. The Ouija is a tool, no more or less dangerous than any other method mentioned in this chapter.

Let the Spirit Move You!

I first met my friend Robert Murch in 1998 when he came to me with an idea for a talking board called Cryptique.® Murch wanted his board to be known as "A spirit board from Salem, Massachusetts." What better place to host the birth of such a board—the Ouija was made during my youth at the former Parker Brothers factory here in Salem.

I found Bob a fantastic designer, another friend of mine named Deborah Norris, who gave Cryptique a moody feel reminiscent of the graveyards of Salem. The planchette was shaped like a gravestone and featured the winged skull motif so commonly found carved on the headstones of New England cemeteries. I made some modifications to the design, built a website to promote the game that included an interactive version of the board, and offered writing and marketing help. At one point, even Toys "R" Us sold Cryptique on its website!

The high point of Cryptique was appearing with Bob and Shawn on Penn & Teller's show, *Bullshit!*, on the Showtime cable network! Sure, Penn & Teller made fun of us like they would any practitioner of the psychic arts, but we gave an accurate and positive portrayal of the Ouija board, and particularly of Cryptique, which host Penn Jillette described as "the perfect blend of death and the mall." Shawn and I used the board on the show, and the spirit of 1692 Witch Trials victim Bridget Bishop came through loud and clear. My favorite part of the evening was that the film crew's equipment kept breaking down, something that I had warned them would happen, and it did so in spite of the crew's response to my warnings that "this stuff never breaks down." Bridget had other plans, apparently.

Sadly, Cryptique is no longer produced, but Bob remains the world's foremost Ouija historian and continues to educate the curious about this fascinating parlor game.

My Own Experiences with the Ouija Board

I have fond childhood memories of Ouija boards, playing with my friends when the adults weren't paying attention. My mom hated them, and even threw away one that I had bought with my allowance. Like many moms, she had bought into the hype. She probably should have known I would turn out like I did when I was saving my weekly five dollars towards Ouija boards instead of comic books. When I began to study the Craft in my late teens, the Ouija made a return. My mentor Shawn Poirier and I sometimes used the board together, but it wasn't until Cryptique that the Ouija became a much larger part of my life.

In 2005, Shawn and I offered a Ouija workshop at *Contact*, a paranormal conference held at the Houghton Mansion in North Adams, Massachusetts, by author and ghost hunter Ron Kolek. After an enlightening workshop where Shawn and I both shared our perspectives on the board, he and I sat to use it. This notorious mansion is haunted by a number of people associated with the house who had died during accidents and suicide. The word S-W-O-R-D kept coming out on the board, and experts at the house told us that a sword had been missing from the home for some time. It was at that point that I began to slip from consciousness. I had been feeling very tired that day and should *not* have been using the board in that state. I began to feel like every muscle in my body was no longer under my control, some outside force directing my movement. Worse, my mind felt as though a dark, malevolent consciousness was layering itself over my own. I was quite scared! Luckily for me, Shawn was there to force whatever spirit was doing this away and bring me up out of the blackness. This was the closest I have ever come to possession and, to this day, I am extremely careful to only work with the spirits when I'm not tired. I'll still use a Ouija board, but tend to shy away from trance mediumship, preferring to remain in total control of what's going on around me. While the visionary state necessary to psychic work will relax you, being deeply relaxed is not the same as being tired. In the latter state, you place yourself in more danger of spirit meddling.

Perhaps my favorite experience using the Ouija board was when I first met paranormal author Rosemary Ellen Guiley. She was staying at an historic home here in Salem while researching a book. She asked me come over to conduct a Ouija séance to contact my departed friend, Shawn Poirier. I brought Robert the skull, my yew wand, and an old Ouija board of Shawn's that I figured might help in contacting him. Rosemary had a device I had never seen before called a ghost box, which cruises through the spectrum of radio waves looking for voices of the dead. She intended to use it after we used the Ouija, but I suggested we combine the two. I figured, what the heck—if Shawn decided not to come through the board, maybe I could hear him on the box. I try to always have a Plan B. The planchette zipped quickly around the board to spell out answers to our questions. But more exciting were the times when the planchette pointed to "yes" or "no" and the ghost box spoke those words at the very same time! We also experienced poltergeist effects manifesting throughout the room, including loud bangs and popping noises.

Rosemary and I felt the results were the product of a combination of factors: the place, with its haunted history; the instant rapport between the two of us; and the combined energies of the board, the skull, and the ghost box. I truly hoped to make contact with Shawn, and really thought having his board might facilitate the connection. Sadly, Shawn didn't come through, but other spirits did. This is typical of any spirit session: you don't always get who you ask for, and the reasons may depend simply on the conditions of the moment as well as factors we do not understand about how the openings between worlds occur. Towards the end of the session, I began to get direct mental messages from spirits; the use of the board helped to catalyze the spirit energy of the room and helped me to create a direct channel.

Proper Use of the Board

If you approach the Ouija respectfully, as you would any spirit communication tool, you will have few, if any, difficulties. Any such device can attract low-level entities who wish only to engage in mischief, and the talking board is no different in that respect. Follow the same guidelines that I recommend for all spirit communications. Be rested and well grounded; invoke spiritual protection; set a purpose for the communication; and do not tolerate interfering presences. If the spirits become belligerent or you feel the energy take an angry or unsettling turn, end the session at once.

Always work with one or more partners (two at a time is ideal; if you have a small group, participants can trade off). It also helps to have a person taking notes. People who use the board alone tend to become obsessed with it, which can lead to spiritual disturbances and mental problems.

Always begin using the board by descending into a visionary state (see chapter 2). You and your partner(s) should each place your fingers lightly on the planchette, ask the question, and wait for response. Allow the planchette to glide around the board without trying to direct it, even if it spells out nonsensical words. What may seem like gibberish can actually make sense later. It may take a while—or even several sessions—for a "breakthrough" communication to be established from the Other Side.

The Ouija can be a tedious method of communication, since responses are spelled out letter by letter. Much as I love the idea of the Ouija board, I often find using it to be the psychic form of cell phone text messaging, and I can't imagine how Pearl Curran turned out several books with one. Still, because one employs a lot of body action when using a board, the Ouija can also be more productive than some other methods, with fast contact. Two persons who are well tuned to the spirit world and to each other can often have amazing sessions. The board also can be combined with other tools, such as EVP recording, ghost boxes, and skulls. If you choose the Ouija as a method of spirit communication, just remember to approach it as any other tool, with respect for the process and for the spirits who come through.

Spirit Scrying

I saved my favorite tool of spirit communication for last. Scrying is a most ancient form of divination and spirit contact that involves gazing into a shiny or polished surface, such as a crystal ball, mirror, stone, or vessel of water or liquid. *Scrying* comes from the English term "descry," which means "to succeed in discerning" or "to make out dimly."

I use the classic concave (curved inward) black mirror, a large crystal ball, and water divination in my own scrying practices, but any shiny surface works. If you want to learn to scry, you might want to experiment until you find what works best for you. The oldest and most common method of scrying is to gaze into the water of a lake, pond, or dark bowl; the necromantic lakes of the ancient Greeks probably served such a purpose in conjuring up the dead. Spring water was particularly sacred to the dead, coming as it does from deep within the Earth where the underworld is said to be. Ancient Egyptians preferred bowls of ink, blood, and other dark liquids.

Nostradamus used a bowl of water set upon a brass tripod. He would dip his wand into the water and anoint himself with a few drops, and then gaze into the bowl until he saw visions of prophecy. John Dee, the royal magician and astrologer to Queen Elizabeth I, used a crystal egg and a black obsidian mirror to see the angels that would come to form the basis of his teachings.

There are many techniques for inducing visions. Whatever surface you use, it should be as blank as possible, and the device should be positioned so that you never see yourself in the reflection.

EXERCISE: SPIRIT SCRYING BY CRYSTAL BALL OR MIRROR

For this form of spirit scrying, I use a concave (curved in) black glass mirror (though some prefer convex or domed), or a crystal ball. Always bless and prepare your scrying devices by washing them in a tea of the divinatory herb mugwort. When scrying the dead, sit in a chair facing west with your scrying mirror or ball on a table covered with a black tablecloth. Place the device so that your reflection does not appear in it and place a white candle to the left of it so that just the smallest point of light appears within. This provides you with a focus point. Now, enter into your visionary state and allow the Death Current to flow through your body, so that the dead may hear your call and come forth.

The dead may show themselves as visions in the surface of the device or appear in the mind's eye. I have experienced both, but most of my scrying visions appear directly on my mental screen, the scrying tool itself becoming more of a focal point. You may only hear their voices in your mind but those messages are still valid, for it then becomes a form of mediumship, which we will explore more fully in the next chapter. Either way, when the dead arrive, be ready with serious questions so that you do not waste their time.

• • •

Exercise: Spirit Scrying by Bowl Divination

In the magical papyri of the ancient Greeks, there are powerful recipes for scrying in a bowl—referred to as lecanomancy. I have taken the best of these and boiled them down (no pun intended) to what I felt worked the best for spirit contact.

You will need a bronze bowl for this exercise. Any size will do; just make sure it's wide enough to see images within. You will also need a white candle, spring water (the waters of the dead), and the finest extra-virgin olive oil. Fill the bronze bowl most of the way with the spring water and be sure to have the olive oil nearby in a glass cruet.

Sit in a comfortable chair with the scrying bowl before a table covered with a black tablecloth. Enter your visionary state. Now, pour a small amount of oil into the water and say, *I conjure thee, oh spirit of [name of spirit]! Manifest yourself before me on this very hour and reveal to me the truth I seek!*

Watch the formations of the oil in the water. The patterns may form the faces of the spirit you have conjured, symbols that relate to your question, or outright visions of what you seek to know.

• • •

Exercise: Spirit Scrying by Candle Flame

Also contained within the Greek magical papyri are formulae for lychnomancy, or lamp divination. Rather than use a lamp, I prefer the candle, one of the most magical of all the sacred tools of the Witch. Shawn always taught me that the blue at the center of the candle flame was not only the hottest point; it was a doorway to spirit. Gaze into that point, he said, and your mind would travel to realms of the dead where all questions could be answered.

To perform this style of spirit scrying, place a white candle on a table covered with a black tablecloth, and make sure you anoint the candle with spirit oil. Sit in a comfortable chair and enter your visionary state. When fully relaxed, stare into the candle flame, directly at the blue center. Do this for a time until visions begin to appear. You will see things in the flame that seem to expand to fill your entire mind's eye. You may also hear voices and see the faces of those you hope to make contact with. Candle divination is an easy, powerful way to communicate with the shades of the dead!

• • •

7

Spirit Mediumship:
Speaking with the Dead

My first experience with spirit mediumship, the practice of receiving messages from the dead, was at nineteen years old when a friend and I attended a gathering at the local Spiritualist church here in Salem. This church specializes in mediumship and spirit communication and, instead of the style of worship you see at most churches, the dead are the focus of communion. Spirit mediums stand at the pulpit and point at people for whom they have messages and deliver them so that all can hear. The first woman who spoke on the night I attended pointed to a man who must have been ninety years old and said, "You there. You knew a Charlie once." I had to hold myself back from snickering, because I imagined the man must have known a hundred Charlies in his day. So far, I wasn't impressed.

But then, a woman came to the pulpit and pointed to me. She said that she felt the presence of a man who had died in violence and feelings of cold. Then she named a date in April. None of this made any sense to me, so I figured we were now running at two strikes. My friend, however, was white as a ghost. After we left, I asked her what was wrong, and she informed me that she had had a boyfriend several years before who had been murdered on the date the medium spoke of. I was truly shocked and wondered aloud how the medium would have chosen me to receive the message. I asked my friend more about the situation, and came to discover that my mother and I were living in the same apartment building as her boyfriend when he was murdered. While this incredible experience should have led me to explore the art of mediumship further, I actually stayed away from it.

For most of the first ten years or so of my twenty-three years of Witchcraft studies, I rarely dealt with the dead. The idea scared me, especially after my experience at the Spiritualist church—so my spells and rituals centered on more common magical methods and I would never have dreamed of conjuring the dead to aid me in any of it. That is, until 1998.

In 1995, I joined Shawn Poirier's Raven Moon Coven, which Leanne Marrama and I now keep alive in Shawn's absence. Shawn's family had taught him folk charms, spells, and psychic ability from a young age, but he also trained in the Spiritualist method with a gifted medium named Dottie. In 1998, I finally attended Shawn's annual Salem séance, "Messages from the Spirit World."

The event began with an introduction to spirit mediumship. Then, Shawn led everyone in an exercise of table tipping, an old Spiritualist technique for demonstrating the presence of the dead that involves the table moving, tilting, and even levitating off the ground by solely spiritual means. The participants in the séance got up in groups of three to try their hand at it, and most of them were successful in bringing the spirits through. When it was my turn, it was me, Shawn, and Salem Witch Jody Cabot with our hands on the table. Being a skeptic, I looked at the table to see if the other two were moving it, much like I did when my friends and I played on the Ouija board as children. It wasn't long before the table was coasting across the floor, tipping, and even bouncing. I turned white as a ghost. Up until this point, magic had been a very safe and regimented process for me. This was the first time I had personally experienced the physical manifestation of spirit. I was a believer. It was not until a few years later that I wholeheartedly embraced the spirit world, but I'll talk about that in chapter 10. After the table tipping, Shawn began to deliver the messages from the dead to each participant. I was absolutely blown away by Shawn's gifts. Shawn left no person without a message, and each was astounded at his accuracy. At the end of the event, we had to carry him out because he was so tired from communicating with so many spirits. Shawn had made a convert of me. I now knew the powers of the dead.

Styles of Mediumship

Spirit mediumship is the ability to communicate directly with the dead using your mind and body as the tools. It takes a variety of forms, and has most recently been popularized by such shows as *Crossing Over* with John Edward, books by Sylvia Brown, and the fictionalized television show *Medium* starring Patricia Arquette.

Most mediumship is mental; that is, the medium, in an altered state of consciousness, tunes in to the dead and receives words, images, and impressions that she then imparts to the living. Those who come to consult the psychics at OMEN, one of my shops here in Salem, often seek to contact their departed loved ones. This is the type of mediumship that my staff generally offers and also the type typically practiced by the popular mediums mentioned above. When this type of mediumship is done in a séance setting, it is referred to as "gallery style."

Less common is trance mediumship, a much more intense practice during which the medium goes into a deep trance and allows her entire body to become temporarily possessed. This is the type of mediumship most often depicted during the séances (or spirit sittings) featured in movies and television, probably because it has more dramatic effect. For this method, the spirits speak through the medium's vocal chords, and use her body to make gestures and movements. Sometimes a medium's actual appearance will change, and her face can even contort to mimic the shape and manner-isms of the spirit coming through.

Even more rare is physical mediumship. In these cases, truly wondrous spectacles may manifest in the physical world, such as ectoplasm, a viscous substance exuded from the medium's body that enables spirits to take on temporary form. Physical mediumship was quite popular during the peak of Spiritualism in second half of the nineteenth century. It declined during the twentieth century, but has been making a comeback in popularity in recent decades. Mediumship is still very much a part of many Spiritualist religious services; a Spiritualist minister is increasingly expected to have mediumistic abilities of mental, trance, and physical sorts, and to deliver messages from the dead to the congregation as part of the weekly worship service–though it is still primarily the mental style of gallery mediumship that you see at the churches now. During a séance held at OMEN, psychic medium Debra Free-man saw a strange, ethereal fog emanate from the back of the room and drift out of the workshop space and into the front of the shop! Participants were terrified, and Debra had to perform a spiritual cleansing to calm them down. Lorelei, a clairvoyant Witch who owns Salem's oldest Witch shop, Crow Haven Corner, did a circle to honor both my mother and hers in spirit the year my mother died. She was photographed just as she was calling the spirit and you can see a clearly visible, solid ring of ectoplasm hovering above her head in the photo.

While mediumship once seemed to be the domain of the Spiritualist church, many Witches today are mediums, and offer mediumistic services along with their traditional tools of Tarot, palmistry, runes, and clairvoyant visions. While it may seem that the Witch has adapted this practice into her repertoire–something Witches are known to be very good at–it is actu-ally the other way around. Witches have always been spirit communicators, going all the way back to the shamans and medicine people of the ancient world.

Ancient Mediums

The first mediums were the magicians and medicine people of early tribal cultures, who traveled between the realms of the living and the dead as one might walk from one room in the house to another. Masks and costumes were worn to embody the spirits, while strange potions and ointments were used to facilitate the shift in consciousness required to swim in the tides of the Death Current. Later, when such practices became frowned upon, mediumship became the domain of the Witch, conjuring the mighty dead in the dark of night, for those who dared seek her out. Scholars usually refer to such ancient mediumistic practices as necromancy because there are often complex rituals involved in the conjuring of the spirits.

The necromantic oracles of the ancient world were essentially mediums who specialized in communicating with the dead. Throughout ancient Greece, where the practice of spirit conjuration was not as prohibited as it was elsewhere, there were temples of spirit communication known as Nekuomanteions, where oracles would conjure the dead that they might share their wisdom with the living. The oracles who served at such temples were not called Witches per se, mostly because they were part of an accepted priesthood and not practicing their arts outside of the umbrella of authority. However, the basic structure was quite similar to the mediumship practiced by Witches throughout history.

Today, spirit mediumship has largely replaced the ritualistic arts of necromancy in common spiritual practice. Witches, who traditionally have always had the power to journey into the realm of spirits, have now embraced modern mediumship as yet one more way to aid in their travels between the worlds.

The Witch as Spirit Medium

During the Witch persecutions that took place over several centuries of the last millennium, the accused "Witches" were often associated with worshipping devils and consorting with demons. However, scholarship also suggests that there were a number of alleged Witches who were accused largely for their work with the dead, proving further the enduring connection between the Witch and the souls of the departed.

The Soulmother of Küssnacht, a part of Switzerland, was burned at the stake in 1577. For the thirteen years prior, the Soulmother, whose real name has been lost in the tides of history, was a professional spirit medium who read for people far and wide. Often, when a person died, those left behind would pay a visit to the Soulmother—quite literally, for her trade was apparently rather lucrative. Visitors would stay at a nearby boarding house (owned by a friend of the Soulmother), which suggests that the seer's reputation extended far beyond her village. The Soulmother mixed both Christian and Witchcraft symbolism to summon the dead. She would draw a magic circle and invoke the sacrifice of Jesus. Then, the spirits of the dead were said to appear, and the Soulmother would share their wisdom with her well-paying clients. Finally, the priests of Küssnacht, probably fed up with the spiritual competition, complained to the local bishop that the Soulmother was practicing Witchcraft. The bishop later referred her to the court of Schwyz, where she was tortured into confessing to the crime of Witchcraft, found guilty, and then burned alive. While the Soulmother probably didn't see herself as the devil-worshipping style of "Witch" that lived only in the fantasies of the Witch hunters, this story shows how mediumship and Witchcraft were perceived by the authorities to be one and the same.[8]

Born in Gerresheim, Germany, on May, 1722, Helena Curtens was one of the last Germans to be burned as a Witch. Helena was sickly from birth, and she and her father sought out places to find healing from her illnesses. At the age of fourteen, after making a pilgrimage to Kevelaer, Germany, where Catholics by the hundreds of thousands still travel today to honor the Virgin Mary, Helena began to tell those around her that she was seeing ghosts—probably of the dead, given Mary's long association with the martyrs. Soon her tales caught the attention of authorities, and under terrible torture, her story soon changed to the more traditional accounts of devil worship. After a lengthy imprisonment and trial, she was burned at the stake at Gerresheim in August of 1738 at the age of sixteen.[9]

According to Hungarian historian Éva Pócs, there are Hungarian Witch trial documents that refer to accused Witches who used ritual initiation and techniques of seership to communicate with the dead and other supernatural beings. These practices were collectively referred to as "Saint Lucy's Stool Techniques," named for a ritual performed on Saint Lucy's Day during which the seer would sit on a wooden stool before a fire and see visions of the dead. Granted, those accused generally insisted that they were performing such rites for benevolent purposes, including the detection of Evil Witches, but it doesn't seem to have stopped these well-intentioned seers from being dragged to the stake for burning.[10]

Spiritualism and the Resurgence of Mediumship

In Western culture, mediumship fell into obscurity during the Witch persecutions due to fear of torture and execution. It never disappeared, of course, but went underground, its practices kept hidden by secretive magical families, the wealthy, and even the clergy. The Christian church discouraged any form of contact with the dead, except through the veneration of saints. But in the mid-nineteenth century, mediumship roared back to life, fueled by a renaissance of interest in occultism, ceremonial magic, mesmerism, and a popular fascination with talking to spirits. Mediumship became the primary focus of Spiritualism, a new religion that openly embraced the practice of speaking with the dead.

The modern religion of Spiritualism was born here in America, where the Fox Sisters of Hydesville, New York, created a media sensation with their spirit rappings. The Fox family lived in a house they believed to be haunted because of unexplained thumping noises at night. The story goes that teenagers Maggie and Katie discovered that the presence seemed to be intelligent and would respond to their own knockings. Soon they were channeling messages through a tedious process of rapping the letters of the alphabet—sort of like a cross beween the Ouija board and Morse code. Their older sister, Leah, saw a marketing opportunity, and soon the Fox sisters were doing platform demonstrations and readings everywhere. Surely this emerging phenomenon was tapping into a desire of the masses, long subdued as they were by the so-called Ages of Enlightenment, to again believe in the spirit world and the hope of an afterlife.

Spirit mediumship became all the rage. There were other factors behind the explosion in popularity, but in short, mediums became the new darlings of every social class. Home séance circles sprouted everywhere on both sides of the Atlantic, and public demonstrations were given to sold-out theaters. Rapping gave way to voice mediumship, in which mediums delivered messages; and to physical mediumship, in which mediums put on displays of phenomena ranging from floating trumpets to the shocking appearances of ectoplasm. Of course, the emergence of modern Spiritualism also brought with it plenty of fraud—there are always greedy people who cast aspersions on the truly spiritual arts to take advantage of the gullible—but this new religion also made it possible for those with the real ability to communicate with spirits to finally find a place that accepted their unique gifts.

Mediumship grew even more popular in the wake of World War I, as the grieving sought to find their loved ones in the afterlife. By the mid-twentieth century, however, public interest dropped considerably, and mediumship fell back into the dark séance parlors, occult classes, and psychic readings where it had thrived before. It remained a focus of Spiritualism, but that religion, too, waned in popularity.

Its popularity may wax and wane, but mediumship will never disappear. As we have seen in our tour of Witches in history, those who can talk to the dead are always in demand.

Spirit Medium Helen Duncan Frees the Witches

Helen Duncan, born in Scotland in 1898, was a popular physical medium in Britain in the mid-twentieth century. She was arrested, charged, tried, and convicted under old anti-witchcraft laws that were still on the books in Scotland.

Duncan worked as a medium and gave readings involving messages from the dead. During World War II, Duncan was sought out by the grieving, and she traveled all over Britain to conduct séances. In 1941, an innocent reading landed her in legal trouble. She made contact with a dead sailor and identified his ship by name: the HMS *Barham*. This was a blow to the family, for they did not know that the ship had been sunk—the government had kept the news silent in a misguided effort to keep public morale high.

Duncan's news leaked out, and the embarrassed Admiralty was finally forced to admit that the ship had been lost. As a result, Duncan was monitored by the government for the next two years. During the secret planning of the Allies' D-Day invasion at Normandy, France, the British authorities decided to rein her in—just in case she blew the whistle at another séance. She was arrested and charged under the Vagrancy Act of 1824, which outlawed fortune telling, astrology, and Spiritualism. Convictions usually carried only fines. Seeking more severe measures, the government also charged Duncan under the Witchcraft Act of 1735, which carried the potential of a prison sentence.

Duncan and her three assistants were accused of faking the conjuration of the dead, and of fraudulently taking money for doing so. Duncan went to trial at the Old Bailey in London in 1944. Despite forty witnesses who testified on her behalf, she was convicted and sentenced to nine months in prison. Led away to her cell, she could only mumble about the piles of lies that had been told about her by the authorities.

The media attention on her case captured the interest of Prime Minister Winston Churchill, who demanded to know why the Witchcraft Act of 1735 was still on the books, and why the government was wasting money on "such tomfoolery." The law was repealed, but not until 1951. Duncan was the last person in Britain to be prosecuted under it. The repeal paved the way for Witches to come out into the open, and the modern religion of Wicca was born.

Duncan may not have called herself a Witch, but she has a unique role in the evolution of modern Witchcraft due to the laws used against her. The intersections between Spiritualists and Witches are common. I often hire Spiritualists for my annual psychic fair here in Salem for one reason: they are among the best psychics! Like Duncan, many spirit mediums have been persecuted and punished under this law or that, and always by authorities who are afraid of the vast power of seers and sorcerers.

Basic Mediumship

You've already learned the most important piece of mediumship in chapter 2: the visionary state. When you can alter your brainwaves to reach into deeper states of consciousness, you are essentially tuning yourself into the spiritual currents that exist just outside of our own—including the Death Current where the spirits dwell. It can be such an incredible experience to tap into the realms of the dead. By doing so, we can feel the joy of knowing that the soul goes on and that death is but a doorway through which we all pass. The technique of mediumship that Shawn taught me was quite simple, so it's something you should be able to use whenever you need to contact the dead.

Before you begin performing any kind of mediumship, you must understand the principles of banishing and exorcism explained in chapter 5. This is no joke! Mediumship opens doorways that must be respected; without that respect, the only doorway you'll be opening is one that leads to trouble.

Exercise: Meditation for Mental or Trance Mediumship

Find a comfortable chair and light a white candle that has been dressed with your anointing oil (see appendix A). Keep your spine aligned as upright as you can; this creates a flow of energy that runs from deep within the Earth up into the universe itself. Good posture is important for psychic work.

Close your eyes and relax into a deep visionary state. Breathe deeply. Feel the Death Current moving through your body. Become one with the vibrational energies of the dead.

If you are conducting mental mediumship, speak aloud or to yourself, *I prepare myself for mental mediumship. I am a beacon to the spirits of the dead. Let them trust me and speak to me and share their wisdom.*

If you are conducting trance mediumship, speak aloud or to yourself, *I prepare myself for trance mediumship. I am a vessel for the spirits of the dead. Let them speak through me and share their wisdom.*

If you have someone you wish to reach, say aloud or to yourself, *Spirit of [name of spirit], come forth and share your wisdom with [me/us] here.*

Be patient and continue to remain in your visionary state until the spirit comes. This process simply must be *experienced,* for mediumship begins by passively waiting for the spirits to come to you and through you. You may not get results on the first occurrence, but you must not give up. Keep trying over a number of nights, perhaps each Monday night—it is the night of the moon and perfect for psychic work.

Write everything down that you hear, see, or sense. Sometimes, the spirits will show you symbols, visions of things to come, words played across the mental screen of your mind; you may smell unusual scents, hear actual speech, and even feel the sensation of breath or touch. Mediumship can manifest through all of the senses as it is truly the sixth sense.

• • •

8

Necromancy:
The World's Most Forbidden Practice

Even more than the word "Witchcraft," the word "necromancy" conjures all sorts of imagery, much of it terrible—from commanding spirits to digging up corpses, conjuring demons to burrowing through rotting cadavers in search of secrets. The word has evolved over the centuries to include everything from speaking with the dead to summoning the ambassadors of hell. However, the root meaning of necromancy is not so terrible. It comes from the Greek words for death (*necro*) and divination (*mancy*) and most properly refers to prophecies and predictions by means of the dead. But even this definition is as murky as the waters of the river Styx—that fearsome boundary between our world and the realms of the dead. Some describe necromancy as divination via the splaying open of actual corpses. I know many people who hold to this repugnant definition today, and it is certainly not without mythological precedent, as you shall see below. Others point to ancient stories that show necromancy as a form of communication with the shades—or spectral forms—of the dead, where no corpses are involved. In medieval times, the word "necromancy" became conflated with the word "nigromancy," or black magic, and so came to represent all manner of the dark arts.

Like the words "Witch" and "Warlock," necromancy has so many negative connotations that one has to wonder why anyone would use it. I use it for the same reason that I use both Witch and Warlock: It's ballsy. It pushes buttons. It implies something that we have to muster up some courage to use. Besides, I tend to interchange words like "Witchcraft," "sorcery," "necromancy," and even "wizardry." Each word has unique etymologies that differentiate one from the other, but they all, ultimately, point to one thing: magic-makers. People can call me a Warlock, a Witch, a magician, a wizard, a necromancer, an enchanter, or a sorcerer. It matters little to me what label they give me since they're all calling for the same thing—the power of magic to aid them in their lives. For, ultimately, all of these titles can be traced back to the earliest magical people who were spiritual guides, drawing on the wisdom of the dead to help light the way for their tribes.

Necromancy in Greece

Necromancy, like other magical arts, was practiced widely throughout the ancient world. Since the word has been traced to ancient Greece, it seems wisest to begin by focusing our attentions there, for that land's beliefs about the dead and its necromantic rituals profoundly shaped the practices of Western magic and occultism.

The early Greeks had varying beliefs about death, the dead, and the afterlife, just as modern people do today. We are probably most familiar with the Grecian view of the afterlife as a dreary and dismal place because of descriptions in literary works such as Homer's *Odyssey*, said to be first written as early as the seventh century BCE.

The Greek realm of the dead was the gloomy underworld of Hades. Originally, Hades was not literally beneath the Earth, but across the ocean, beyond the Western horizon as realms of the dead so often are; in the *Odyssey*, Odysseus sails his ship west to the edges of Hades in order to perform a necromantic ritual to consult the dead at the very edges of the underworld. He never entered, but rather conducted his rituals where the rivers Acheron and Cocytus met. By the sixth century BCE, however, Hades was usually thought to be a subterranean realm. There were also different divisions of the underworld; distinctive places such as Elysium for honored heroes and other blessed souls; and Tartarus, a hellish place where the wicked were punished for their sins against the gods and mankind.

Hades was bounded by five rivers. The best known is the river Styx ("Hate"). The others are the Acheron ("Woe"), the Cocytus ("Wailing"), the Phlegethon ("Flaming"), and the Lethe ("Oblivion" or "Forgetfulness"). From the names, this underworld doesn't sound like a vacation resort. The dead were shepherded to Hades across one of these rivers by Charon, the dreaded ferryman, for a price; hence the custom of burying the dead with a coin under the tongue. They had to pass by the most terrifying guard dog ever known, the mighty Cerberus. Usually said to have three heads, it was Cerberus's job to make sure that only the dead came in, and none of the dead went out. Exceptions were made for heroic journeys, special petitions to chthonic deities, and for the practice of necromancy. When summoned by Witches and other necromancers, the shades of the dead were like prisoners on leave: at the end of their duties, they had to return.

The Greek underworld was named for its master—the god of the dead, Hades. He ruled with his melancholy wife Persephone, daughter of the fertility goddess Demeter, whom he very likely stole at Acheron in Thesprotia. There were other chthonic, or underworld, deities as well, including Thanatos, spirit of death; his twin, Hypnos, the spirit of sleep; and Oneiros, the spirit of dreams. Hermes, who escorted souls to the underworld much like the Egyptian Anubis, had chthonic aspects as well. Hecate, goddess of magic and queen of all witcheries, became known as a chthonic deity in her darker guise. Among the most fearsome of all the denizens of the underworld were the Erinyes, or Furies, named Tisiphone, Megaera, and Alecto, who were born of the blood spilled from the castrations of Uranus, and who relentlessly pursued and punished the souls of the wicked.

Some of the early Greeks believed that the departed acquired special knowledge in death, especially regarding future events, and could be summoned forth by dark ceremonies that they might impart this knowledge to the living. Necromancy was practiced, but with neither universal acceptance nor approval. In fact, necromancy remains the most forbidden of all magical arts.

Necromancy usually was accomplished with the help of an intermediary, such as an oracle, a priest or priestess, or a Witch. These experts of the unknown often resided in remote locations where openings to the underworld were known to exist. The more well-known oracles acted as mediums and channels for the gods, but the dead were the source of information for some. All oracles of the dead were ruled by the chthonic gods, and prayers and sacrifices were always made to them. Consulting an oracle was a widely respected practice in the classical world—and it was also considered to be serious business. Matters of state were always presented to oracles, as were preparations for battles and wars. Great leaders usually sent emissaries to the oracles, but sometimes they went themselves, especially if the need was grave. The dead were sometimes consulted through oracles for advice in life's decisions, to solve murders and crimes, and to provide guidance about what was to come in the afterlife. Generally, the Greeks believed that the dead were compelled to tell the truth, though accounts of false information exist. When dealing with the dead, or any spiritual being, discernment is a must.

The ancient classical world featured four primary oracle sites of the dead: Acheron in Thesprotia; Avernus in Campania, Italy; Heracleia Pontia on the south coast of the Black Sea; and Tainaron on the tip of the Mani Peninsula. Ghost-layings were also performed at these sites to exorcize the spirits of the dead who were attached to people and tormenting them.

The Greeks used several terms to describe these oracular places. *Nekuomanteion*, or "prophecy place of the dead"; *psuchagogion*, or "drawing place of ghosts"; and *psuchomanteion*, or "prophecy place of ghosts"; were in use in the fifth and fourth centuries BCE. The term *psuchopompeion,* or "sending place of ghosts," was recorded around 100 CE, and in the fifth century CE we find the term *nekuor(i)on,* "seeing place of the dead," with a variant *nekromanteion.*[11]

Actually, any place featuring a cave or lake could serve as an oracular site of the dead in the classical world, and probably many such places were used that have not been recorded in surviving literature. Caves especially were seen as natural openings to the underworld, and thus were an excellent place to summon up the dead. Literary references to sites were sometimes vague, and so distinguishing the details of one site over another has been open to interpretation by scholars.

The necromancers altered their physical appearance and behavior in order to meet the dead, in a supernatural place we would describe today as being between the worlds. They favored dressing in black, much as Witches have often dressed, made their complexions pale, and talked in squeaks, chirps, mutters, and howls.

Heracleia Pontia

The city of Heracleia Pontia was named after the hero Heracles, who, according to lore, descended into Hades from there, bringing back the fearsome guardian of the gates of the underworld, the three-headed dog Cerberus. When struck by sunlight, the beast foamed at the mouth in fury, spewing saliva on the ground, from which sprouted the poisonous aconite plant. A cave near the city was used as a *nekuomanteion* by the fifth century BCE. The third-century Greek poet, Quintus Smyrnaeus, said it was immense in size and that nymphs dwelt in its crystal-clear water.

The entrance to the cave was only three meters wide. A stairway descended to a central chamber measuring forty-five by twenty meters, supported by stone pillars. It was flooded with a calm pool of the crystal-clear water. A rough tunnel led to a small, unhewn chamber where human bones were found.

Heracleia Pontia was said to have been where Pausanias, the renowned Spartan general and regent of the fifth century BCE, came for a ghost-laying.

According to Plutarch, Pausanias ordered a Byzantium virgin from a prominent family, Cleonice, to come to him for sex, which would disgrace her family. She reluctantly entered his bedchamber in the dark, and stumbled over a lamp. The noise startled him awake. Thinking he was under attack, he drew out his dagger and fatally stabbed the girl. Her ghost began to torment him, telling him to "go to justice." At the *nekuomanteion*, he begged her to go away. Cleonice came in a vision and said that he would soon find relief in Sparta, a veiled but accurate prediction of his impending death, which would come at the hands of the Spartans.[12]

Pausanias was buried in the forecourt of the temple, and his ghost haunted the place, frightening people away. The Spartans turned to an oracle to ascertain how to get rid of the ghost. They were told that the temple was polluted with his body, but if they erected two bronze statues of the regent at the temple altar, his ghost would leave. They did, and it left.

Tainaron

In myth, Tainaron (now Cape Matapan) has a long reputation as an entryway to the underworld. Heracles dragged Cerberus up there too, and the dog may have poisoned this area with aconite as well. The small cave that was the oracle site was located below the temple of Poseidon on the cape promontory. It once measured ten to twelve meters wide and fifteen meters deep, and was fitted with a door and walls; the roof collapsed in long ago.

Acheron

Located in Thesprotia at the confluence of the real rivers of Acheron and Cocytus, this oracular site is documented as a place to seek out the dead for prophecy. Ancient references make no mention of a cave; the actual oracular site appears to have been the Acheron lake itself, formed beyond the river confluence as the Acheron river spread out into a marshy area. Adding to the atmosphere were mysterious noises created by spring water in the soil, which were believed to come from the presence of the subterranean dead.

Several mythical descents into the underworld were said to have taken place there: Orpheus in pursuit of Eurydice; Theseus; and Heracles, who seems to have gone down twice, once for Theseus and again for Cerberus. Acheron was dedicated to the underworld god Hades and his wife Persephone and the underworld was very likely the place he kidnapped her from. Historian Daniel Ogden suggests that the underworld versions of Acheron and Cocytus spoken of in Homer's *Odyssey* may be based on this very real place. The mythical counterparts were where Odysseus was sent by Circe to summon the spirit of Tiresias. [13]

The Greek historian Herodotus told the story of Periander, a despotic and greedy ruler of Corinth, who sent one of his men to Acheron to ask the ghost of his wife, Melissa, where she had hidden some money from a guest prior to her death. Periander had accidentally killed the pregnant Melissa by kicking her in a fit of rage. The shade of Melissa was summoned but gave no answer, complaining that she was cold and naked in Hades because Periander had not performed the proper ritual of burning her clothes at her funeral. She also gave proof of her identity by providing a gruesome fact that only Periander could have known: she told the emissary that her husband had put his loaves into a cold oven; that is, he had sex with her corpse. In response, Periander summoned all the women in Corinth, stripped them naked, and burned their clothing with a prayer to Melissa. He sent another emissary back to Acheron, and this time, the dead Melissa revealed the location of the hidden money. [14]

Plato portrayed the Acherousian Lake as a repository of souls of the dead. Those who came for consultations poured their libations of milk, honey, oil, and wine, and the blood of sacrificed animals into pits dug beside the lake or into the lake itself. The dead were said to rise up out of the waters to answer the questions put to them.

Avernus

Located near Cumae in Campania, the site of Avernus features a large lake formed in a flooded volcanic crater; volcanos are often thought to be portals to the underworld. The ancients referred to the lake as "birdless," for the waters emitted toxic gases that killed birds, which was seen as evidence for its underworld nature. There are no historical records of necromancy being performed there, but ancient writers attested to the existence of a chamber below the lake that served such a purpose. As at Acheron, the dead were believed to rise up out of the water.

Avernus was another site associated with the rituals of necromancy performed by Odysseus, such as in Sophocles's *Odysseus Acanthoplex*. The reputed underground chamber also was associated with a Cumae Sybilline oracle, who used mirrors in her summoning of the dead. Images of the oracle show her seated with her mirror, or holding the mirror up in front of her, and with an altar of offerings of eggs and other food for the dead.

The Necromantic Rituals of Greece

In literature's most famous rite of necromancy, Homer's Odysseus was directed by the Witch Circe to journey to the underworld to consult the ghost of the blind seer Tiresias. After disembarking his ship, Odysseus walks through a grove dedicated to Persephone, full of willow and poplar trees, to where the rivers of Acheron and Cocytus meet—the place designated by Circe for the ritual. As the valley bound by the real rivers of Acheron and Cocytus at Thesprotia "is clothed in poplars and willows even today," historian Daniel Ogden suggests that the Greeks based these underworld rivers on their real-world counterparts. [15]

Odysseus and his men brought out their sheep for sacrifice and dug a pit in the ground, pouring in libations of milk, honey, wine, and water, and sprinkling white barley. Odysseus made prayers to the ghosts and promised that when he got back to Ithaca, he would sacrifice his best heifer to them, and offer Tiresias his best black sheep. He slit the throats of two sheep and let their blood pour into the pit. The Greeks believed that blood especially was desired by the hungry ghosts and would give them temporary form in order to speak.

The shades of the dead did indeed arise, including those of old men, soldiers killed in battle, young women, and more. Odysseus was afraid and drew his sword to keep them back; he would not let them near the blood until Tiresias appeared to answer his questions. The first to approach was the ghost of his fallen comrade, Elpenor, whose body remained unburied; Elpenor, of course, asked for proper burial. Odysseus's own dead mother, Anticleia, appeared. Then the blind seer Tiresias came, and Odysseus allowed him to drink the blood. The seer told Odysseus that any shade who drank the blood would speak the truth, but if the blood was denied, the shade would withdraw. He prophesied the perils that awaited Odysseus on his return home to Ithaca. Then Odysseus allowed his mother to drink the blood, and she, too, made prophecies of days to come. He tried to embrace her but could not, for she was without substance. After that, Persephone sent numerous ghosts who were the wives and daughters of famous men. He also let them drink, and questioned each of them in their turn. The ghost of King Agamemnon appeared, weeping at the circumstances of his murder. Odysseus attempted to embrace him, too, but his arms went right through him. There followed ghosts of Odysseus's comrades who were slain in the Trojan War, among them Achilles, Ajax, and Patroclus.

Finally, Odysseus was granted visions of heroes who were the children of the gods; Heracles was the last. Odysseus lingered to see more of the heroic dead, but then he was swarmed with thousands of shrieking ghosts. It was believed that Persephone chased off necromancers who stayed too long by sending a gorgon, a hideous female with hair made of poisonous snakes, whose gaze turned mortals to stone. The dreadful Medusa was just such a creature. Odysseus feared that a gorgon would not be far behind the screeching spirits, and so he quickly ushered his men back to the ship.[16]

Blood was not offered to the shades in all necromantic rituals. Ogden describes the use of sweet libations to evoke ghosts of the dead in Aeschylus's *Persians*. Atossa, the widow of King Darius and mother of Xerxes, the successor, was troubled by the ghost of her husband in dreams. She and a council of Persian elders evoked his ghost for prophecy. To soothe the soul of her husband, Atossa offered libations of

... white milk, good to drink, from an unyoked cow, the
secretion of the flower-processing bee, gleaming honey,
offerings of water from a virgin spring, and an unmixed
drink from its mother in the field, this restorative from
an ancient vine. The fragrant fruit of the light olive tree,
which always luxuriates in leaves, is here too, as are woven garlands of flowers, children of the earth that bears
everything. But, my friends, sing hymns in support of
these libations to the dead below, and call up the demon
Darius, while I pour these honors to the gods below into
the thirsty earth.[17]

The ghost of Darius appeared and solemnly–and accurately–predicted that
Xerses's military campaign against Greece would be crushed.

The Greeks believed that restless ghosts were effective candidates for
necromancy. The victims of murders, suicides, tragic accidents, and battles
were unhappy in their deaths and probably are unhappy in the afterlife. Such
spirits are hungry for attention and are quick to offer answers.

The Greeks also favored battlefields and tombs for necromancy, for they
believed that ghosts lingered around the places of their burials. Battlefields
were said to be full of the angry dead, some buried only partially and not
properly, and some thrown irreverently into mass pits or not buried at all.
This also extended to tales of the Roman necromancers. The Witch Erichtho, whom I refer to later, wandered battlefields looking for fresh corpses to
reanimate.

Battlefields are heavily haunted, with the ghosts of the slain soldiers
still fighting and making a horrible racket. Spectral armies and soldiers make
spontaneous appearances at such sites, to make prophecies or to reenact
their last battle. The Greeks used their necromantic rituals to summon ghosts
from battlefields and tombs. Corpses and bones were not necessary, for even
the ashes of the cremated could yield up ghosts, and rattle and groan in their
prophetic answers.

When summoned in rituals, the ghosts of the dead appear in visions, and often in dreams. The funerary altar of Ammias, a priestess of a mystery cult in Thyateira (Asia Minor) in the second century CE, bears the following inscription: "If anyone wishes to learn the truth from me, let him put what he wants in a prayer at the altar and he will obtain it by means of a vision during the night or day."[18] The night vision refers to the spirit coming in a dream. To summon dreams of the dead, necromancers sometimes slept at gravesites or on top of tombs after doing their rituals.

While divination by necromancy was an acceptable practice in ancient Greece, there may have been laws and prohibitions against conjuring the dead for curses and binding spells.

The prominence of Greek oracles diminished between the third and first centuries BCE, in part because the country suffered the effects of continual warfare.[19] The Romans, rising in prominence, had different ideas regarding the dead, followed by the Christians, who sought to either shut down all oracular sites or convert them into shrines dedicated to saints and angels.

Roman Necromancy

The Romans considered the dead to be dangerous and had a more negative view of necromancy than the Greeks. For many Romans, the dead were useful for binding curses against the living, but if they escaped the grave those same dead were likely to terrorize the living in monstrous forms. During the days of the Roman Republic, necromancy would have fallen under the proscriptions against the practice of magic and sorcery in general. Roman accounts of necromancy were gruesome, lacking even the macabre grace of Greek accounts. The Romans believed necromancy to be the domain of horrid Witches who were virtually bestial in their depraved rites.

Erichtho

A chilling description of necromancy performed by the Thessalian Witch Erichtho is offered by the poet Lucan in *Pharsalia*.[20] The necromancy of

Erichtho is not a vision in a dream or a mirror, but a reanimation of a fresh corpse, and her story influences many of the terrifying images found in the ideas of necromancy today.

Corpse reanimation was held to be one of the most powerful forms of necromancy. To be successful, the corpse was fed blood and propped upright on its feet to symbolize its impending resurrection. Herbs were placed on the chest and head to magically restart breathing. The corpse could also be anointed with the necromancer's own blood. The necromancer then uttered powerful incantations to command the ghost of the dead person to reenter its body. If the ghost failed to respond, the necromancer threatened it with untold tortures in the underworld.

The poet Lucan, who lived from 39 to 65 CE, wrote a long account of the Roman civil war that erupted during the time of Julius Caesar, nearly a century before. One of his chapters tells about the necromantic undertakings of Roman General Sextus Pompey, son of General Pompey the Great, who was fighting the forces of Julius Caesar in a civil war. Lucan described Sextus Pompey as an unworthy man with a shameful past. Fearful of a violent fate in an upcoming battle at Pharsalus, he sought the magic most forbidden, believed by the Romans to be hated by the gods: necromancy. And Thessaly, long known for its Witches, was a mysterious and perilous land "full of violence to the gods."[21]

Erichtho was the fiercest of her race, a grisly, unkempt hag with skin as pale as bone, who knew the veiled secrets of the river Styx, dwelled in deserted tombs, and dragged the dead forth from the shadowy underworld. Her very breath poisoned the air. She savagely mauled corpses, gathering their dripping slime and gore; dug through the gruesome cavities of bodies, plucking out eyes; and wildly tore cadavers apart limb by limb. Even vultures and wolves fled from her. If her rites called for the blood of the living, she did not hesitate to murder, carving fetuses out of women and stabbing even dear friends. She would then proceed to sever a head, forcing its lips apart that they may speak with the voice of the grave, and begin her conversation with the Stygian shades. It is hard to imagine a more horrific being.

However, no matter how terrible the Witch is portrayed in these gruesome tales, there's always someone willing to go there. When Sextus Pompey, camping with his troops in Thessaly, heard about Erichtho, he thought she was just the girl he needed to tell him about the future. He snuck out at night and tracked her down in the midst of broken tombs. She agreed to help him by reanimating a corpse.

Erictho wandered a desolate battlefield in search of the ideal fresh corpse that had no wounds to the lungs that might impair proper speech. She carefully selected a corpse with its throat cut and dragged it to a cave. She donned her ritual clothing and tied her stringy hair back with writhing vipers. Then she forcefully pried open the chest of the corpse and let it fill with its own blood. She rinsed the cavity with moon juice, a foam left on plants by the full moon believed to have magical properties. She poured in a mixture of foul ingredients that included the frothy saliva of rabid dogs, lynx guts, hyena hump, the bone marrow of a deer fed on serpents, pearl oyster, various snakes, stones incubated by an eagle, and the ashes of a phoenix. Then she shrieked her incantations, working herself into such a frenzy that she literally foamed at the mouth. Erictho uttered a horrible incantation sounding like the howling of wolves, the hissing of snakes, the barking of dogs, and the screeching of owls. It penetrated into the very depths of Tartarus. She invoked Pluto and Proserpine (the Roman names of Hades and Persephone), Chaos, Hecate, and the ferryman of the Styx, bidding them to send her the shade of the dead soldier. The ghost appeared but was loathe to reenter its corpse. You can't blame the poor soul, given that worse company probably couldn't be found; but it mattered little, for Erictho whipped the body and screamed at the gods until the ghost obeyed. This is an excerpt of Ogden's translation of when the Thessalian Erictho reanimates a dead soldier for Sextus Pompey (65 CE, Lucan Pharsalia 6.588-830. Translated from Latin):

> At once the congealed gore warmed up, soothed the black
> wounds and ran into the veins and the extremities of the

limbs. As the blood struck them the organs beneath the chill breast quivered, and life, creeping anew into the innards that had forgotten it, mingled itself with the death. Then all the dead man's limbs shook, and his sinews flexed. The corpse did not raise itself from the ground gradually, one limb at a time. Rather, it shot up from the earth and was upright in an instant. The eyes were laid bare, the mouth an open grimace. His appearance was of one not yet fully alive, but of a man still in the phase of dying. He was still pallid and stiff, and in consternation at being brought back into the world.[22]

The reanimated corpse begrudgingly answered the questions put to him and forecast Sextus Pompey's defeat, finishing: "Europe and Asia and Libya's plains, which saw your conquests, now shall hold alike your burial-place—nor has the Earth for you a happier land than this."[23]

When it was done, the corpse looked dejected, begging for death again. Even the underworld had to be preferable to this. Erichtho performed a magical spell to make the corpse fall. Sextus Pompey returned to his men as the Witch burned the corpse in the fire. At least she had the courtesy to grant the poor soldier an eternal peace from ever being defiled in this way again.

Sextus Pompey lost the battle at Pharsalus, and was forced to flee for his life. In 35 BCE, he was captured by his enemies in Miletus, Anatolia (now Turkey), and was executed without trial.

During the Roman Empire, necromancy fell even further into the realm of undesirable activities, becoming associated with imperial insanities and vanities, and paranoia that enemies would call up the dead to find out the death dates of emperors and use the ghosts to conspire against them. Necromancers were rumored to sacrifice young boys in order to conjure their ghosts for prophecy, spells, and curses. Given the imperial intrigues, assassinations, and murders, not only of rivals but family members and spouses, it is no wonder the dead evoked terror, but in these tales, we also see the old pattern of sorcerers and Witches being forbidden for what they might do to those in power.

Canidia

Even more loathsome than Erichtho are the Thessalian Witches Canidia and her cohorts, portrayed by the poet Horace in *Epodes* ("Incantations") and *Satires*. Both works were completed around 30 BCE, during the reign of Emperor Caesar Augustus. Modern scholars have speculated that Augustus, who was planning to execute severe laws against Witchcraft, enlisted the aid of the two reigning poets of the day, Horace and Virgil, to portray Witches and Witchcraft in a disgusting light as part of a propaganda campaign. Though little is known of the laws against magic, they were influential for a couple of centuries in the prosecution of sorcery and Witchcraft, proving that Witch persecutions existed long before Christianity came into power.[24]

Horace's Witches appear more like denizens of the underworld than anyone you would meet on Earth. They are dressed in tattered black clothing and have wild, unkempt hair; Canidia's hair is entwined with small vipers, and Sagana wears a wig that bristles like a sea urchin or a boar. They are extremely pale, their teeth are blue, and their nails are worn and ragged from digging in the Earth. Canidia, however, keeps a thumbnail long, presumably to act as a spade. The Witch Folia howls the moon down from the sky and enchants the stars.

Epodes 5 tells how these three Witches, along with a fourth, Veia, kidnapped a young boy from a wealthy family and sacrificed him in order to procure body parts for a love potion to lure Canidia's estranged lover back to her. They buried the boy up to his chin and callously placed food in front of him several times a day. As he wasted away, his longing for the food was transferred via sympathetic magic to his liver and bone marrow, which the Witches intended to harvest for their wicked potion. Sagan sprinkled about foul waters from Avernus, the toxic necromantic lake in Campagnia.

The boy begged for his life, but when he realized that the Witches would show no mercy, he angrily spat a curse at the haggard crones, declaring that his ghost, accompanied by the Furies, would attack them at night with curved fingernails and sit upon their chests, depriving them of sleep and filling them with terror. He proclaimed that the Witches would be stoned to death by an angry mob, and wolves and birds would scatter their unburied bones. Despite the seriousness of a curse laid by the dying, the Witches carried out their evil deed.

The stories of Erichtho and Canidia, while fictional, show how far the authorities would go to paint those who communicated with the dead in a negative light. What were once the sacred rites of the noble shamans of old now became the grisly rituals of evil hags, bent on defiling both the dead and the living.

Emperors and Necromancy

Nero, who ruled from 54 to 68 CE, epitomized everything negative perceived about ghosts and necromancy. He had his mother Agrippina murdered in 59 CE for her intrigues against him, and gave her a minimal burial. He was soon pestered relentlessly in dreams by her ghost and also the Furies, who whipped him for his crimes. He dreamed of wails issuing from her burial place, and of a mausoleum opening its doors to him and bidding him to enter. Plagued by these horrific visions, Nero consulted Persian necromancers to summon forth his mother's ghost and beg for her mercy. According to Ogden, Pliny described Nero as having no respect for the dead. "With all too much cruelty did he fill our city with ghosts," said Pliny.[25]

Other Roman emperors, both Christian and non-Christian alike, were said to practice necromancy, and never for good purposes. Some, like Nero, were terrified by the shrieking ghosts of their murder victims. Hadrian (r. 117-38) lost his favorite youth, Antinous, to drowning in the Nile, but it was rumored that he had instead sacrificed him for the purpose of necromancy.

Hadrian did construct a *psuchomanteion* at his villa, perhaps to commune with the ghost of Antinous.

By the fourth century, Rome had strict laws that banned all forms of divination, and especially forbade necromancy for the purpose of harming one's enemies—probably an attempt to protect the emperors from their conspiring rivals. In doing so, they set the stage for how the later Church of Rome would deal with those who dared consult with the dead.

As an aside, history often repeats itself. Author Peter Levenda points out that during the rise of the Third Reich, Adolf Hitler and Heinrich Himmler (himself an occultist) instituted laws against astrologers, occult lodges, Freemasons, and other magical practitioners. However, when these individuals were rounded up, some were forced into service for the Reich. By now, you should have no question as to why. Those in authority have always feared the magical arts, for these powers are real and they put strength and knowledge into the hands of individuals.[26]

Early Christians and Necromancy

The early Christians in the Roman Empire had divided views on necromancy. On one hand, Justin Martyr, a Father of the Church, thought that it proved the immortality of the soul. Others, such as Saint Basil, denounced it. The debate would go on for centuries, with all forms of magic and divination eventually earning official condemnation.

In the first centuries after Christ, wonder working and miracles, including communing with the dead, were performed by Christians and non-Christians alike, in keeping with the model set by the Acts of the Apostles. Some of the wonder workers competed with Christianity. One was Apollonius of Tyana, a neo-Pythagorean philosopher whose reputed necromancy eschewed the blood and horror of earlier practices for the more genteel method of prayer. This hearkened back to the more peaceful, shamanic practices of tribal societies.

Apollonius of Tyana

Apollonius was a neo-Pythagorean and reputed magical adept of the first century CE. He was said to have acquired many of his supernatural abilities during a sojourn in India. The miracles attributed to Apollonius paralleled those of Jesus and the apostles in many ways, and it is possible that some of those stories were retrofitted onto him. As a neo-Pythagorean, Apollonius condemned blood sacrifice, and so would not have used blood in a necromantic ritual.

In Philostratus's account, *Life of Apollonius of Tyana*, as referenced by Ogden, Apollonius desired to speak to the ghost of Achilles to ask him questions about the Trojan War. He traveled with his companions to Ilium, and wandered about the tombs, making speeches and offering "bloodless and pure sacrifices." Reaching the mound of the warrior Achilles, he told his companions to return to their ship, for he wished to spend the night alone on top of it, perhaps implying that he may have intended to discover the spirit of the warrior in dreams. Later, in telling his companions what transpired, he said, "It was not by digging a pit as Odysseus did, or by evocating ghosts with the blood of sheep, that I managed to speak with Achilles, but by using the prayers that the Indians claim to use for their heroes."[27]

Apollonius's bloodless sacrifices and prayer-based necromancy were marked departures from earlier Greco-Roman rites, even those that did not involve blood sacrifice. In effect, they initiated a new stream of "kinder, gentler" necromantic practice. In reality, Apollonius was very likely scraping away much of the veneer of evil grafted onto necromancy over the centuries by authorities seeking to discredit its practice.

The Christian Church ruthlessly attempted to stamp out the magical arts, and although it successfully suppressed magic, it could not eliminate it altogether. In many cases, the Church absorbed magical practices and converted them into acceptable religious traditions, just as they did with the spiritual beliefs of most of the places they conquered. And, in some cases, the Church simply turned a blind eye. Most magical rites went further underground, hidden in families of Witches and occultists, while others were practiced openly, though thinly veiled in Christian symbolism. Necromantic rituals, forming part of the darker side of magic and in constant collision with Christianity's teachings on death and the afterlife, remained underground but never truly went away.

9

Oracular Necromancy:
Divination with the Dead

Some years ago, when my friend and mentor, the late Shawn Poirier, told me he was buying real human skulls on the Internet, I was pretty freaked out and thought he was diving off the deep end. Mind you, I'd been practicing Witchcraft for years, but I'd never heard in any book or from any teacher that a skull would add value to the nature-loving, tree-hugging ways of Wicca. Shawn often poked fun at both my naïve idealism and my cynical skepticism, and while it took me years to understand, I know now that it was because these things he was teaching me—they were the real deal. Magic isn't always safe. It doesn't always fit in. And it definitely doesn't always conform to nature. It is supernatural and has the power to direct the tides of nature in ways that most magical practitioners only scratch the surface of.

Shawn purchased two skulls. One, an adult that lacked a lower jaw, Shawn said was named Robert. I asked, "Did *you* name him that?" Shawn replied, "No. That's what he says his name is." I scrunched my face up, skeptically. The other skull, to my horror, was that of what must have been a seven-year-old child. "They *sell* these? And what's *her* name?" I asked. "Claudia," he replied, without missing a beat. "And just what do you plan to do with them?" I demanded. Over the next few years, up until the time of Shawn's passing in 2007, I learned just that.

What Shawn knew instinctively, and what I discovered when I inherited Robert after Shawn's death, was that this skull was better suited for necromantic magic than for divination. I later found out through more scholarly practitioners that this was due to Robert not having a lower jaw. To be sure, Shawn really didn't get much more than a name out of him. Claudia, on the other hand, was a true necromantic skull. She had both the upper and lower jaw, and all her teeth. Shawn used to have quite the conversations with her, and my coven-sister Leanne Marrama continues to do so as Claudia's current guardian.

You've learned about why you would contact the dead, how to make offerings to them to begin a relationship, and some of the more common methods of spirit communication. You've also learned how the ancient world called upon the dead in ritual. And while many of the specifics of those practices are enshrouded in the depths of time, there are rituals you can perform today that will aid you in bringing the dead in for contact.

In some ways, necromancy is not all that different than spirit medium-ship. In fact, necromancy is very likely its ancestor. The primary difference is that modern mediumship has been stripped of most of the ritualistic elements, while necromancy often involves complex rituals, tools, offerings, and other physical practices designed to help facilitate the process. Another difference is in the intent. Modern mediumship was promoted to a far broader audience and often lacked purpose other than to prove to an increasingly skeptical society that there was, in fact, an afterlife. It was often done simply to bring closure to people hoping to make contact with a particular spirit. Necromancers have no doubt that the spirit world is real, and they approach their work with a definitive purpose. This usually involves a question that the necromancer wishes to have answered, such as a portent of the future, where treasure may be hiding, or the intent of an enemy. Such criteria are why the Witch of Endor is usually considered a necromancer and not a medium, but it is important to understand that these lines are often blurred. Some might argue that mediumship should replace necromancy. I feel that both have their place and that ritual and ceremony can often bring spirits into far clearer presence. Some have even told of seeing the spirits manifest into near-physical form as a result of their necromantic arts!

Defining Your Purpose

Necromancy is *not* a parlor trick. It should not be used like the Ouija board to call up spirits to impress your friends at parties. Even more than mediumship, this is a very ancient art that the spirits of the dead have learned to recognize as the dinner bell for returning to our world, so you'd better take it seriously or you might just end up wishing you had!

It is important that you employ the arts of necromancy for significant reasons. Yes, the spirits will tell you of things to come in the future and they will also reveal hidden secrets, but you should not waste their time or yours with trivialities. Some years ago, I stopped offering psychic phone readings regularly because the same people would call almost nightly asking, "When's my man gonna call?" Inevitably, after I told the client when, and the client got the call from her enamored when I said it would happen, my phone would ring again and I'd be asked, "When's my man gonna call?" These people never seemed to want to just wait for the man in question to call. Granted, sometimes the man was never going to call, and sometimes, clients would call about men they hadn't seen since 1973. Regardless, the questions always seemed to me to be so trivial, and I quickly became frustrated at my inability to convince these people to simply let life happen, and that psychic readings are meant to help us through milestones in our lives. I can only imagine what these individuals would do with the power of necromancy, but please, I implore you to take this more seriously. Imagine yourself after your death. You're in a serene place of spiritual bliss, exploring fantastical realms inaccessible to the living. You don't mind returning to your former world to visit loved ones still living. Until, that is, your cousin Mildred suddenly starts summoning your poor soul to her boudoir nightly to ask, "When's my man gonna call?" I'm sorry, but I think I'd rather be in the Christian hell than deal with that! So please, do the dead (and your own sanity) a favor and don't bother them with frivolous questions.

It's a good thing to build a daily relationship with the dead, with offerings, communications, and the like, but spirit work is a two-way street and the dead should be getting as much out of the relationship as you are! Always approach such work with a sense of purpose. Know what question you want to ask, whether it is if you'll get married, if you're going to get hired for that new job, or even if it's the combination to your safe that you forgot. Just please make sure your purpose is one that truly justifies calling the spirits away from their other pursuits.

Choose the Appropriate Spirit

When deciding whom to contact for your necromantic inquiries, be sure to choose the spirit that best fits your purpose. If you're looking to know the best path to take in your career, you don't want to call on your uncle who spent half his life on unemployment. You'll want to call on the spirit of your brother, the successful executive. When you want to know if love is coming, call upon that big sister who really understood the inner workings of love, not your second cousin who spent her life in a convent. Now, mind you, all of the dead have access to some information, but it's just easier to get someone to help you who is better equipped for the cause!

Don't Diss the Dead!

For anyone who has studied some form of necromancy in the past, this is perhaps one of the most important sections you will read. Some practitioners of necromancy, including the ancient Greeks and many medieval authors on spirit conjuring, would recommend commanding the spirits by threatening them with torment and harm, promising an offering only after a question is answered or a task is complete. In doing so, they would often call on the lowliest of the unquiet dead, lost souls with little intent other than to cause mischief and misery. I repudiate this method wholeheartedly.

First of all, would you really look forward to an afterlife that resembles Guantanamo Bay, with greedy necromancers summoning you back to this plane with threats of spiritual waterboarding? If that's not enough to make any decent person stop and think before going that route, then at least consider the vast dangers involved in this method.

Perhaps it is empowering to an inflated ego to think that we might be able to order the spirits around like they were mere slaves awaiting our every command. I guess it could be appealing to wonder what it might be like to have an army of the dead ready to act on our every whim. But this is foolhardy, arrogant, and highly dangerous. Anyone who ever had an Italian grandmother like mine knows that you aren't going to tell grandma, "I command you to stand in that triangle over there while I decide what you should do for me!" I don't know about your grandmother, but mine, from everything my mother told me about her, would step out of that triangle and hit you with a wooden spoon. And what about those spirits whose intent is purely hateful? Such souls can be very strong willed and can sometimes overpower the living because the dead have learned to tap into energies that the living are often unaware of. Some spirits may pretend to cower before your every command simply because they might find you interesting, but the moment you are at your weakest, they will strike.

While I understand that the forceful method is very old, it is not the oldest. One has only to look to the medicine people found among the tribal cultures of Africa and the remote areas of the world to see that a far more respectful tone is taken with the beloved dead with offerings made before the question is answered or task undertaken. This is how the earliest Witches dealt with the dead, and it is how truly wise Witches deal with them today.

It is far more sensible to call on the spirits who truly cared about you in life, such as family, or on your ancestors, who have an interest in seeing their bloodline continue unfettered. When you draw in spirits with whom you already have a connection, and who care about your cause, they will *want* to help you because this is, in part, why they still partake in this plane of existence.

Finally, consider this. Think of your coworkers. Isn't it safe to assume that those around you who truly care about their job perform better? The spirit world is no different, which is why I choose to work with the spirits of those who loved me in life—those who would have cared about the particular reason I have for calling a spirit up. I would never dream of threatening the spirits except in the most extreme of cases—when the spirit has a malefic intent and is trying to harm either me or those I care about. But other than in those most dire of circumstances, I maintain a relationship of love, respect, and admiration with all of the spirits I call on.

The Skull: Portal to the Spirit Realms

In chapter 3, I described the skull as among the most important tools of the Witch. This most ancient tool of divination and magic is a fundamental implement of necromancy and has often been referred to as the oracular head. The Witch of Endor would likely have had one—known as the Oboth to the Hebrews. As stated before, if you cannot obtain one from a reputable place like *BoneRoom.com,* then substitute with a skull made of bronze, resin, or quartz crystal. These are not quite as powerful because they do not contain the energy of the species, but they will work as a strong symbolic link to the dead. As mentioned previously, a skull used for divinatory practices should probably have a lower jaw since, traditionally, this meant that it was able to communicate. If yours does not have one, not to worry, for it will still be a fantastic energy conduit to the Death Current, that vibrational plane of existence where the spirits of the dead reside. However, you will probably not receive much communication from the skull directly and may want to use another method of actual contact such as a scrying mirror or cauldron of fire.

To energize the skull, you'll use your other tools and a willing sacrifice of your own blood. Don't worry; you won't have to slice your hand open or anything weird like that. Three drops of blood, taken via a sterile medical lancet available at any drug store, should be more than enough to satisfy the spirits. In ancient times, animals were sacrificed. We don't even need to approach the ethics of this, for while there is strong magical force in the blood of any creature, it is missing the emotional component of sacrifice, at least outside of truly poor countries. When you can buy ten more chickens down at the grocery store, you're not really giving much up.

Rjtual: A Rjte of Necromantic Divination

The following ritual is the perfect basis for your work with divinatory necromancy. The tools involved will almost always facilitate the presence of the dead, and I personally do this whenever I want to be sure that the dead will show up. My coven-sister Kelly Spangler and I performed a variation of this ritual during a lockdown at the Salem Witch House for an episode of the Travel Channel's *Ghost Adventures*. We simply would not allow the hosts of the show to come to Salem and not have a truly paranormal experience, and this ritual guaranteed that the spirits would be on the guest list!

You will need:
- Human skull (or substitute)
- Yew wand
- Bronze dagger
- Pentacle of protection
- Chalice of libation filled with spring water—*not* tap
- Offering cauldron
- Spirit powder (see appendix A)

- Spirit incense and burner (see appendix A)
- A spirit rattle or bell
- Medical lancet (available at drug store)
- Jar of honey
- Additional offerings of olive oil, milk, wine, and barley, all kept in separate containers until needed. If you do not have all of them, please have at least the spring water, honey, and olive oil.
- Anointing oil (see appendix A)
- A black candle and a white candle
- A piece of parchment paper and pen

Be sure to place all of the tools and offerings upon your altar of the dead and fill your chalice with fresh spring water—*not* tap water. Stand before the altar, and relax yourself into a visionary state (see chapter 2).

Ring the spirit bell or shake the spirit rattle to create sacred space and let the dead know that you are ready to make contact with them.

Light the black and white candles, saying, in turn, *This black candle shall draw the spirit of [name of spirit here] that [he/she] may provide the answers I seek while the white candle shall share with [him/her] the energy raised here.*

Write the name of the spirit you wish to call on the piece of parchment paper and place it on the pentacle of protection, saying, *By the power of the written word, I do stir and summon the spirit [name of spirit here]! Come forth and provide the answers I seek!* Anoint your wrists, heart, throat, forehead, and the crown of your head with anointing oil, saying, *I consecrate myself as a creature of spirit that the spirit of [name of spirit here] will come forth and provide the answers I seek!*

THE WITCHES' BOOK OF THE DEAD

Sprinkle the spirit powder in a circle, counterclockwise (the direction of the dead), around your area of working. Be sure to include the altar. If your altar is against a wall, sprinkle behind it as best you can. Say, *This powder shall serve to protect me from all evil and harmful energy. Let no spirit or force enter here who would speak untruth!*

Take up the bronze dagger with your right hand and trace a circle three times around you, counterclockwise, and say, *By bronze blade of the ancients, I cast this circle to defend me from all evil and harm. Let all spirits who enter here speak only truth and be of pure intent!*

Light the charcoal (or stick incense) and sprinkle the spirit incense upon the charcoal. Raise the incense to each of the four directions, North, East, South, and ending in West before the altar, each time saying, *Let this sacred smoke stir and summon the spirit [name of spirit here]! Come forth and provide the answers I seek!*

Open the lid of the honey pot and say, *Let the sweetness of honey please the spirit of [name of spirit]. Come forth and provide the answers I seek!*

Using your right hand, tap the crown of the skull three times with the yew wand and say, *I hereby conjure the spirit of [name of spirit] to come forth and provide the answers I seek!*

Now you must make the offerings to the dead by pouring them into the offering cauldron. Pour some of the spring water from the chalice of libation. Pour in some honey from the honey jar (make sure it isn't crystallized—reheating it helps with that). Pour the olive oil, milk, and wine into the cauldron also. Finally, sprinkle in the barley, saying, *Let these offerings appease you, spirit of [name of spirit here]! Come forth and provide the answers I seek!*

Take the sterilized medical lancet and prick the index finger on your right hand and place three drops of blood into the offering cauldron. Now, say, *I make this offering of my blood, of my volition, that it may feed you, spirit of [name of spirit here], of my life force! Come forth and provide the answers I seek!*

With this said, place your left hand, palm downward, on the top of the skull, and breathe deeply. Ask the question you want answered aloud. Continue to breathe deeply and wait. The answer can come in a number of ways. The most common begins with a vibration of energy moving from the skull into your left hand and throughout your body. This is the energy of the Death Current moving through you. Once you feel this vibration, it will typically be accompanied by a voice that seems to emanate telepathically from the skull directly into your mind. Listen for what the dead are saying, for you will most likely get your answer in this way. In some instances, you may actually see visions of things that are to be within the smoke of the incense. Pay very close attention to your dreams on this night, for you will almost certainly receive more visions there. In the rarest of instances, the spirit will manifest as a vision before you, speaking directly to you as the prophet Samuel did before the Witch of Endor. Do not be alarmed if this happens. Simply listen to what the spirit tells you and be respectful.

Once you feel that you wish to close the ritual (this is always at your own discretion), take up the yew wand in your right hand and tap the crown of the skull three times with it, saying, *I give you thanks, spirit of [name of spirit], for the wisdom you have shared with me! May you depart in love and joy, and return when I have need of you again!*

Place the yew wand back upon the altar and take up the bronze dagger with your right hand. Draw a circle, clockwise this time, around the space three times, saying, *I hereby close this sacred rite. As rising moon, and setting sun, it is done!*

. . .

Ritual: The Rite of the Mirror of the Dead

If the skull you use is not of the divinatory kind with the lower jaw, you may not be getting much communication directly from it. Because it is such a powerful portal to the realms of the dead, the skull should always be present for the ritual, no matter what kind it is. But there are other methods you can use that might better facilitate contact. One such method is to use a black scrying mirror, washed only in an infusion of mugwort. See chapter 6 for more on the scrying mirror. Everything about this ritual is the same as the Rite of Necromantic Divination above with the following exceptions:

As you are actually scrying for this version of the rite, it might help to be seated with the mirror placed at eye level across from you on the altar.

Be sure to place the incense near enough to the black mirror so that it is partly veiled in smoke but not so close that it is enshrouded in it. The mirror should be angled slightly so that nothing, including you, is reflected in it. You may want to keep just the black candle lit for this version of the ritual, making sure that the candle flame is not reflected in the glass either.

Once you have made your offerings in the cauldron, gaze into the mirror and say, *Into this mirror, I conjure the spirit of [name of spirit] to come forth and provide the answers I seek!*

Stare into the blackness of the mirror and wait. It may take a little while to see a vision of the answer you seek, but it will come. Images can be literal or symbolic. Sometimes, the spirit will answer with mental pictures of things it understands, so this process can sometimes play out like a game of charades. You may also hear whispers from the mirror telling you the answer to your question. Yes, that's right: hear. The Wicked Queen of the classic tale *Snow White and the Seven Dwarfs*, didn't invent that trick. Messages from the spirit world can often take the form of all five senses of sight, sound, taste, smell, and touch! Pay close attention and also be sure to pay attention to your dreams as well.

Once you feel that you wish to close the ritual, complete it as you would with the Rite of Necromantic Divination above. After the rite, you may want to write your impressions in a special journal that chronicles your spiritual adventures.

As a final note, you may also perform this version of the ritual, simply substituting the mirror with a copper scrying bowl filled with spring water, also mentioned in chapter 6.

• • •

Ritual: The Cauldron of Fire

In some forms of necromancy, a copper tripod was used to make a fire of cypress wood, long a tree of the dead, and olive wood with incense sprinkled into the flames. The three legs of the tripod are important, as the number three has long been a number of the dead, dating back at least to the story of Christ's resurrection on the third day, and perhaps even further. For safety reasons, I recommend using a three-legged cast iron offering cauldron on top of a ceramic tile to protect the altar from heat. Everything about this ritual is the same as the Rite of Necromantic Divination above with the following exceptions:

This version of the ritual should be performed outside. Even with all of your windows open, this could set off your smoke detectors, or worse, cause a fire.

When you place your offerings in the cauldron, you should place very little liquid. Otherwise, you will not be able to light a fire within. Once you place all the offerings, including the blood, in the cauldron, fill the cauldron halfway with bits of cypress wood and/or olive wood, both effective for this purpose. Light the fire and sprinkle in some spirit incense (stick incense will not work for this method), saying, *Into this flame, I conjure the spirit of [name of spirit] to come forth and provide the answers I seek!*

You should add more incense at intervals to continue the smoke and the scent. Traditionally, the incense was added a total of seven times, but I add it as needed throughout the rite. Meditate on the flames and the smoke of the incense. You will likely see visions of things to come. Both the flames and the smoke may contain symbols similar to what you see during scrying (see chapter 6). Watch and listen carefully, for you may also hear whispers within the crackling of the flames that may answer your question. Again, pay close attention and also be sure to be mindful of your dreams.

Again, when you wish to close the ritual, complete it as you would with the Rite of Necromantic Divination above. Once the rite is complete, be sure to write down your experiences in a journal.

• • •

Going to the Graveyard

Graveyards are among the best places to perform necromantic rituals. Unfortunately, you really aren't supposed to enter most of them at night, and doing so could be both dangerous and in violation of the law. So I don't recommend doing this often, but if you have the opportunity to do it even once in your life, it's an extremely powerful way of tapping into the spirit world.

The ancient necromantic rituals have given way to modern rituals, such as the one offered below, that are just as effective. They are often comprised of verbal or written requests to the dead that include offerings, such as flowers, coins, and so on. Customs vary by region. In New England, cemeteries are typically adorned with flowers or the occasional American flag. In New Orleans, amongst their "cities of the dead," there are many tombs, crypts, and graves featuring piles of colorful offerings of all sorts, including written prayers, alcohol, toys, photographs, statues, personal items—just about anything you can imagine. At Holt Cemetery, a burial ground for the poor and one of the Crescent City's rare belowground graveyards, the resting places are adorned with a wondrous blend of folk art, offerings, and magic.

Ritual: Graveyard Necromancy

Since it is simply unwieldy in this day and age to traipse into a graveyard with all of the implements of necromancy, I recommend not bringing any tools, though you might want to wear a pentacle pendant or other symbol of protection. For this simple necromantic ritual, you are going to visit the grave of someone you love and lie upon it to receive the answers you seek. As mentioned previously, the spirit you choose should be someone who would understand the particular question you want answered.

The only thing you should bring with you is an offering of food, drink, or other gift that the person you are calling on enjoyed. Short of that, an offering of money always works. Usually, the poor will later pick up the money and so you'll be helping someone in the process. And when all else fails, leave flowers, as they have been more than acceptable offerings to the dead for millennia. Before entering a graveyard, always knock at the gate three times and ask that the spirits of the dead open the way to the other realms.

Place your offering on the grave with respect, reverence, and love and say, *I give you, [name here], this offering to honor your contribution to my life. May your energy continue to shine down on all those who knew and loved you. Please, come forth and provide the answers I seek! Blessings of gratitude!*

Now, lie down upon the grave, head closest to the tombstone or grave marker, close your eyes, and relax into a visionary state. Feel the Death Current flowing up from the ground and into your body. Sense the spirits throughout the graveyard and know that you are in their world now. After a time, you will begin to see visions, hear voices, smell scents, and experience other sensations. Listen closely. The answer you seek may come as a mere whisper on the wind, but it will come!

When you are ready, offer a last word of thanks and leave the grave-yard. Remember to always exit a graveyard backwards. This helps you to keep any unwanted spirits from following you home!

• • •

10

Necromantic Magic

I had my first real foray into working with the dead in 2003 in a class on necromancy taught by Shawn Poirier. We cohosted our first Festival of the Dead that year. After many years of practicing much softer forms of Witchcraft, I cautiously decided to experiment with something bolder.

Up to that point, I had tended to play in the shallower end of the magical pool. I've always been a bit of a skeptic; plus, living in an occult magnet like Salem for over twenty years has exposed me to all manner of frauds and freaks. When Shawn suggested this necromantic event, I was both cynical and perhaps just a little bit nervous about the issues it might raise for me.

I participated in the ceremony with a raised eyebrow. Shawn created a circle of spirit powder on the floor in the middle of the function room of one of Salem's swankiest restaurants, surrounding an altar set with necromantic tools, including two human leg bones and, of course, Robert the skull. Only in Salem could you have a human leg bone in one hand and a piece of chicken satay in the other—but then this was a restaurant after all.

Each participant was asked to go up to the skull on the altar, place his right hand on it, and project a magical wish into the world. The spirits, according to Shawn, would then act to make those wishes happen. I was skeptical. If it were that easy, I asked, wouldn't they be selling skulls at Walmart? Still, I put my skepticism aside and, in my turn, knelt before the altar. I made an offering to the spirits and placed my hand upon Robert the skull . . . to discover it was vibrating. I lifted it up. No joy buzzer was present. Yes, it was vibrating to a very pulsing hum. Upon projecting my manifestation, the vibrating stopped. It was an intense milestone in my personal development. The spell itself soon came to fruition and I became a convert to the ancient ways of the necromancer.

Employing the Dead in Magic

In the previous chapter, you learned to work with the powers of oracular necromancy—divination with the dead, which is what the word "necromancy" means at its core. However, over the centuries, necromancy came to refer to the general practice of magic with the dead—which is no mystery, given the propensity of Witches to call on the spirits for both divination and magic. Necromancy was also confused with black magic, and thus the word began to refer to all manner of magical practice whether the dead were involved or not. In my own practice, I use the word "necromancy" to refer to both the oracular and magical kind; I do not use the word to refer to any form of magic that does not involve the dead.

If the Witch did it, the powers that be either found a way to make it illegal or severely limited its practices to narrow, official boundaries. As I mentioned in chapter 7, necromantic sorcery has usually been so feared by authorities that they tried to dissuade people from pursuing this form of magic by legislating against it and portraying Witches as agents of evil. We have to strip away the hyperbole and libelous attacks to get to the core of what Witches really did and why it made the authorities fear it so deeply. The most obvious reason is that taking power into one's own hands denies the supremacy of the God king, the Pope, the divinely ordained leader. To walk the path of the Witch is to reclaim your inner power!

If the practice of necromancy seems antiquated and odd, know that it is still going on today, largely kept alive by Catholics and other, more orthodox religious traditions. All but a handful of the Catholic saints are the spirits of the dead said to intercede on behalf of the living by virtue of offerings and prayers. If this isn't necromancy, I don't know what is. Mary Magdalene, Saint Francis, and other Catholic notables are often shown holding a skull, which in these cases symbolizes hidden knowledge. While many of the Catholic traditions are based on older, pre-Christian magical practices, we owe them a great debt of gratitude for keeping these beliefs alive, especially considering that many modern pagans and Witches have shirked the dead in favor of mythological deities.

Heart, Will, Intention, and Action

Before beginning any magical working, be sure that your heart is in it. Without true heart—and by this I don't just mean the physical muscle but rather the central core of spiritual being that radiates from within you—magic doesn't work. The Egyptians took the connection between the physical and spiritual heart very seriously, which is why the heart was the only organ they left in the body at the time of embalming. They believed that the heart contained the soul. Without the heart, magic will not flow through you. You must radiate the joy and love of the universe for others—including deities and spirits—so that they want to lend their strength to your cause.

Bring your will into the act, for it is your strength of determination— your iron will—that will make the magic happen! Your will is that pure focus that empowers you and connects you with the reservoirs of energy weaving throughout the universe. Without that focus, your magic is nothing but dust particles blown this way and that upon the wind.

And you also must figure out what it is you want to accomplish. Too many aspiring sorcerers attempt to practice Witchcraft without any sense of what they want to get out of it, whether spiritually or materially. Intention is a huge part of the battle. Do you want that new car? Well, project for it! See yourself driving it! Manifest that car into reality. If it's a lover you want, whether it be a specific lover (see below for a note on ethics), or just the best person out there for you, then make sure you get specific about the person or traits you want. Don't be wishy-washy!

Yes, you may be reading between the lines at this point. Watered-down versions of Witchcraft are heavily practiced and promoted today in the mainstream. Even Oprah does it. It's called "The Secret."

Well, the real secret is that to do magic, you've got to not only put your heart, will, and intention into it; you've got to take action in the real world as well. As I often tell my clients looking to do love magic without leaving the house, "the pizza delivery man is probably not going to propose, so get the hell out of the house and put yourself out there!" With real action, magic is allowed to do its work! My father always referred to this most powerful form of magic as the "magic of *do*."

A Note on Magical Ethics

As we're talking about using magic, the question may arise: What should we use magic *for*? Some say that one should never use magic to do anything manipulative, such as forcing someone to love you. However, *all* magic is manipulative by its very nature. The guidelines are not so cut and dry. Still, you might not want to turn the object of your affection into a walking zombie—especially since you may never get rid of him, which you may want to do when you get tired of things. It is okay to ask the spirits to give a little nudge to a person so that he notices you more, thinks to give you a call, or perhaps makes a date with you. I call this "psychic perfume." It's okay to make yourself more alluring to a person or send a message in dreams as long as you recognize that it's not a good idea to force people to conform to your will. Love cannot be manufactured, so at best you'd only end up with someone who has an unhealthy obsession for you, and at worst you could end up being pursued by someone with serious psychological problems who is now fixated entirely on keeping you in his life. As they say, be careful what you wish for.

This brings us to the idea of hexing and cursing. Contrary to most modern books on Witchcraft, Witches have always hexed and cursed, but the vast majority of them have done so ethically—*in the name of justice!* In times when justice was often available only to the wealthy, ordinary people would seek the Witches out to help them take action against those transgressors who had raped and murdered, stolen property, or hurt the community in some way. The Witch would absolutely curse such people to be brought to justice, but she would typically do a reading of some kind to see whether a person was guilty. In most cases, finding this out didn't matter, since the Witch did not need to know exactly who the perpetrator was in order to bring him to justice. She merely had to know that there was one. If all you're doing is hexing and cursing people, you may want to seek therapy, since such pursuits denote an unhappy life.

And finally, as we discussed in the previous chapter, magicians can overestimate their own power to subdue and control spirits, often at their own peril. Spirits can often become dangerous when approached with threats and abuse. If you approach the spirits from a place of respect, make them appropriate offerings, and treat them well, they will *want* to help you.

Using the Skull in Magic

You've learned to use the skull as a communication tool in oracular necromancy. Now you're going to use it, and the other tools introduced in chapter 4, to conjure the spirits to aid you in manifesting your needs and desires. Necromantic magic is much simpler than you might imagine, requiring a basic assortment of tools and, if you can obtain one, a human skull. Again, a skull made of bronze, resin, or quartz crystal can be an effective substitute. The skull will be your focal point in rituals with the dead, for it is your doorway to spirit. You will direct all your heart, will, and intention through the skull, creating waves of energy through the spirit world by which the dead shall manifest your desires.

The skull you employ for magical purposes does not have to have a jaw in the way that a divinatory skull does. In this case, since you're using it to call on the dead that you may send them out to perform tasks, it is not necessary for the skull itself to be able to communicate.

As in the previous chapter, you will also need to charge up your skull with your necromantic tools and with a sacrifice of your own blood. Again, just a few drops will do, and they should always be drawn with a sterile medical lancet, found at any drug store.

Ritual: Necromantic Magic with the Skull

The following spell is a powerful means of using the skull to employ the dead in necromantic magic. I use this method more than any other to send my will into the world. Using the skull to cast spells is documented as far back as the magical papyri of ancient Greece in 200 BCE, so this form of magic has been around for a very long time—and with good reason. It works.

You will need:
- Human skull (or substitute)
- Yew wand
- Bronze dagger
- Pentacle of protection
- Chalice of libation
- Spirit powder

- Spirit incense and burner (see appendix A)
- Honey pot
- A spirit rattle or bell
- Medical lancet (available at drug store)
- Anointing oil (see appendix A)
- A black candle and a white candle
- A piece of parchment paper and pen

Make sure your tools are set upon the altar of the dead and that your chalice is filled with fresh spring water—*not* tap water. Stand before the altar, and relax yourself into a visionary state (see chapter 2).

Ring the bell or shake the rattle to create sacred space and let the spirits know that you are prepared for the work at hand.

Light the black and white candles, saying, in turn, *This black candle shall draw the spirit of [name of spirit] while the white candle shall help [him/her] to usher my will upon the spectral winds.*

Write the name of the spirit you wish to call on the piece of parchment paper and place it on the pentacle of protection, saying, *By the power of the written word, I do stir and summon the spirit of [name of spirit]! Come forth and aid me in my task!*

Anoint your wrists, heart, throat, forehead, and the crown of your head with anointing oil, saying, *I consecrate myself as a creature of spirit that the spirit of [name of spirit] will come forth and aid me in my task!*

Sprinkle the spirit powder in a circle, counterclockwise, around your area of working, including the altar. Say, *This powder shall serve to protect me from all evil and harmful energy. Let no spirit or force enter here with malice and may only those forces who hold me dear come forth!*

Take up the bronze dagger with your right hand and trace a circle three times around you counterclockwise and say, *By bronze blade of the ancients, I cast this circle to defend me from all evil and harm. Let only what is true and pure enter this space!*

Light the charcoal (or stick incense) and sprinkle the spirit incense upon the charcoal. Raise the incense to each of the four directions, North, East, South, and ending in West before the altar, each time saying, *Let this sacred smoke stir and summon the spirit of [name of spirit]! Make manifest my desires and usher them into reality!*

Open the lid of the honey pot and say, *Let the sweetness of honey please the spirit of [name of spirit]. Come forth and aid me in my task!*

Using your right hand, tap the crown of the skull three times with the yew wand and say, *I hereby conjure the spirit of [name of spirit] to come forth and aid me in my task!*

Now, make the offering. Take the sterilized medical lancet and prick the index finger on your right hand and place three drops of blood on the skull as an offering. You're not using the cauldron to make the offering for this spell, but instead you are making a direct offering of blood to the spirits through the skull itself. Say, *I make this offering of my blood, of my volition, that it may feed you, [name of spirit], of my life force! May you now go forth and execute my will!*

With this said, place your right hand, palm downward, on the top of the skull and, with all your heart and will, visualize that thing you desire most. Channel that thing into the very fabric of the Death Current that the spirit you have called will take hold of it and make it real. See it in your mind's eye so strongly that there is no room for doubt or failure. Your goal *will* be achieved. Your *desires* will be had. You *will* succeed! This could be the new job you've wanted. It could be the vacation you've been hoping to take. Or, it could be getting a certain object of your affection to think about you a little more. The dead are fantastic at bringing dreams to the living, so asking the spirits to help a lover to dream of you is an excellent use of this ritual.

When you wish to close the ritual, take up the yew wand with your right hand and tap the crown of the skull three times with it, saying, *I give you thanks, spirit of [name of spirit]! May you depart in love and joy, as you go to complete my task. May you return when I have need of you again!*

Place the yew wand back upon the altar and take up the bronze dagger with your right hand. Draw a circle, clockwise this time, around the space three times, saying, *I now release the energy created here tonight. May it join the spirit of [name of spirit] in manifesting what I desire into reality! As rising moon, and setting sun, it is done!*

• • •

Ritual: The Graveyard Ritual

The second most-visited grave in America (number one being that of Elvis Presley) is the tomb of Marie Laveau, located in St. Louis Cemetery #1 on the outskirts of the French Quarter of New Orleans. The aboveground Greek revival family crypt where she and many of her family are interred is noted for being covered with X's, drawn in graveyard brick three at a time by those seeking for their wishes to be answered. Marie is an unofficial saint in New Orleans—a Loa, or intermediary spirit of the Voodoo traditions of the Crescent City. When visitors make offerings of rum, flowers, cigars, money, and food, Marie is believed to answer prayers and exert her magical influence from beyond the grave. As Marie Laveau is my personal favorite contact in the spirit world, I keep a statue of her on the altar of the dead at my shop, HEX, and I make an annual pilgrimage to her tomb in New Orleans, where I perform a ritual of offering and reverence and ask Marie to aid me in keeping magic alive here in Salem.

You can do this kind of magic just by visiting a graveyard where someone you love or admire is buried. Graveyards are very powerful conduits of the Death Current, for obvious reasons. The best time to visit is at midnight (or, perhaps, at the "soul's midnight" of 3 AM), but the daytime can work as well. If you do go at night, be sure to find a cemetery where you will not be arrested for trespassing. Most are quite strict about visiting after dark, but some are more lax than others. As mentioned in the previous chapter, you should always knock three times at the gate of a graveyard before entering and ask the spirits to open the way to the realms of the dead. You should also come with an offering of food, drink, flowers, or something else that the deceased preferred in life. If you don't know what that is, bring some of the traditional food for the dead in appendix A, or, as mentioned before, an offering of money is wonderful since the poor might later take it and this is pleasing to the spirits.

Leave your offering at the intended grave with respect, reverence, and love and say, *I leave you, [name of spirit], this offering to honor your contribution to my life. May your energy continue to shine down on all those who knew and loved you. I come to you for help with [situation or task]. Please assist me as only you can and help me to change things for the better. Blessings of gratitude!*

When you are ready, offer a last word of thanks and leave the graveyard. As you learned in the last chapter, always exit a graveyard backwards to keep the spirits from following you home!

• • •

Ritual: The Ritual of the Crossroads

The crossroads are among the most magical of places in cultures around the globe. The meeting of roads symbolizes the meeting of worlds and thus the crossroads become a place between the realms of matter and spirit. The Witch goddess Hecate was said by the ancients to guard the places where three roads meet, though she is ultimately present at every crossroads, and one can find offerings to her at such places if you know what to look for. In the Voodoo traditions of Haiti and New Orleans, Papa Legba (or, as they say in Old Nawlins, Papa Lebas) is the keeper of the crossroads, guarding the way to all other spiritual forces. He is identified with Saint Peter, who can often be seen holding a cross of keys . . . again the crossroads.

Visit a crossroads at midnight (or at 3 AM), bringing an offering for Hecate and for the dead. This can be as simple as pouring honey wine upon the ground. Appendix B contains an expanded list of offerings for Hecate and other deities of the dead. Hecatean priestess Mulysa Mayhem taught me that it is important to invoke the goddess Hecate at the crossroads, for it is she who shall mediate and protect you against those among the dead that would bring you harm.

You will also speak the ancient Greek prayer of protection: *"Aski kataski haix tetrax damnameneus aision."* The prayer dates back to the time when Diana was worshipped at Ephesus and it was said to be associated with her. Some say the meaning is undecipherable, and some say it means "Darkness, Light, Sun, and Truth."[28] Whatever this phrase truly means, it has been used for more than two thousand years as words of power to protect against evil. It is one of the greatest of spells.

Stand at the center of the crossroads and enter into a visionary state. Call out the prayer with all the fire of your heart and strength of your will: *"Aski kataski haix tetrax damnameneus aision."* Do not be a wimp about this. Too many Witches fail in their magic by bringing no life to their words of power. Pour or lay your offering for Hecate on the ground at your feet, and say, *Mighty Hecate, may you guard me here at the crossroads as I call upon the powers of the dead. Bless us in this rite!*

Wait a few moments for the energy to shift. You will feel a change in the air when the shades of the dead begin to emerge from the shadows and the Death Current is flowing through the very Earth beneath your feet. When you can feel its power, pour or lay your offering for the dead alongside Hecate's offering and call out, **Let those among you who would aid me in my cause. Join with me now to [task to be done]. Let nothing stand in your way as you bring this to be. Let mighty Hecate bear witness to this bond, so mote it be!**

What you have just learned is a variation on one of history's most ancient spells. The crossroads have meaning to so many cultures and traditions that merely to stand in one is to swim in the tides of magic.

• • •

Ritual: A Ritual of Dreams

It has even been suggested in such popular blockbusters as 1999's **The Sixth Sense** that the dead can better communicate with the living while the latter are asleep. Witches and sorcerers have always known this, and have taken advantage of it from ancient times. If the dead could invade the dreams of the living, it was supposed, then perhaps the Witch could employ those spirits to influence the living while they slept. Having used dreams to communicate information to others many times over the years, I find it works even better when the dead are involved, since they can keep doing the work when I've moved on to other tasks.

To perform this form of magic, you will want to get a comfortable chair and set it before your altar of the dead. Be sure to do this at a time when you know that the person you seek to influence will be asleep. You will need a black and white candle, your incense, and an offering for the dead, preferably honey wine or a blend of milk and honey, in your libation chalice (see chapter 4).

Go into a visionary state and light the black and white candles and the incense, saying, *This black candle shall draw the energy of spirit while the white candle shall help to usher my will upon the spectral winds. Let this sacred smoke lift my desires and make them reality.*

Pour half of the contents of the offering from the libation chalice into the offering cauldron, for the dead are always served first. Drink from the chalice and say, *As I drink from the wine of the dead, so I shall go into the realms of the dead, to return later to the living when my work is complete!* Pour the remaining offering into the cauldron, for the dead are also served last!

Sit in the chair before the altar of the dead with the skull across from you on the altar. Gaze into the eyes of the skull as long as you need to in order to create a bond with the spirit and connect to the realms of the dead. When you can feel the shift, say, *I ask of the spirits of the beloved dead! Go into the dreams of [name of person you wish to see visited]. Let him/her dream of [your message or imagery you wish for that person to experience]. Let these [visions/words] burn into his/her mind that my will be known!*

Now, sit back in the chair and close your eyes. If you would like to participate in the work of the dead, this would be a good time to meditate and journey with them on the spirit winds to the place where your intended is sleeping. With the spirits at your side, go into the dream world of the individual and work with the dead to help in bringing the messages you wish to impart. When you come out of the dream-state, the dead will still be working long into the night.

• • •

Creating Your Own Rituals

The rituals above represent but a few powerful examples of the many ways one can call on the spirits of the dead in necromantic magic. Some of the most powerful rituals will be those that you create or modify yourself as they come from the heart. Just as I have taken ancient ceremonies and adapted them for modern use, over time you will infuse these practices with your own soul's voice. And so the legacy of magic will continue to grow and evolve through the ages with creative new ways for reaching the spirits.

11

Dreaming the Dead

For those of you who are still reluctant to interact with the dead, don't be. You've almost certainly already experienced them. In fact, you're probably experiencing them nightly, whenever you drift off to sleep. Yes, the most common way we experience contact with the dead is in our dreams. Spirit visitation dreams are often so realistic that people who experience them question whether or not they were actually dreaming. Such nocturnal incidences typically involve meaningful communication, intense emotions, and sometimes even physical contact. Modern therapists are inclined to explain these lifelike "dreams" as merely the result of wish fulfillment. However, in ancient times people knew such visits to be true encounters with the dead.

Witches have always been masters of dreams, and have always known the ancient truth that dreams are a crossroads between the living and the dead and that, by dreaming, we can actually travel into the Death Current, communicating with spirits on their own vibrational plane of existence. As you learned in chapter 2, bringing yourself into a visionary state allows you to reach into supernatural worlds. Well, in dreams you're already there, so it's not something you have to work at. Dream visits seem to depend heavily upon conditions on the Other Side rather than on our ability to make them happen. Such visits are usually spontaneous, occurring within a few days or weeks after a person dies. They provide an opportunity to say good-bye, to bring closure, to impart advice, or perhaps to issue a warning of things to come. While it can be difficult to summon the dead in dreams, an understanding of such visitations is useful, because your ongoing work with the spirits will increase the likelihood of these experiences. It's important to prepare your dreaming consciousness, especially at times when a friend or loved one has passed away. As you advance in skill, you will be able to call the dead to visit you in your dreams.

Ancient Legacies

The ancients placed a great deal of importance on dreams and their ability to build bridges between the worlds of the living and the dead, the gods, totem animals, and other inhabitants of the unseen realms. Many early cultures, including the Greeks, Hebrews, Africans, and Native Americans, made almost no distinction between dreams and other kinds of visionary experiences that happened during the day or night, while sleeping, in trance, or even in waking consciousness. For them, dreams were yet another facet of reality. The emphasis was placed on the content of the experience, and on the ability of the dreamer to perceive and communicate with otherworldly realms of existence.

When we refer to our dreams today, we simply say that we "have" them, as though they belong to us and arise from within us as a part of our own psyche and subconscious mind. The ancients had a much different view: dreams were real experiences that the dreamers witnessed. Thus, they did not "have" dreams but rather saw them. The gods, the dead, and other supernatural beings made real visits to the dreamer, emerging from their hidden domains into the realm of mortals.

We see the great significance of dreams in the pages of classical Greek literature. Various Homeric epic poems and tragedies tell of the dead appearing in dreams to offer instructions and impart warnings. Such dreams are said by the storyteller to be objective events that happened independently of the dreamer, and do not arise from within. Spirit visitation dreams were a serious matter and were initiated by supernatural forces outside of the dreamer's own consciousness. In some tales, they entered a person's bedroom through the keyhole and stood at the head of the bed while they delivered a usually somber message.

The Greeks believed that if you were not properly buried when you died, your spirit could not pay the ferryman to cross the river Styx to the realm of the underworld and would be doomed to wander the Earth until proper burial rites were performed. Under such circumstances, you were allowed to return to a living person in a dream and ask for burial.

The Greek dead also appeared in prophetic dreams, usually to warn a person against a dire fate much like the ominous portents heard during necromantic practice. In Aeschylus's tragic trilogy, the *Oresteia*, Agamemnon, the King of Argos, comes home from the Trojan War and is murdered by his wife, Clytemnestra. Later he returns from beyond the grave to appear in a dream to warn Clytemnestra that she will be killed by their son, Orestes, to avenge his death at her hands. Despite Agamemnon's warning, Clytemnestra is unable to avoid this act of vengeance and is killed.[29] While prophecy can sometimes allow us to change the course of fate, seldom do we have the courage it takes to alter our path and manifest a new destiny.

Around the seventh century BCE, Greek culture absorbed an Eastern idea about dreams: that instead of being visited, the dreamer traveled out-of-body at night to visit the realms of spirit in order to receive important information. Such visions could be of a direct or symbolic nature. This concept was embraced by Orphism, a Greek religious movement that influenced many of Greece's later great thinkers, including Pythagoras and Plato.

Plato referred to dreams as "the between state," a real place where the human soul went during sleep to meet the gods and supernatural beings who are otherwise inaccessible. He said that dreams are another way to experience the world besides through sense and experience.

Plato keenly observed that dreams embody the heights and the depths of human consciousness. The heights were the revelations of the gods and the depths were dreams emanating from our dark, instinctual side. Dreams provide an outlet for instinct, "the lawless wild-beast nature" that exists in all of us, said Plato—centuries before Freud would make the same observations. Furthermore, Plato believed that dreams could be controlled in order to discover hidden truths. If we go to sleep with the "appetites" under control, and if our lives are in harmony and balance, then the rational side of the soul would be free to experience the mysteries of the divine, know the truth of the ages, and peer into the past, present, and future.

Saint Augustine believed that only a holy person could receive dream visits from the dead, like his friend Saint Ambrose, who was visited by saints Gervasius and Protasius. Augustine said this was God's will. Less saintly people were not considered to be so favored, and were thought not to be able to receive such visits, nor were they thought to be able to return after death to appear in dreams.

Once Christianity supplanted virtually all other religions, dreams as a method of spirit interaction became isolated to incidences of saintly intervention. Although the Bible tells of important dream events (but not involving the dead), dreams largely lost their importance in favor of the Church as the medium to the divine. Manifestations of the dead in any form, including dreams, were not to be trusted because they were masquerades by the Devil. An exception was made for dreams about the lamenting dead who appeared to ask for prayers to ease their time in Purgatory, or of those of the saints.[30]

However, the idea of dreams as a means of spirit communication was kept alive. Professor of Hebrew Literature Galit Hassan Rokem makes mention of sixteenth-century rabbis who are said to have been asked how to handle a situation in which "a dead person comes in a dream and asks to be removed from his grave because he is buried next to a heavy sinner."

Another of the deceased "asked in a dream that his clothes be buried with him." In that particular instance, "the rabbi showed special resourcefulness by suggesting that the clothes be distributed to the poor, so that the dead man's soul be clothed with charity in its eternal abode." While there is nothing specific in the Hebrew Old Testament about the dead communicating through dreams, Professor Rokem offers a number of examples from the Talmud.[31]

The Dreams of the Necromancers

The connection between sleep, dreams, and death has always been strong. Sleep has been referred to as the "little death," and dreams have been seen almost universally to be links to the underworld, for the dead often appear in dreams.

The Greeks and Romans were among a number of earlier cultures that consulted dreams for certain purposes. Especially important were dreams for healing, and seekers made pilgrimages to remote sites where priests assisted them in summoning the gods for help with all manner of ailments and injuries.

The art of calling the dead into dreams, a form of dream incubation, was an important rite at ancient *nekuomanteions*—temples where oracles would divine hidden wisdom from the whispers of the dead. In fact, the surviving accounts of necromancy at the Greek oracular sites point to ritually incubated dreams as the primary means of communication with the dead.

After powerful rituals were performed with offerings made and prayers spoken, the necromancers slept on the skins of sacrificed animals and expected to see the dead in their dreams. They believed that the spirits would appear to answer their questions, prophesy the future, and warn of imminent danger. Upon awakening, the priests would aid the dreamers in interpreting the messages received from the Other Side.

Witches and Dreams of the Dead

As this is a book about Witchcraft, we cannot neglect the role of the Witch when discussing dreams of the dead. The archetypal, mythical Witch was long considered a nocturnal creature, creeping into the dreams of her victims to torment them, and sometimes sexually molest them, stealing their seed and causing impotence. I'm sure psychiatrists could have written volumes had they been practicing in the time of the Witch persecutions that plagued Europe over several centuries. Instead of hanging trees and stakes, we'd have had many a couch occupied by terrified villagers whose dreams included the spectral forms of Witches seeking to terrorize them in the shadowy night.

The connection between Witches, dreams, and the dead goes as far back as the Fertile Crescent, woven into the beliefs of Mesopotamia. Originally, the Mesopotamians believed that there were both good Witches and evil ones, and that to be a Witch alone was not worthy of persecution. Later, Witches became scapegoats and the domain of temple exorcists who specialized in banishing their powers, further demonstrating my point in chapter 1 that spiritual power became consolidated to priesthoods while practitioners of natural magic were demonized. Among the powers of these dark Witches was the ability to send dreams to their prey in the form of clouds. Often, those enchanters who do appear in the dreams of the tormented are thought to be the shades of Witches who have died, having assumed a nearly demonic presence in death, existing only to assail the living. Magical rituals known as the *Maqlû*, meaning "burning," were conducted during festivals of the dead to help banish these villains of the night. [32] In my own research into ancient sources for the archangel Michael, I came across a reference for Mukhla, the Sumerian archangel of the Sun-God. [33] I cannot help but wonder if this reference to the ritual of fire known as Maqlû ties in somehow to the great archangel who represents the element of fire to both Witches and ceremonial magicians.

The Italian benandanti were a cult of sorcerers who professed to protect the fertility of the land from being blighted by the malandanti—or evil

Witches. This didn't stop them from being charged with the crime of Witch-craft themselves, since the priestly authorities of the Church typically didn't differentiate between good magic and bad—unless they themselves were the ones doing it. The benandanti were accused of attending the infamous Witches' Sabbath, a feared event where Witches were said to meet at festive bacchanalias in celebration of the Devil. True Witches know that this was actually a time for gathering and bringing life to the land through ceremony and magic, so the benandanti were not so far off in their practices. It took decades of torture to convince the benandanti to "admit" to participating in the Witches' Sabbath, as stories can certainly be altered under the duress of untold agonies. However, before this point, the men of the benandanti claimed to battle Witches and wizards for the supremacy of the crops. The women of the benandanti claimed to witness "processions of the dead." Both men and women claimed that they entered into a dreamlike trance during which they left their bodies in the form of animals to enter into the otherworld. The benandanti compared their journey to a "temporary death," and it is likely that they entered the spirit realms with help of the various fly-ing ointments often associated with Witches. The benandanti claimed that they had this power because they were born with a caul—a thin membrane that can sometimes cover the face of a baby as it emerges from the womb, also often associated with natural Witchcraft and the second sight. Historian Carlo Ginzburg theorizes that the so-called sorcerers who the benandanti fought against were in fact the "unappeased dead," spirits only blighting the land because they have not been honored.[34]

While the benandanti are perhaps the most obvious example, scholar Éva Pócs, in her groundbreaking work, *Between the Living and the Dead: A Perspective on Witches and Seers in the Early Modern Age*, refers to many exam-ples from European trials where the dead factor into the work of the Witch. The appearance of both Witches and the dead in dreams occur in a number of these trial accounts.

Bringing it back to my home here in Salem, we have only to look to the first Witch accused—the slave woman Tituba. When asked by Judge John

Hathorne what sort of apparition had persuaded the slave to give herself over to Witchcraft, Tituba replied, "One like a man just as I was going to sleep came to me."[35] This blurring of the lines between dreams and waking consciousness, the living and the dead, is prominent in the story of Witchcraft through the ages.

Finally, my mentor, hereditary Strega Witch Lori Bruno, pointed me to my favorite tale of dreaming Witches, a magical community that Lori's Sicilian family has long believed they were descended from. In 500 BCE, along the southern slopes of Mount Etna in Sicily, was Hybla Geleatis, a town "dedicated to the cult of a pre-Greek goddess, a chthonic or underworld divinity." The people of the town of Hybla Geleatis, and Lori's family in particular, earned fame "throughout the whole of Sicily and beyond" not only for remaining devout to their uniquely non-Greek religion, but for their masterful ability as dream prophets. It is likely that the prophecies of these seers were deeply connected to the spirits of the dead; not only was their deity a goddess of the underworld, but also the crater of Mount Etna itself, long a center of volcanic activity, was believed to be a direct entrance the underworld. This ancient legacy survives in Lori and in all of the Witches today who have learned to listen to the whispers of the dead in the shadowy currents of their dreams.[36]

Tribal Dreams of the Dead

Many of the tribal cultures existing in remote areas today hold the legacy of the ancient shamans and medicine people from whom Witches also evolved. To further see how the Witches and sorcerers of earlier European cultures may have viewed the dead in dreams, we have only to look to some of those tribal groups still practicing the ancient magical ways.

When a person dies among the Yoruba of Nigeria—whose ways came to America long ago in the form of Cuban Santeria and other Afro-Caribbean magical traditions—attendees of the funerary rites will often tell the deceased that, from now on, they shall see him in their dreams. Among the

Zulu tribes of Southern Africa, the people embrace the ancestors into their dreams. Among the Tiv people of Nigeria, the people are more apprehensive of dreams of the dead. But there is a thread that runs through all of the peoples of Africa who believe that the ancestors can come to us in dreams, and that is that the dead are able to "offer advice to the living, warn them, give them insight into the future, correct their conduct, and admonish them for neglecting spiritual duties." [37]

Native Americans of the southwestern United States, such as the Zuni and the Navajo tribes, have a deep-rooted fear of the dead. However, the medicine people of these tribes will often seek out the dead in their dreams, trances, and shamanic journeys. Like the ancient Greeks, the Zuni believe that the dreamer journeys outside the body and is not bound by time or place. Able to travel through past, present, future, or anywhere he wishes to go, the dreamer is able to join the dead in the realms of spirit that he may receive the imparted wisdom of his beloved ancestors.[38]

The people of the Xavante tribe of Brazil perform their own variation of dream incubation through sacred cylinders of polished wood believed to have the power to make contact with the dead. A tribal elder hangs the cylinder over the grave of the person with whom he wishes to communicate and, as he sleeps that night, he will meet the spirit of that person in his dreams. The Xavante express their dreams differently, depending on gender and age. While women will tell of their dreams of the dead in songs of lament, adolescent boys will observe the dead from a distance, and old men will communicate with the dead directly, narrating the images of the dead into stories for their people.[39]

Spirit Visitation Dreams in Modern Times

The emergence of psychology and psychotherapy restored the dream to importance in so-called modern society. Sigmund Freud and Carl Jung were the primary pioneers, and Jung especially reestablished the otherworldly and mystical nature of dreams. Dreams were seen as highly symbolic and compensatory; that is, they were expressions of the deep part of the Self that sought a balancing out of the stresses of life. Even dreams of the dead were interpreted in symbolic ways, or viewed as part of a grieving process that enabled people to have closure.

Spirit visitation dreams, however, resist complete assignment to symbolic interpretation. Freud himself even acknowledged this difficulty, stating, ". . . dreams of dead people whom the dreamer has loved raise difficult problems in dream-interpretation and that these cannot always be satisfactorily solved."[40] As researchers delve deeper into the study of consciousness, the afterlife, the soul, dreams, out-of-body experiences, near-death experiences, and the like, the evidence points to spirit visitation dreams as truly genuine experiences. If the dead do come to you in a dream, it is important to consider the symbolic meaning of the experience, but you should also regard it as an actual visit, and one with purpose, be it a message, a warning, or merely an opportunity to be close to you.

Characteristics of Dream Visits by the Dead

As I mentioned earlier, there is a sharp reality to dreams of the dead that sets them apart from ordinary dreams. The dreamer usually feels a heightening of the senses. The dream environment often manifests as a bridge, a crossroads, a strange landscape, or a meeting place on the Other Side, all suggesting that the dreamer is now between the worlds of the living and the dead. The atmosphere of the dream is likely to feel highly charged, almost electrical, while colors, scents, and even touch are enhanced, and the overall tone may seem quite surreal.

The ancient Greeks typically saw a more somber dead in their dreams, reflecting their beliefs in the afterlife as a gloomy place. The dead would appear as they had looked at the time of their death. If a man had been killed in battle, by murder, or in an accident, his appearance would be wounded, mangled, and bloody. In modern experiences, the dead are usually related as being radiant, vibrant, happy, youthful, and, if they had been ill or injured, are completely healed. People who die old often appear younger. This is generally my own experience, though I have found that those who died when they were older sometimes come to me in that form, perhaps to seem more relatable as this would be how I most recently remember them.

Communication with the dead in dreams can be verbal or telepathic. Often, the visiting dead say they have only a limited time, or that they had difficulty getting through, implying that the conditions of such a dream visit might be hard to arrange.

Who do the dead tend to visit in dreams? It might seem obvious that those closest to the dead—spouses, family, lovers, and good friends—would be the most likely people to see their departed in dreams, and that is usually the case. But sometimes spirits will visit people who know them but were not particularly close to them. Such people are left to wonder why they were visited. No one knows the exact mechanics behind spirit visitation dreams, but they may follow a path of least resistance, reaching out to whom they can.

Paranormal author Rosemary Ellen Guiley recalls a woman who received a vivid spirit visitation dream from her dead mother-in-law, who had a message for her son that she was always with him. The wife said she would be happy to relay the message, but asked why the mother did not tell her son directly herself. The dead woman replied, "I can't because of the way that he dreams." She could get through to her daughter-in-law, but not to her son. I love Rosemary's example here because it confirms, once and for all, that you can never truly escape your mother-in-law.[41]

When the dead come to call in dreams, there is generally a purpose for doing so. Proper burial has remained a theme since ancient times. The dead can be restless without having had a ceremonial sendoff to the afterlife. Even when there isn't a body—such as in natural disasters, disappearances, wars, and so on—a memorial service is often still required to bring closure, for the dead need it as much as we do. Other common purposes are to say a final good-bye and to reassure those left behind that they have survived death and are doing okay. The dead also return to address unfinished business, especially concerning their estates, and to offer advice and guidance to the living. Sometimes, the dead can come for vengeance against those who have wronged them, so remember, those you do evil to may have the last word in the spirit world. Once you begin to honor the spirits at your altar of the dead, those you honor will likely make more frequent appearances in your dreams, sometimes with messages, sometimes with warnings, and sometimes just to help maintain the relationship that you are mutually building.

Ritual: Summon the Dead in Dreams

Most spirit visitation dreams seem to originate from the realms of the dead, but sometimes it is possible to summon the dead to your dreams with ritual, just as the Greek necromancers, the Xavante elders, and countless other magical people have done through the ages. Here is a simple yet effective ritual to do so. I created this ritual with Rosemary Ellen Guiley, combining my knowledge of ritual magic with her extensive research into dreams. It draws on both the wisdom of the ancients as well as sound methods of modern dream incubation popularized by such films as the 2010 blockbuster, *Inception*.

You will need:
- A white candle
- Anointing oil (see appendix A)
- A human skull or substitute to act as a catalyst (see chapter 3)
- Bronze dagger
- Yew wand

- Spirit incense and burner (see appendix A)
- Spirit powder (see appendix A)
- Jar of honey
- Chalice of libation filled with spring water
- Dream journal (can be a writing journal or even a simple notebook)
- A photo or memento of the person or persons you wish to contact

Before you conduct such a ritual, it is important to know whom it is you wish to contact. I cannot stress this enough. If you go into your dreams with a psychic neon sign saying, "come one, come all," you may not be happy with who shows up. The inexperienced can sometimes be weaker in dreams, and there's no sense in opening the doorway to the spirits of serial killers, rapists, and other such ne'er-do-wells.

If you have specific questions for the spirit you're calling, it's important to know those as well. In your dream journal, write the name of the spirit you wish to contact as well as any questions you may have at the top of a blank page. That page will be dedicated to any visions, messages, or other perceptions you experience during the dream, which you should write down immediately upon waking. You may want to write these in the journal the morning of the day you plan to perform the ritual so that you can take the day to think about whom you wish to contact and what questions you might ask.

You should also write the name of the spirit and your questions on a piece of paper and place it on your altar of the dead along with the photo or mementos. This will form a connection between the altar and your dream space.

Before you begin the ritual itself, it is best to take a ritual bath with a palm full of kosher salt added to purify and protect your body before proceeding. While in the bath, meditate on the spirit you wish to meet in the dream and contemplate the questions you wish to ask.

Create an altar on a small table near your bedside with all of the tools listed above. Anoint the candle with oil and light it, softly saying, *As the candle flame is a doorway to the other worlds, let it open the way for [speak name here] to join me in my dreams this night.*

Lightly sprinkle spirit powder around your bed and softly say, *By the Earth of the grave and the sweet scents, let no evil spirit enter here.*

Light the charcoal and sprinkle a bit of incense over it—or, light a stick of incense, softly saying, *The smoke of this incense becomes as the mists of the underworld, through which the shade of [speak name here] will enter, to join me in my dreams this night.*

Take up the bronze dagger in your right hand and pass it through the smoke. Then, draw a circle of protection around your bed, three times counterclockwise, and softly say, *Let this circle become a doorway between the living and the dead. Let no evil enter here! Let only spirits who are pure of intent join me in my dreams this night.*

Return the dagger to the altar and take up the yew wand in your right hand and pass it also through the smoke. Tap the wand on the crown of the skull three times and softly say, *By my will, I do stir and summon the shades of the dead, that [speak name here] shall join me in my dreams this night, bringing wisdom, truth, and visions of what is to be.*

Place your left hand upon the skull and softly say, *Through this portal, I join myself to the energies of the Death Current, that [speak name here] will hear my call and join me in my dreams this night.*

Hold the chalice of spring water up above your head with both hands and softly say, *I make this offering to the spirits, that they may infuse it with the wisdom of the dead. By drinking from it, may I swim with them in the sacred waters of the dreamtide.* Now, drink half of the contents of the chalice, leaving the rest for the dead, and place the chalice on the table.

Snuff the candle out, as it is unsafe to fall asleep with it burning.

Get into bed. As you are falling asleep, visualize the spirit you wish to communicate with as vividly as you can. Imagine talking to the spirit and obtaining the answers you seek. Affirm to yourself that you will see the spirit whom you wish to see and affirm that you will remember the dream when you awake.

Upon awakening, record as much detail as you can in your dream journal. Dreams can evaporate with astonishing speed, so if you cannot write it down or record it, then repeat it to yourself so that it becomes set in your memory.

After you've had your coffee and you're more awake, or perhaps later in the day, take some time to analyze the dream. Think about the messages you received. Sometimes, the words might sound like gibberish, but after you ponder them for a while, they may become clearer. Did the spirit appear alone, or were there others with him or her? Were you taken to specific places that might have had importance?

It is important to note that you may not experience a literal visit and conversation with the dead, but your answer may have been delivered in other ways: through visions of specific places or things, words, and even symbols. There may be elements in the dream that have associations with the person you were hoping to contact, and so there may still be meaning behind them even though you did not actually see the person.

If you get no results, do not be discouraged. You can repeat this ritual until you get the hang of it. If you still feel unanswered after several nights, give the process a break for a few days and then try again. Keep in mind that answers may not be obvious and literal. It is helpful to have some experience in dream work, and I encourage you to study more on the subject. Answers can even come outside of the dream, such as flashes of intuition or strange coincidences that happen even days after the ritual was performed. Dream magic manifests into the universe in a way that unfolds in its own course and at its own pace.

• • •

12

Ghost Hunting: Seeking Out the Dead

I have been present for a number of ghost hunts through the years. I participated in one during a conference at the Houghton Mansion, a highly active haunted site mentioned in chapter 6. I've investigated the infamous Danvers State Hospital, a former insane asylum at which strange phenomena continue to occur. Shawn and I joined psychic medium Chris Fleming in his search through Salem for the spirit of Bette Davis that was featured on the Biography Channel show *Dead Famous*. But my absolute favorite ghost experience was when I filmed with the Travel Channel's popular show *Ghost Adventures* at a lockdown in the Salem Witch House, home of former Witch Trials judge Jonathan Corwin.

Ghost Adventures

In late 2010, my friend and paranormal author Jeff Belanger invited me to perform a spirit blessing ritual for an episode of *Ghost Adventures* set to air in

February 2011. I had never seen the show, but it was my coven-sister Kelly Spangler's favorite, and since she is a powerful spirit medium, I invited her to go along. The choice of sites was between the Witch House and a local restaurant that I really didn't want to film at because, however many times I had brought TV crews to their location, the owner and staff had always told me they didn't like the "kind of tourists" that my publicity attracted, and so I saw no reason to go somewhere that wouldn't appreciate my work. After seeing what had shown up at the Witch House during the show *Dead Famous*, I felt that it was a much more interesting site with much more potential for paranormal phenomena. There was just one tiny problem: the restaurant had a longstanding association with the spirit of Witch Trials victim Bridget Bishop, which meant that the restaurant's segment of the show might actually get as much activity as the one filmed at the Witch House. This would not do at all.

Kelly and I showed up at the Witch House with my favorite tricks of the trade: Robert the skull, the yew wand, the bronze dagger, the jar of honey, a chalice of libation, my Anubis spirit rattle, and a medical lancet to draw blood. The manager of the historic building told us that the hosts of the show were already locked inside, so we waited for one of the producers to come around to let us in. While we were waiting, I looked at Kelly and said, "This will be the only place they will get anything." I pointed my right hand in the direction of the restaurant and said "Bridget, I ask that you give them no audience this night. Give them no show at all. Depart from that place and let them discover nothing!" Yeah, it was catty, but I didn't want anyone, living or dead, to steal the spotlight from the Witch House.

The producer let us in and we met the hunky paranormal investigators that host the show: Zak Bagans, Nick Groff, and Aaron Goodwin. Being locked in a house with them was hardly what I would call work. Kelly and I set up a temporary altar of the dead, complete with fake candles and no incense—for this was a very old historic home and nobody wanted to chance a fire. Our hosts brought out a variety of strange equipment including a PX box, which converts electromagnetic fields into one of over 2,000 words that sound like they came out of an old Speak & Spell, giving voice to the dead, and a "spirit box," a tool that allows the spirits to communicate by traversing through a spectrum of radio waves. The team mentioned recording some strong activity on the second floor, but their machines really started to get going once we arrived. Real Witches are magnets for the dead. We proceeded with our necromantic blessing, knowing that when you perform the proper steps, the spirits will come forth. We went into a visionary state and I made an offering of three drops of my blood. No sooner had I done so than the PX machine went really wild, spewing out a torrent of words and, in particular, repeating the word "apple" several times. I was elated that such a timeless ritual would continue to produce such dramatic results.

Once Kelly and I had blessed the space, I then called Zak, Nick, and Aaron up to the altar, each in their turn, to place their right hand upon Robert and declare themselves creatures of spirit, equal to, and able to protect themselves from, anything they might encounter. We were only supposed to be there for this initial blessing, but they were getting so much activity from their machines that they decided to keep us for the remainder of the filming. Kelly and I continued to channel the flow of the Death Current so that the spirits of the place would come through. The team began to listen for voices on the spirit box. It was incredible. So many different energies seemed present, but one, a woman's voice, rose above the din of the rest. The voice called out the name of Robert the skull (so Shawn was right about what his name was) and then called out my full name. I'm still a skeptic after all these years, and so this just blew me away. Then the team asked for the name of the spirit. The spirit replied with a first name. They then asked for the last name. Again, a reply came. The full name of the spirit present was Bridget Bishop. The PX machine saying "apple" made much more sense now. Bridget Bishop once owned an apple orchard in Salem on the site where the restaurant now stands. That she came that night to the Witch House, a place her spirit had never been associated with in the past, proved the power of the magic I did before entering the building.

Kelly and I didn't know quite how to tell the team that we had done a little hocus pocus to ask Bridget to leave the restaurant so that the film crew would find nothing there. And we certainly had no idea that she'd be joining the spirits already present at the Witch House that night! When we finally got to see the show, very little happened in the second lockdown at the restaurant. In fact, the only voice to appear on the ghost box was "Mary," so my spell to draw Bridget away from the site worked like a charm and made for quite a spectacular experience. This has definitely become one of my favorite stories of the powers of spirit conjuration. It not only proved the existence of the dead, but the existence of magic as well!

What Is Ghost Hunting?

Ghost hunting is a popular pastime that anyone can undertake. There are countless paranormal groups in every state that organize hunts and investigations, many of which are open to the public, and television shows about ghost hunting are among the most popular. Ghost hunting largely involves the collection of evidence to determine if spirits are present, and a significant part of it involves communication with the dead. I have participated in my share of ghost hunts and séances over the years; have seen, heard, and felt apparitions; and have experienced many communications from the dead. While I do not consider myself a ghost hunter, per se, I love to join in on such paranormal investigations when I can, and I believe that having a Witch on board can guarantee that you not only detect the spirits, but also encourage them to show themselves.

Ghost hunting can be exciting and even unnerving, for you never know what you are going to experience, but you must also be patient. If you are new to this field, keep in mind that much of what appears on ghost hunting television shows has been edited down from many hours of tape. Ghosts do not always show up immediately, and so you should not always expect to experience paranormal phenomena right away. Ghost hunting is a truly scientific process that can take time, but the results are worth the effort!

Before we consider the ways of ghost hunting, let's take a look at our targets: what exactly is a ghost? Is it really a manifestation of a dead person? What are we hunting?

What Is a Ghost?

The broadest definition of a ghost is that it is unexplained phenomena associated with the dead. The dead can include people, animals, and anything in the natural world, as well as the "dead" past—buildings, vehicles, and objects that no longer physically exist. Do the dead really stay behind and haunt us in homes and other places?

As we discussed in chapter 5, most of what we call ghosts are actually *residual hauntings,* which are energy imprints on the spirit of place that either the living or dead have left behind. It is like a psychic photograph or video that plays over and over again, and is experienced when the conditions are right. There is no intelligent awareness to them. Examples of imprints are ghosts that always walk the same corridor, smells that always occur in the same room, and so on. Most imprints are comprised of smells and sounds; seeing a ghost is often the least likely way for most people to actually experience one—unless, of course, you have the psychic ability to see the spirits on their own plane of existence.

Other hauntings involve *interactive intelligent presences.* These ghosts tug your jacket, pull your air, brush by in a breeze, move objects about, and make noises, such as footsteps, when no one is present. They may be some form of shell energy also left behind by the living, but they are capable of interacting.

Still other hauntings involve *earthbound souls,* the ghosts of those who got stuck in their transition to the afterlife. Sometimes they died suddenly and do not even know they are dead. Or they have unfinished business and somehow were able to remain behind, but are stuck in a twilight world between the living and the dead. Earthbounds can also interact with the living, and sometimes ask for help moving on.

Finally, there are those souls who freely choose to travel back and forth between the planes of spirit and the world of the living. These souls are not bound to the Earth, but, like guardian angels, they are able to intercede in our lives much like the Saints of the Church. It is these spirits that are called on most at your altar of the dead and in rituals of necromancy.

How Hauntings Happen

Hauntings can arise simply from what the living leave behind. Many hauntings are created by emotionally charged events, especially unhappy ones such as accidents, murders, suicides, natural disasters, wars, and so on. Some hauntings are related to neutral or happy events, such as taverns that are haunted by the ghosts of their prior patrons, but negative emotions account for most recorded paranormal phenomena. Still other hauntings are tied to legends that have become embellished over time.

Any place can be haunted: houses, buildings, landscapes, places in nature. Houses do not have to be old to be haunted. A new house can have paranormal activity. The spiritual residues of the dead can linger in psychic space or even within the land itself.

Hauntings are not always permanent. It is possible that the interest and attention of the living can perpetuate hauntings by acting as an energy source. The phenomena often respond to certain individuals: some people stir up activity unconsciously wherever they go, especially those who are eccentric, outlandish, or larger than life. As Kelly and I demonstrated during the filming of *Ghost Adventures*, sometimes you can stir that activity through ritual.

What Ghosts Do and Where to Find Them

The kinds of phenomena you are likely to experience in a haunted place include being touched by invisible presences; weird smells; unexplained sounds and noises; hearing voices; seeing apparitions that seem either filmy or solid; movements of objects; lights and even appliances going on and off by themselves; equipment failing; and batteries suddenly draining. How do you know if a place is haunted? Repeated phenomena such as described above, for which *no natural explanation can be found*, indicate that a place is occupied by residues, ghosts, or other spiritual entities. Of course, seeing an apparition is the best evidence of all. Some are both filmy and transparent; others seem solid as though they are living people; others are dark and shadowy. A dark spirit form is not necessarily bad or evil—it is just the way it chooses to manifest.

We stress the importance of eliminating natural explanations first, which we discuss in more detail in chapter 5. Too often, people eager for paranormal experiences misinterpret mundane events and see them as evidence for spirit activity where there is none.

Most casual ghost hunters go for a thrill, to gain proof of the afterlife, or to collect evidence that ghosts are present in a particular location. The messages that the spirits are trying to communicate usually take a secondary role. Some ghost hunters, on the other hand, seek specific information from the dead, especially pertaining to the future.

As I discussed in chapter 7, restless ghosts can often be quick to provide you with information. However, as I've also discussed, I rarely work with the spirits of the unquiet dead as they can be unpredictable, mischievous, and dishonest. I only do so when trying to gather evidence in ghost hunting or while investigating a murder or other crime. While this method of paranormal investigation can be effective, it should also be done with much care and protection.

Spirits of the dead can be found anywhere, not just in graveyards or haunted houses. Research sites before you visit them for ghost hunting. Try cemeteries, battlefields, and places where tragic deaths have occurred, especially places known to be haunted by specific personalities. Try other, more benign haunted places for comparison. And look in your own home.

Wherever you go, obey access restrictions and do not trespass. Most cemeteries and battlefields have hours of public access. Do not deface monuments, tombs, crypts, and headstones. Use modern equipment and methods described below.

The Role of Spirit Mediums and Witches

Some paranormal groups arm themselves to the teeth with ghost-hunting equipment and avoid the use of mediums and psychics—insisting that they are trying to be "scientific." Others prefer to bring a Witch or psychic medium along. I believe in the latter. The perception of ghosts is mostly a subjective experience—much of what can be found on record are anecdotal accounts rather than photos, videos, and recordings. As our technology advances, that is changing, but there remain phenomena that science simply cannot measure as of yet. To rely solely upon equipment means you would likely miss 90 percent of the action.

Psychic mediums, and especially Witches, have a great deal to offer, because they can fill in many blanks that equipment cannot. They can often detect phenomena more easily than equipment, and instruct those using it where to direct their work to record the phenomena. My favorite example of this happened during a ghost tour in the French Quarter of New Orleans with my dear friend and magical teacher Bloody Mary, who is a Voodoo priestess, psychic medium, and paranormal investigator who inspired me to write this book. Mary brought our group to the infamous LaLaurie mansion, one of America's most haunted houses and site of the alleged torture of numerous slaves on the part of their mistress, the Madame Delphine LaLaurie. Mary was looking up at a corner of the mansion and said, "I see two spirits up there. Let me see if I can catch them." She whipped out the digital camera, snapped the picture, and, sure enough, there were two distinct energy formations captured on film. Bloody Mary is one of the most powerfully spirit-connected people I have ever known, and she is the perfect type of person to bring on a ghost hunt. Such seers save those with the equipment a lot of time by letting them know just where to look for spirits!

Witches and mediums can also get impressions and information about history, events, names, dates, activities, and so on. In some cases, the information can then be validated through research of historical records or by interviewing people. This can often make the process of documenting the evidence of a site take far less time as well.

Your own mediumistic ability—and everyone has some—is going to come into play in ghost hunting. You learned about mediumship in chapter 7, and you'll want to practice your gifts regularly if you want to play the role of seer on a ghost hunt. You are attempting to experience the unseen and unheard, and those phenomena are going to register on your subtle senses. The more you participate in paranormal investigations, the sharper your own psychic ability becomes. I have heard many a "scientific" ghost hunter say they have no psychic ability, but this is not the case; they are just not acknowledging it. Yes, just like some have a greater aptitude for singing or mathematics, there are some who have a greater natural ability to be psychic, but every one of us has at least a little bit of the second sight.

Just as a spirit medium is important to ghost hunting, so too is the Witch, and often the same person plays both roles. Practitioners of the ancient craft understand the powers of protection magic, banishing, and exorcism, and are able to raise the energy necessary to keep angry or hateful spirits from causing harm. Ghost hunting can be spiritually dangerous, and as you learn the techniques in this book, you may just find yourself very valuable to your local ghost hunters. Just as noted paranormal expert Hans Holzer long worked with famed Witch and psychic Sybil Leek, the paranormal investigation groups of today could benefit from having a Witch onboard!

Ghost-Hunting Gadgets

The very best piece of equipment you can bring to a ghost hunt is yourself, for your senses, including your psychic awareness, do most of the work. However, it is helpful to use at least some technical equipment. Ghost hunting really didn't develop as a pastime or even a professional pursuit until the late nineteenth century, when attention was focused on evidence for survival after death. People wanted to experience and study mediums and haunted places, and societies of experts formed dedicated to those activities. The Society of Psychical Research in London and the American Society for Psychical Research in New York City are the most prominent of these.

In the early days people had little in the way of equipment, and ghost hunting was largely based on personal observations. People had film cameras and magnetic tape recorders. Sometimes they brought along thermometers, for rapid and extreme changes in temperatures are characteristic of many haunted places. They often spread flour or talcum powder on floors to try to capture ghostly footprints. For the most part, early ghost hunting consisted of doing a vigil in the dark, waiting for something unusual to happen.

Some of that still holds today. There's much more gear, but after it is set up, you will probably still have to wait hours in the dark for things to happen. Sometimes you'll be rewarded and sometimes you'll go home with little to show.

Today, the average person can buy an astonishing array of equipment for a modest investment of money. Websites tout "must-have" gear, and the various ghost hunters on reality shows are often so outfitted with gadgets that they end up looking like the men from the film *Ghostbusters*. While the spectacle probably makes for entertaining television, perhaps we can credit these ghost shows for increasing the kinds of equipment available, since the shows have inspired an entire subculture of ghost hunters across the world. However, you do not need to arm yourself to the gills or outfit a van to do good ghost hunting.

What Gadgets Should You Get?

Good digital cameras and video cams are important, and so are digital recorders. Some ghost hunters prefer film cameras and magnetic tape recorders, but the digital ones will give you good results and are much easier to deal with in files that can be uploaded to your computer or the Internet. Some investigators experiment with infrared and ultraviolet photography, and there are filters, film, lights, and internal modifications that can be done to cameras to suit those purposes. Bloody Mary has always told me that an 800-speed disposable camera can do the trick quite well in a pinch—and I've seen some pretty amazing spirit photos captured that way.

Thermometers are effective but not essential. If you experience sudden drops or spikes in temperature, you must be able to rule out *all* possible natural explanations to have useful data.

EMF meters are very popular and relatively inexpensive ghost-hunting tools, but not really necessary when starting out. EMF stands for "electromagnetic fields." An EMF meter measures electromagnetic energy present. It is a popular belief among ghost hunters that high readings, or especially spikes in energy levels, indicate ghostly presences. However, these devices will pick up any source of electromagnetic energy, such as electrical wiring behind walls and outside sources. The meter can also be set off by cell phones and walkie-talkies, so you want to be very careful about how you use one. No one gadget is going to measure everything you need to know, so it is always best to test phenomena with more than just one. I rarely use my EMF meter, and feel it's probably something you can save for when you're working as part of a larger investigative team.

Thermal cameras that register either heat or cold are also popular with ghost-hunting teams, but most of them are quite expensive, so make sure that this is something you're really serious about before grabbing one of those. I personally wouldn't use one. They look great on TV, but they are not practical in the field. Heat signatures of the living can linger quite a while in a place, so determining the source of a reading can be difficult. For example, if you press your hand against a wall, some heat traces of that can still be picked up long after you are gone. There have definitely been some interesting videos out there of unexplained masses registering on thermal cams, but their overall practicality, weighed against their cost, makes them nonessential for most ghost-hunting adventures.

See how easy it is? A couple of cameras and a digital recorder, and you're good to go! If you decide to go deeper into paranormal investigation, you can always add more gear later—preferably after you have had a chance to see it in action with others and evaluate its practicality. Rosemary Ellen Guiley keeps her gear to a minimum: cameras, recorders, and a fascinating device called a "ghost box," similar to the one the *Ghost Adventures* team used when I filmed with them and one we will discuss later on in the section on electronic voice phenomena. Rosemary uses her own psychic sensitivity and always welcomes the input of psychics and mediums, which is essentially how we became friends. She asked me to use my own psychic ability to help her investigate a house.

You may get evidence quickly, or you may have to take hundreds of photographs and spend many long hours recording in order to get something truly "unexplained." Beware of fuzzy round balls in your digital photos. These are called "orbs," and some people believe them to be spirits. Orbs are usually explainable: most are objects such as dust, moisture, bugs, and so on that were very close to the camera lens. We can't rule out a possible paranormal orb, of course, but don't put too much weight on them. Sometimes people will show me orbs in digital photographs that turn out to be nothing more than JPG compression artifacts, something I'm familiar with as I was a professional Web developer and designer for many years. If you're going to use a digital camera, please set your camera's JPG quality to the highest setting so that it compresses the image as little as possible and you don't get those pesky artifacts. When ghost hunting, I typically set my camera to "Raw" file format, so there is no chance of them.

You must look diligently for natural explanations in all your evidence before you consider the paranormal. My paranormal investigator friends often get frustrated as they are frequently asked to comment on photos that show orbs, clouds of moisture, camera straps, explainable shadows, lens flares, and so on. Remember, you can see just about anything in a cloud if you truly want to.

Despite all the hunting and investigating going on, no one to date has come up with hard proof of survival or existence of ghosts that science will accept. However, piles and piles of *unexplained* photographic and audio evidence have accumulated over the years. For many, the reality of ghosts and an after-life are articles of personal faith, often based on personal experiences.

Electronic Voice Phenomena

One of the easiest and best ways to communicate with the dead is through electronic voice phenomena, commonly known as EVP. And what's best about it is that the only tool you need is a digital or tape recorder.

EVP involves the capture of mystery voices that cannot be heard by the human ear. Turn on your recorder, ask a question, leave a space of about ten to fifteen seconds for an answer, and remain quiet. On playback, you may hear an answer during that quiet gap. Sometimes the responses are clear and some-times they're less distinct, and you may need to use software to edit or aug-ment them in order to understand them. It is not unusual to receive no replies.

No one has an explanation for why EVP happens, but the phenomena have been noted since the turn of the twentieth century. Recording equip-ment has become increasingly sophisticated and sensitive, making EVP ob-tainable by just about anyone who has the patience to experiment. The ghost-hunting TV shows portray EVP within the context of investigating haunted locations, but in truth these voices can be captured anywhere. Many of the thousands of dedicated EVP researchers around the globe work right within their own homes. These voices can often be the whispers of the dead seeking communication with the living.

A Short History of EVP

The invention of the phonograph in 1877 by Thomas Alva Edison marked the beginning of our awareness of mystery voices. The phonograph could play recorded voices, music, and sounds, which in the late nineteenth century seemed miraculous to many. Even more astonishing was the discovery that the phonograph could also record unknown voices of invisible presences.

The first known demonstration of that happened accidentally in 1901. An exile in Siberia, Waldemar Borogas, set up a portable Edison phonograph to record the trance rituals of a Tchouktchis tribe shaman. The shaman beat his drum and chanted to enter a trance. On playback, Borogas's recording picked up strange mystery voices joining in the ritual, as though invisible presences were chanting along. Shamans, like Witches, are known for standing at the thresholds between the worlds, and so it comes as no surprise to me that such voices would show up.

Some may have considered Borogas's results to be a weird fluke, but others who were experimenting with the new technology also got mystery voices they could not explain. Serious research of EVP got underway in the 1930s, but little headway was made with the limited technology of phonographs. In the 1950s, magnetic tape recorders enabled better recordings, and led Friedrich Jurgenson, a Swedish opera singer, painter, and film producer, to become convinced he was talking to the dead while casually recording bird songs. Jurgenson devoted the rest of his life to investigating the mystery voices contained within his recordings. His work captured the attention of a man named Konstantin Raudive, a Latvian who was living in Sweden. Raudive met with Jurgenson and was so intrigued by the voices that he launched his own research.

Raudive in turn recorded over 100,000 electronic voice words and phrases during the course of his research. The voices spoke in different languages, some very clearly, others sounding like bad long distance telephone connections. Some of the words and phrases were clear, while other messages seemed to be delivered in code.

Raudive's work gained widespread attention, and soon the mystery voices were labeled "Raudive voices." When his work was translated into English in the 1970s, his London publishers coined the term "electronic voice phenomenon," which became known over time as "electronic voice phenomena" or EVP.

EVP research expanded rapidly in the wake of Raudive's work. On the heels of Raudive came Sarah Estep, a Maryland woman who was convinced the voices were explainable—in fact, Estep firmly believed that there was no survival after death at all, negating any possibility of communication with the dead. Her own experiments to disprove EVP, done with a reel-to-reel magnetic tape recorder in the basement of her Annapolis home, sent her into a life-changing spin. Instead of silence, she recorded voices with messages and specific answers to questions that she could not deny. Estep became an EVP convert, a believer in life after death, and one of the leading EVP researchers in the world, founding the American Association of Electronic Voice Phenomena, now called the Association for TransCommunication.

Experimenters discovered that voices could be captured using a variety of techniques. Especially helpful was the presence of a background noise, such as static, radios tuned between stations, fans, running water, electrical humming, and so on. It seemed the noise—called "white noise"—provided undifferentiated sound that could be manipulated into words by spirits.

EVP remains scientifically unproven, but hundreds upon hundreds of thousands of recordings have been made over the years that cannot be explained naturally. The field has become quite sophisticated with equipment and techniques, including the capturing of real-time, audible mystery voices—more about that later on.

Friends of mine who specialize in EVP have yielded tantalizing messages from a variety of communicators. I definitely believe they've been in contact with the dead, and also with unknown beings in other dimensions. One of the factors that makes EVP so exciting is the hard evidence of a recorded voice—and it gives such tangible weight to much of the occult work that Witches do.

The Characteristics of EVP Voices

The voices that come through during EVP sessions are rarely like those you speak to over a telephone. They are often faint and hard to understand; sometimes headphones or excessive amplification are necessary. The average EVP lasts two or three seconds—hardly a chatty conversation. What's more, the voices have their own peculiar characteristics: they are compressed, have odd cadences, and often sound robotic or tinny. Nonetheless, it is often possible to distinguish gender and age; that is, the voice of an adult versus the voice of a child. Some people who attempt to connect with a specific individual on the Other Side say they can recognize the identity of the communicator by her voice.

Jurgenson was startled to hear the voice of his dead mother. So was one of the English editors of Raudive's work. Peter Bander was a skeptic, not inclined to purchase the translation rights of Raudive's research—until he listened to one of Raudive's tapes and heard his own deceased mother with a personal message for him. She said in German, "Why don't you open the door?" For Bander, there were two meanings to the message: she was referring to his habit of keeping his office door closed most of the time, for which he was teased by his colleagues. He also thought the message to be a veiled reference to "opening the door" to Raudive's work. Bander went from skeptic to believer, and joined the growing ranks of prominent EVP researchers in his own right.

It also seems that the voices coming through are always understood by at least one person present for the session, regardless of the language spoken. And yes, voices do speak in different languages, sometimes changing language in mid-reply. It is possible to ask a question in one language and get an answer in another. For example, Rosemary told me about how she took a trip to Mexico to engage in some EVP research; she asked questions in English and got answers in Spanish!

Researchers have attempted to explain how EVP occurs, but the process remains as mysterious as the voices themselves. How do disembodied entities without physical vocal cords make sounds at all? And how are the voices impressed upon recording devices? The "how" behind EVP may have to do with conditions we do not yet understand.

How to Do EVP

Recording EVP is easy. Like all forms of spirit communication, repeated practice brings better results. Nonetheless, some individuals seem to be EVP magnets and get more results than others. Don't be discouraged if you get little or even nothing in the beginning; most of the world's foremost researchers were frustrated with their initial results. Estep was on the verge of quitting before she got her first voice.

Get a good quality recorder. Almost any equipment can record EVP, but since many voices are faint, quality equipment will improve your odds. I favor digital recorders that have built-in USB plugs, which make the transfer to computers quick and easy. In that way, you can set up files of a permanent EVP library. Most record in one or more of the MP3, WAV, WMA, or AAC formats. Just as I prefer to take digital spirit photographs in as high a quality as possible, I also recommend recording your EVP with your device set to its highest quality. Just as JPG compression can affect what you see on a picture, the compression of sound can do so even more, since it is even harder for the human ear to fill in the blanks of audio recordings than it is for the human eye to do so with pictures. As with all forms of spirit communications, you must try a variety of approaches until you hit the ones that work best for you. Some experimenters swear that magnetic tape is better than digital, but that is not the case for everyone. You might also experiment with using background noise to see if it enhances your results.

Frequency and consistency are important, especially in the early stages of your EVP work. Set aside a regular time and place for recording. You do not have to devote a great deal of time; even a few minutes a day or evening can be productive. In fact, many experimenters hold sessions of only ten to fifteen minutes. Some experimenters, however, conduct long sessions. First they ask a few questions, and then leave the recorder running for a few hours. Prepare your questions in advance, especially if you are intent on contacting someone specific.

Build ritual around your session. Work in a visionary state, use your altar of the dead as the recording place, and invoke the participation of the spirits that you work with regularly, as they will want to help you succeed. Keep a log and note conditions or circumstances that seem to affect results, such as time of day or night; weather conditions; significant dates; lunar phases; astrological aspects; planetary hours; and even your emotional state of mind. *Manifest* good results and you will get them!

Because of the brief nature of EVP responses, don't ask questions that require long and complex answers. And be sure to leave gaps of about ten to fifteen seconds between questions.

Play back your recordings over quality speakers, or use headphones. Understanding EVP is an "ear" that you will develop with practice. Good EVP should be fairly easy to understand. You can augment your listening with an audio software program that can enhance faint voices. Adobe Audition and the freeware application Audacity are two programs popular with EVP researchers; both are available for Mac or PC—but I use Apple's GarageBand and I only add amplification and very careful equalization. Be careful not to manipulate your files to the point where you are creating EVP rather than enhancing it.

How Should You Talk to the Dead?

The Greeks and Romans said that ghosts muttered, moaned, howled, squeaked, and chirped, and their necromancers imitated them when trying to evoke them from the underworld. The rituals must have been frightful spectacles indeed, with the blood sacrifices, howling necromancers, and gloomy shades of the unquiet dead.

The voices we hear via our modern technology are closer to ordinary, conversational ones. As noted, they have odd cadences, accents, and tonal qualities, but they are a far cry from ancient descriptions. I recommend talking to the dead as you would talk to a living person.

Evaluating Identities

It is often hard to know for certain who is speaking from the Other Side. Sometimes a voice is recognizable as the individual spirit you're trying to contact or the communicator gives information that validates that identity. Sometimes there are "drop in" communicators that, for unknown reasons, are able to briefly come through and interrupt the prevailing voice; they may or may not identify themselves before dropping back out.

Regular sessions are likely to connect you to repeat communicators; in fact, one of your familiar spirits, those that you work with at your altar of the dead, may make frequent appearances with advice and suggestions. Communicators who are rude, abusive, or manipulative should be ignored or instructed to stay away. Please see chapter 5 on how to banish such mischievous entities.

Real-Time EVP

Nearly all EVP is collected passively by asking questions and listening for voices on playback. Around 2005, however, some interesting devices made their way into public use that enable *real-time* EVP: the voices are heard live, not just on playback. Real-time EVP is sometimes referred to as "instrumental transcommunication," or ITC, a field of research that involves high-technology spirit communication. ITC was an outgrowth of EVP research, developing first in Europe in the 1980s and then spreading around the globe.

Real-time EVP has been documented for decades, but it is only in recent years that it has found its way into the mainstream. The chief method for real-time EVP employs radio sweep: a device that rapidly scans up and down the radio bandwidth to create a jumble of noise. The effect is like having a radio tuner on permanent scan. As the sweep hits and moves past a station, you hear a word or two from the broadcast or a note or two of music. The scan becomes background noise for real-time EVP. Mystery voices may speak on top of the scan.

These devices go by various names, including "ghost box" and "Frank's box." The name "ghost box" comes from the fact that such devices were popularized by paranormal investigators and especially by such shows as *Ghost Hunters* on SyFy and *Ghost Adventures* on the Travel Channel. The latter show used one to detect the spirit of Bridget Bishop when I filmed with them. "Frank's box" is named after Frank Sumption, one of the early makers of these devices. Since sweep devices to date are built individually and by hand, not many have been offered for sale commercially, but I have seen a number of them available online, especially on eBay. However, you can also alter an inexpensive radio to produce a rudimentary scan, and so for a very modest investment, you can capture real-time EVP without paying top dollar. You can find instructions online for modifying certain radio models.

Once you experience live voices, it is hard to be content with only passive EVP. It is interesting to get a mix of both. Once, Rosemary brought a ghost box to our séance at an old house in Salem. When the planchette on the Ouija board pointed to "yes," the box would sometimes say "yes" as well! I was really blown away.

Real-time EVP is like passive EVP: sometimes you get great results and sometimes little or nothing. Responses are short and clipped, and often are hard to understand. A real-time device is dependent on the radio stations in any given area; AM works better than FM. Too few stations cannot produce a good scan, and sometimes the proximity of a single, powerful station can overrun a scan. The EVP does *not* come from broadcast, but from voices that piggyback, or ride on top of the broadcast signal.

A real-time EVP session is productive for an average of thirty-five to fifty minutes. For unknown reasons, links do not hold well much beyond that time frame. It may take up to ten or fifteen minutes for a session to "click" and start to produce voices.

Real-time sessions can be organized much the same as you would for passive EVP. They can be open-ended, seeking communication with whoever might be present, or targeted to specific personalities on the Other Side.

When you use a ghost box, try to work in a visionary state, have some of the tools from your altar of the dead present, or even keep the device on the altar itself. When you turn it on, tap the box three times with your yew wand and state, *This is [your name here], and I call the spirits [or a specific spirit by name] to come forth through this device. This session is now open and I await the voices of the dead.* If you have a question, you may want to consider asking it two or three times, even when responses are heard, as a measure against misinterpreting broadcast snippets. The devices never produce duplicate scans—every time the device sweeps past radio stations, different sounds are being broadcast, so the background noise is in continual change. Answers that are repeated from communicators thus are more likely to be from unexplained sources.

When a session is ended, thank the spirits who have come through. This brings formal closure to the session.

If you have the opportunity to experiment with real-time EVP, record all sessions, for passive EVP often shows up in recordings when you play them back.

Real-time EVP is even more controversial than passive EVP, for skeptics contend that it is much easier to mistake broadcast snippets for EVP. Consequently, real-time EVP does require more stringent evaluation. We are far from having a reliable, on-demand link like a "cell phone to the spirits," but I do believe that technology will someday be capable of uniting the worlds of the living and the dead beyond any doubt.

13

A Festival of the Dead

In early 2003, Shawn Poirier and I were sitting in his living room talking about the fabulous Witches' Ball we had hosted the previous October. The guests who attended loved it, and we wanted to do more for the coming October. Salem had been host to an annual "Haunted Happenings" since the early 1980s, but the festivities were really at a low point at that time. Shawn and I scoured the Haunted Happenings calendar and he remarked that this once-great event had been reduced to "corn husks and dog shows." It was then that I said to him, "Hey, why not bring Halloween back to what it was? Why not host a whole month of events focused on the dead? Isn't that what this holiday is about anyway?"

So began what is now Festival of the Dead, a group of events held each October in Salem that includes a public séance, a ghost-hunting seminar, a course in necromancy, a silent dinner with the dead, a Victorian tea where participants share memories of their loved ones in spirit, a vampire masquerade, and, of course, The Official Salem Witches' Halloween Ball.

Our festival was not well received at first. The mayor at the time treated Halloween and Witchcraft tourism in general with disdain. The official office of tourism wouldn't allow us to join and argued that Salem's tourism should be focused entirely on arts and culture. We thought this insane. The city's attempts to ditch the Witch made international news . . . and people everywhere else thought it was insane too.

Shawn and I persevered. We kept sticking our feet in doors, attending meetings at City Hall and the Chamber of Commerce, and getting involved in any way we could. A few choice publicity stunts along the way—like 2004's bloody bikini vampire poster of the Countess Bathoria, and 2005's serial killer Wanted posters all over town—didn't hurt. We sent a clear message: embrace Witches or we'll find something worse for you to look at. While abrasive, this tactic worked. Shawn and I began to be accepted in more serious circles in town, and, with much effort, helped to bring Halloween—and all of October in Salem—back to its former glory. We have a fantastic new mayor now who cares about the whole of Salem tourism, a rejuvenated tourism office (I'm now on its board of directors!), and a new mission to promote all of the wonderful things that Salem has to offer—including the Witch and the magical holiday of Halloween!

With Festival of the Dead, my new career was born. I had been practicing Witchcraft since I was eighteen years old, but suddenly, at thirty-three, I was walking a magical path unlike any I had traveled before. I remember the appropriately titled post-mortem meeting held after the first Festival ended in 2003. Those of us who hosted events discussed how doing so was transforming our long-held perspectives on death. If death is transformation, then everyone involved in this new exploration of it was changing in ways we didn't yet understand. All we knew was that *this* was Halloween. *This* was the power of the mighty dead. *This* was pure magic.

Celebrating Death

One might ask why anyone would want to celebrate something so dreaded as death, the dead, or anything to do with mortality. On a psychological level, I think it helps us to confront our fears and process the reality that people have left us, others will follow, and, finally, so too shall we travel through that doorway to the Other Side. On a spiritual level, honoring our departed loved ones keeps their energy close to us and invites them to continue to participate in the blessings of our lives. In America, we have the now-secular holiday of Halloween, making a mockery of all that scares us. Yet the roots of Halloween can be found in the sacred death holidays of old, and virtually every society in history has recognized the value of setting aside special times to honor the beloved dead. Such a communion between the living and the dead shows how connected we all are by the true language of spirit.

From their earliest beginnings, humans have faced the great mystery of death, knowing that it came in its own time for everyone. The truly wise learned to understand and honor this most profound of the rites of passage, guiding their peoples to understand its mysteries. These sages knew that even in the brightest of life's moments, Death's face would be peering from just beyond the shadows, waiting to leave his calling card, and so the magical leaders of old helped to prepare their people for the transformation that comes to us all.

Death is humankind's great lover. He courts and pursues us more relentlessly than any mortal paramour. Throughout history, humans have been led in a dance with death that is both fearful and romantic. Digging through the tomes of religion, myth, anthropology, folklore, and literature, we find the grim examples of death's shadows cast over all cultures like funerary shrouds. We discover that countless societies celebrated death, revered the spirits of the dead, and learned to cope with their fears of that inevitable destination.

Megalithic people of Western Europe left dolmens, mysterious chambers of stone. They were often the burial places of great heroes. The dolmens were also seen as doorways to hollow hills, the realm of the faerie—whose tales are often intermingled with those of the dead and the underworld.

In majestic Egypt, the wellspring of much of the magic and mystery that have survived through the ages, festivals were held for the dead throughout the year, one of the most important being the annual Festival of the Valley, held in the city of Thebes, one-time capital of Egypt and situated on the east bank of the Nile River. Across the Nile on the west bank of Egypt was the famed Valley of the Kings, where for centuries the tombs of the pharaohs were built. At the Festival of the Valley, the people of Thebes would cross the Nile in a regal procession of boats to the west bank to honor departed royalty and to visit the tombs of their loved ones in the Necropolis. There, they opened the tombs and celebrated with feasts where the living and the dead shared in the banquet. This helped the living to continue the blessings they received from the dead.[42] Such ritual offerings of food, shared between the living and the dead, can be found in today's Dumb Supper, which you will learn more about later. The Egyptians treated their dead with the utmost respect, particularly those of royalty. They perfected the process of mummification, wrapping the dead in the finest of linens, ointments, and perfumes, and filling their tombs with all of the treasures they enjoyed in the body as well as carved canopic jars to hold the body's organs. As stated earlier, the only organ the Egyptians left in the body was the heart—which they considered the center of the soul.

The Romans honored their ancestors throughout the year, but their reverence for the dead peaked with the aptly named Parentalia. An annual nine-day festival beginning on February 13, the Parentalia was a time when businesses and temples closed and families would hold private feasts for the souls of their parents and other relatives in their homes. The observances culminated in the Festival of the Feralia on the 22nd, when the celebration extended to all the dead and crowds would gather at the tombs of the departed to make offerings of wine, milk, honey, oil, and water, while the tombs themselves were adorned with flowers. These practices endured long after the fall of the Roman Empire, as we will see later.[43]

The Romans also celebrated the other side of death's coin. The Lemuria, held on the ninth, eleventh, and fifteenth days of May, was a festival designed to keep harmful spirits in check. Lemuria derives its name from the *lemures*, the ghosts of those who died without a surviving family, or who were evil or harmful in nature. If evil, they were associated with the *larvae*, nasty spirits who frightened and injured the living. Like the Parentalia, during Lemuria, businesses and temples closed, and rituals were performed—only these rituals were designed to appease and exorcise the dark spirits that they might trouble the populace no more.

The Athenians of Greece had a similar three-day festival of Dionysus known as the Anthesteria, held in the early springtime, when it was believed that the days belonged not only to the gods, but to the souls of the dead as well. Like the Romans at the Parentalia, each family attended to its own departed loved ones with offerings of items such as honey cakes. They prevented the dead from getting too close by smearing their doorposts with pitch and by chewing whitethorn leaves, a type of hawthorn. On the last day, they made offerings of cooked vegetables and seeds to Hermes, the god who escorted the dead to the underworld, and invited the dead to leave with him.[44]

Few celebrate the dead quite like the Japanese Buddhists. At their annual festival of Obon in August, with roots dating back to 606 CE, participants feast and dance to honor their dead. The Japanese believe that the souls of their dead return home for the first two to three days of the festival. Fires are lit in yards to guide the souls of the dead to their homes, and those without yards light candles. In researching this holiday, I could not help but be reminded of the traditional jack-o-lantern—carved pumpkins lit on our doorsteps each Halloween night. Offerings of food and flowers are placed on home altars and the names of the dead are written, much like we do on the altar at HEX. Prayers are spoken and dances held and, on the third and final day of Obon, the spirits return home as lanterns float on tiny barges along the current of nearby rivers or on outgoing ocean tides.[45] This must be a truly beautiful spectacle that I hope to see myself one day.

The Chinese Taoists and Buddhists have a similar holiday in the Hungry Ghost Festival, held during the fifteenth day of the seventh lunar month of the Chinese calendar. Dating back to medieval times, the Hungry Ghost Festival involves rituals of salvation designed to ease the suffering of lost or unhappy souls. Offerings of food are made for the dead either in public ceremonies or within each home, depending on the region. In one area of Eastern China, rice cakes are left as offerings at crossroads, drawing an interesting parallel back to the Greco-Roman and African dealings with the dead.[46] Some things truly are universal.

One custom that I draw from the Chinese in my own practice is the burning of Hell money, also called Hell bank notes. Hell money is burned in bundles to the spirits in a variety of ways: to ask for favors from the dead, to purchase the salvation of lost souls, or simply as an offering. I often use the offering cauldron on my altar of the dead to burn Hell money as a means of buying favors from the spirits, and it's a practice I recommend highly. You can write the names of the dead on the notes or even write out spells for things you're manifesting. Gift shops in virtually any Chinatown offer Hell money for sale, or you could buy it online.

I was raised in a Roman Catholic family, and even though we were not strictly observant, respect for our dead was taught to me from my earliest childhood. This honor for the dead permeates the Church of Rome, rooted as it is in the pre-Christian Empire that nurtured its early development, and so we have the holidays of All Saints' Day (November 1) when the Saints are venerated, and All Souls' Day (November 2) when prayers are said for the suffering souls of the faithful dead. It has been questioned whether the Church placed these holy days at the time of much older Roman and Celtic holidays. Various days dedicated to the martyrs who were killed under the rule of pre-Christian emperors are recorded beginning in 373 CE and included Easter Week, the Sunday after Pentecost, and May 13. The Romans preferred May 13, and Pope Boniface IV codified this in 609 CE at a re-dedication of the Pantheon.[47] For those who have been paying attention, the May 13 date falls within the days of the pre-Christian Roman festival of

Lemuria—when rituals were held to appease the unquiet dead. That this was intentional is a matter of debate for scholars, but I simply cannot believe that this is coincidental. It certainly seems that the Roman Church was hoping to direct the focus of its people away from the appeasement of the "evil" dead and more towards prayer for the exalted saints. The later move of All Saints' to November 1, the date still celebrated today, officially began in 731 CE with a proclamation by Pope Gregory III. Scholars over the last hundred years or so have argued that this was to eradicate another holiday of the dead that we shall explore further on.

Despite the wishes of the Church, people continued to pray for all of the dead at All Saints' Day. The Church just couldn't seem to eradicate the earlier practices of spirit veneration in favor of just the saints. So, two centuries later, Saint Odilo of Cluny established a separate day when all souls of the faithful could be honored, presumably setting aside November 1 for the true saints and martyrs and declaring November 2 a day when we could pray for those souls who reside in purgatory, that their sins might be cleansed and they be ushered to heaven.[48] Thus, the Day of the Dead was born. Of course, this didn't become the norm everywhere, as many Catholics still embark on their graveyard visits on the 1st. As we will discover, the Day of the Dead penetrated most thoroughly in the Americas. Elements of both the Roman Parentalia and Lemuria have survived into the modern Catholic All Saints' and All Souls' Days, as they are both times when families visit the graves of loved ones to leave flowers and other offerings. In particular, All Souls' Day is a time when the more tarnished souls are prayed for.

The attention to the graves is still very much the norm in my beloved New Orleans, where, on *Touissaint*, French for All Saints' Day, people leave immortelles (elaborate mourning wreaths), burn candles, and even dine with the dead at their crypts—legacies of the Romans, Greeks, Egyptians, Meso-americans, and Africans, all blended into modern Catholic beliefs. In New Orleans, where a history of frequent disease and death prompted celebration and festivity, funerals were often accompanied by much revelry, evolving into such customs as The Jazz Funeral, when processions of mourners and musicians parade the streets of the French Quarter and partake in a lively wake, second only to the traditional Irish wake in terms of mirth and cheer. The Crescent City really knows how to honor the dead!

We cannot speak of festivals of the dead without mention of Día de los Muertos, the Mexican Day of the Dead, celebrated each year on November 2, with some practices beginning as early as October 31. Sugar skulls are inscribed with the names of the living and given as gifts; all manner of skull- and death-related candies and foods are shared; toys of skeletons, skulls, and coffins are given as gifts; and offerings to the dead are laid out on elaborate altars typically covered with photos, religious icons, statues, candles, gourds, food, and countless marigold petals. The tombs are washed, repaired, and painted and, like the altars, lavishly decorated with marigolds, candles, and foods.

Seen as an odd and morbid custom by many outside of Mexico, this lively and festive holiday represents the culmination of the old world and new, the natural evolution of European pre-Christian and Christian beliefs as they blended with those of the indigenous people of the region. Spanish Conquistadors arrived in the New World to discover a people who venerated the dead just as their own ancestors had in Western Europe so very long ago, with rituals, chants, and offerings of wine, tobacco, and many kinds of foods. Whether these were direct precursors to later practices remains very much a source of debate, as, at the time of conquest, the Spanish weren't exactly trying to preserve the history or the practices of the natives. There are many examples in medieval European history of soul cakes, sweets, flowers, and other offerings made at the time of All Souls' and All Saints' Day—all pointing to numerous European influences on the holiday.

To see why the collision of the old and new worlds created a holiday so fixated on the dead, one has only to look to the archeological remains of the indigenous people of Mexico. Throughout the region, including in the ruins of both the Aztecs and Mayans, skulls and skeletons abound and are incorporated into both the architecture and statuary, including clay sculptures of either gods or humans with skulls for faces. I was lucky to see the wall of skulls at the Mayan temple of Chichen Itza in 2005, and it was breathtaking to see the ways of death so integrated into a culture. The native peoples of Mexico saw death as the extension of life, a passage to the next world, and so festivities were held to honor the departed. Unable to eradicate these observances, the Spaniards consolidated the various practices that would have taken place over the course of the year to coincide with the Catholic holy days of All Saints' Day and All Souls' Day. While the Aztec religious practices were forbidden, the festivities remained and were incorporated into Catholicism. This must have seemed as an ancestral homecoming of sorts to the Spaniards for European Catholics had inherited their own days of the deceased from the Celts, Romans, Greeks, and Egyptians. The old wisdom never dies, and the Mexican people still honor the festive celebration of the dead inherited from both their Mesoamerican and European ancestors. It has become a time of feasting and merriment that endures today, and now blends many of the practices of the Halloween celebrated by their neighbor to the north.[49]

Halloween: Modern Holiday, Ancient Roots

America being the melting pot that it is, it stands to reason that this is where the modern holiday of Halloween would develop, with its trick-or-treating, costume balls, and spooky fun. Oddly, the holiday had long been forgotten in most of Europe until the Americans made it cool again, and now it's seeing a revival in European countries as well. While the American Halloween has become mostly about begging for candy, bobbing for apples at Halloween parties, and the whimsically scary costumes that I so cherish from my childhood, the holiday has a much deeper spiritual meaning. It is the Witches' New Year, when we gather with our covens to speak with the dead, perform divinations, and cast spells for the coming year, for it is believed that on that day the veil between the worlds of matter and spirit are thinnest and that both the living and the dead can journey between those worlds at will. Thus, on Halloween, Witches are at their strongest. But, where did all this come from? While the stereotypical images of scary Witches flying on broomsticks and frightening children fit with the more secular Halloween folklore, real Witches also hold this day in great esteem. This is because Halloween is far older than the candy corn, plastic masks, Reese's Peanut Butter Cups, or even that cheap, no-name candy that no self-respecting child ever wants in her trick-or-treat bag. Halloween was so named because it occurred on the eve of the Catholic All Hallows, another name for All Saints' Day, and so for centuries it had an association with the dead. But the legacy of this mysterious night doesn't end with the Church. Halloween contains traces of many of the holidays discussed thus far, because there is a silver thread of truth that connects them all, but there is one holiday above all others that the Church is argued to have drawn upon most when they placed All Hallows Eve on October 31.

Yes, the practices of Halloween can be traced back to most of the death festivals we've explored thus far, but the strongest influence is said to belong to the ancient Celtic harvest holiday known as *Samhain* (pronounced sow-en). Samhain, drawn from the Gaelic words *sam* (summer) and *fuin* (end), marked the end of the Celtic summer and heralded the beginning of the new year. Many folklorists argue that this was a time when the Celts believed the veils to the otherworld would part and the spirits of the dead, faeries, and other supernatural beings would maraud the land in a great wild hunt of frolic and fright. The numerous customs of Halloween, from the jack-o-lantern to the festive costumes, are but collective memories of the ancient peoples whose energies still swim in our blood, now blended into a hodgepodge over centuries of cultural assimilation. Old Witchcraft families have kept some of those traditions alive while modern magical scholars have dug into the past to find other pearls of wisdom that might have survived from the ancient worlds, hidden in songs, legends, and old wives' tales.

Samhain is said to have been one of the four great "fire festivals" along with Beltane, Imbolc, and Lughnasadh, held over the course of the Celtic lunar year.[50] It was the last harvest, when it was known that the days ahead would be colder and harsher and that much of the plant life would soon be dying. The herds were culled and slaughtered to ensure that the remaining livestock would have enough to eat for the winter, while foods were stored for the brisk months ahead. It was the perfect time to meet and celebrate one last time before the weather made it much harder to do so. Great feasts were held on hilltops, like the Feast of Tara in Ireland, when the tribal chiefs gathered, games were played, dances held, and the doors to the otherworld were opened that the dead might be consulted and divinations cast for the coming year. Much merriment was made, and the people got drunk on beer. Anyone who has attended an Irish wake knows that little has changed; such rites of the dead are still steeped in both joy . . . and booze. As my good friend Bloody Mary loves to say, spirits *love* spirits, so always remember to have a toast to the ghost!

Costumes were worn and gourds were lit with candles—to frighten away evil spirits, or to light the way home for the beloved dead. I prefer the latter interpretation, especially when one considers the Obon festival of Japan, where candles are still lit to show the dead the way home. Anthropological research reveals that shamans in indigenous cultures still wear masks to become possessed by the spirits and the gods. Either way, these practices endure. Halloween costume balls are held throughout the world, and the jack-o-lanterns are still lit on countless doorsteps, though Americans now use the orange pumpkins indigenous to the new world instead of the original turnips.[51]

While Samhain is certainly the most recognized influence on the modern Halloween, it's not the only one. Scholars have detected the traces of the Roman holiday of Pomona—the early November festival of the goddess of fruits and seeds when apples—long a symbol of Witches—became an offering to the gods, and also the Parentalia, Lemuria, and Anthesteria referenced above, when both the beloved and not-so-beloved dead were honored and appeased. We have no written texts from the Celts themselves, and one of the earliest suggestions to be taken seriously that Samhain was a Celtic "Festival of the Dead" was made by social anthropologist James Frazer in his 1890 classic, *The Golden Bough*. Frazer usually gets the credit for connecting Samhain and the dead, but there was at least one other author before him making the same connection. In 1782, a British military surveyor, General Charles Vallancey, suggested that Samhain fell in the month of November because it was "the season appointed by the [Celtic] Druids for the solemn intercession of the quick, for the souls of the dead, or those who had departed this life within the space of the year" and that souls, "according to their merits or demerits in the life past were, aligned to re-enter the bodies of the human or brute species."[52] Frazer's scholarship has been called into question and Vallancey's even more so, but both make powerful arguments for an ancient Celtic time of the dead.

Historian Ronald Hutton, in his book *Stations of the Sun*, makes a compelling argument that records that prove a connection between Samhain and the dead are scarce. Hutton argues that Frazer may have assumed a Festival of the Dead based in part on the choice of the Church to place All Saints' Day on November 1 and that Frazer's assertion that the Church layered their holiday over an older pre-Christian one was weak. Hutton bases his argument in part on the fact that there were other dates of All Saints' Day prior to its placement on November 1—he focuses particularly on the date of May 13. However, Hutton seems unaware of Vallancey's earlier contributions, and also neglects to mention that May 13 was also the dark Roman festival of the dead known as Lemuria. Moreover, after establishing his point that All Saints' Day originated as a holiday to celebrate first the martyrs and later all of the saints, Hutton then argues that "the dead arrived later" in the form of All Souls' Day, apparently making the argument that All Saints was not a festival of the dead before this point.[53] Yet, when you think about it, the martyrs and saints are all the spirits of people who are dead. While All Souls broadened the types of spirits Catholics were supposed to address in prayer, it certainly didn't alter the original nature of the holiday. As I said above, it makes more sense that the Catholics would have placed All Souls' Day on May 13 to encourage people to stop making offerings to the evil dead of Lemuria and instead honor only the lofty saints.

Regardless, connections between Samhain and the dead remain conjectural, and those connections are often reverse-engineered through the legacy of folklore regarding stories of the Celtic otherworld at that time, as well as surviving folk practices—particularly divination. Raven Grimassi, in his book *Witchcraft: A Mystery Tradition*, draws on serious sources of Celtic scholarship to make a compelling argument that Samhain's obvious connections to the otherworld, and to the Celtic father deity, Dagda, with his own association with cauldrons and sows (both underworld symbols) as well as apples—the fruits of the underworld also seen above in the Roman holiday of Pomona—suggest connections to the dead that cannot be ignored.[54] And, of course, we're still bobbing for apples at Halloween.

Despite the mystery surrounding the nature of Samhain as the end of the Celtic summer and the beginning of the cold winter, it was certainly a likely time for the Celts to honor their dead. I do not think we can discount the folklore of Scotland and Ireland in alleging the supernatural roots of the holiday or, perhaps most importantly, the choice of the Catholic Church to place its own death holiday, All Saints' Day, at the same time of the year. While I personally believe that the Celts absolutely honored the dead at Samhain, it is also my belief that Samhain was not the only influence on the holiday of Halloween. Practices of both Halloween and the religious Samhain observed by most Witches today can be traced not just to the Celts, but also to the ancient Greeks and Romans, whose practices are documented in historical records.

And so we come to the Witches. After the repeal of the 1951 Witchcraft law in England, the father of modern Witchcraft, Gerald Gardner, released his 1954 book *Witchcraft Today*, giving birth to a religion that drew inspiration from the pre-Christian fertility cults and magical folk practices of old, celebrating the full moon, new moon, the four Celtic fire festivals, and the solstices and equinoxes. In Gardner's new faith, Halloween was returned to the Celtic Samhain of old—a festival of the dead held to honor those who have gone before and a time to divine the events of the coming year. Much of Gardner's work has been accused of drawing more from the earlier pre-Christian Witch-cult theories of the 1920s book *The Witch-Cult in Western Europe* by Egyptologist and anthropologist Margaret Murray; Charles Godfrey Leland's controversial 1899 work, *Aradia: Gospel of the Witches*; and the magical writings of infamous twentieth century magician Aleister Crowley, than on any true connection Gardner might have had to the ancient coven he claimed initiated him. However, it cannot be argued that Gardner did not do his research, since much of what is contained within the "Book of Shadows," Gardner's primary religious text, draws from the many of the surviving remnants of ancient magic. Still, Gardner must be credited with having laid the foundation upon which most modern Wiccan and Witchcraft groups are based. While I do not consider myself "Wiccan" per se, even *my* practices cannot escape Gardner's influence. It pervades all that modern Witches do, and his influence in the practice today is unavoidable.

The Witches' New Year

Whatever the true origin of Halloween—and I don't believe there is only one origin—it has become the spiritual heir to all of those festivals of the dead that have gone before: Samhain, Parentalia, Lemuria, and Anthesteria; and it is sister to those traditions still thriving: The Church days of All Saints' and All Souls' Days, Mexico's Día de los Muertos, Japan's Obon, and the Hungry Ghost Festival of China. The dead don't really care about the cultural context in which we show them honor and remembrance—what's important is that we honor and remember them at all. In my years as a Witch, it has always amused me to watch this tradition or that group attempt to find one "true" path to the absolute truth of the past, because virtually all faiths and practices have blended. Moreover, while I feel that history is important, there is something far more important than that: honor and remember the dead for they shall honor and remember you!

Here in Salem, Massachusetts, we're known as the "Halloween Capital of the World," and nearly half of our city's million or so annual visitors arrive during the month of October. They fly in from all over the planet to learn about the infamous Witch Trials of 1692, when nineteen people were hanged and one person crushed because the local Puritan populace thought that some of their neighbors were worshipping the Devil. They come to meet some of the many hundreds of modern Witches who live here today, none of whom worship the Devil because the Puritans were completely wrong about the practices of Witches. They attend our many Halloween parties, including my own Vampires' Masquerade Ball and, of course, The Official Salem Witches' Halloween Ball, which, for Salem Witches, is the party of the year. They get psychic readings to discover their destiny at shops like HEX, OMEN, and others listed in appendix C. And, finally, they attend public ceremonies such as the ritual that Sicilian Strega Lori Bruno and I host on Salem Common on Halloween Night—for this is the most magical and spirit-filled evening of the entire year, and it is a time when the living aren't the only tourists in Salem. The dead come to visit as well!

Since Halloween is a time for the dead, I wanted to end this chapter with some actual rituals that my coven does here in Salem at this time.

The Dumb Supper: A Dinner with the Dead?

Every October here in Salem, close to Halloween, we hold a large feast in the grand ballroom of the Hawthorne Hotel. Participants are each blessed by Witches as they are ushered into the dining area through a 15-foot "veil between the worlds." Dinner is served in reverse order—dessert first, soup last—with the silverware reversed. A large, 12-foot altar crowns the back of the room where participants leave photos and mementos of their dead, that their energy might be drawn to the space. At the center of the altar is Robert the skull, who waiters know must be served each course first. Guests enjoy the sumptuous meal in total silence. Nobody speaks for the duration. Instead, they listen to songs of the dead from many cultures and styles—everything from modern Witches' chants of the dead to Schubert's "Ave Maria," Luther Vandross's rhythm and blues ballad "Dance with My Father," and even a live recording of a New Orleans Jazz Funeral. This is by far my favorite event of the year. It is the Dumb Supper, when each participant remains silent and the guests of honor are our beloved dead.

Over the years that we've held the Dumb Supper in Salem, the spirits have manifested in some rather exciting ways. The most fascinating experiences are reported by those I call "the husbands," men brought by their wives who cluster together in the corner with their cocktails, wondering just what the heck they have been dragged to. Most years there's a husband who comes to me after the dinner, talking about a ghostly experience he had after coming to the event with a cynical attitude. One such guest, a quite respectable man with a civil servant's job in a nearby city, told me how he saw the spectral forms of his grandparents dancing across the ballroom floor and even had a vision of his recently deceased dog. This was a far cry from the skeptical attitude he brought to the dinner. Even the waiters and waitresses, who are also not allowed to speak, get caught up in the spirit of the evening. My coven-sister Leanne once pointed out to me that not only were they serving Robert the skull at each course, taking the obviously uneaten plates away as each next course arrived, but as they went to refill everyone's water, they'd attempt to refill Robert's as well! If nothing else, our annual Dumb Supper has become a powerful psychological journey into our relationship with the dead.

Like Halloween, the modern Dumb Supper features elements of a number of ancient traditions. My own Dumb Supper updates the tradition even further with the addition of music, mainly to aid the many non-Witches present in maintaining silence in a room of nearly a hundred people. While many Wiccan and Witchcraft books imply that the tradition dates to the ancient Celts, my research for this book took me down a different road. I found many references to the Dumb Supper throughout the twentieth century, but few had anything to do with the dead. The story generally involved a group of girls making a dinner of cornmeal and salt and eating it in silence, waiting for the "spirit" of their future husband to appear. If a girl saw nobody, she would never marry. If she saw "a black figure, without recognizable features," it meant that she "would die within the year."[55] Other versions required every step of the meal to be set backwards. None involved the dead. The spirit visage of the future husband is more reminiscent of astral projection, the ability to travel outside the body in spectral form, or perhaps a type of precognitive vision. From what was accessible to me in research, I was able to find only one story prior to the Wiccan revival of the latter twentieth century that involved a woman using the Dumb Supper to call up the spirits of the dead, and it was an African American folktale referenced in 1929.[56] Prior to that point, one 1920 version alleged that supernatural signs might manifest, such as "two men carrying a corpse" or a "large white dog."[57] References to the Dumb Supper go back no further than 1901 with the ritual culminating not in the appearance of the spirit of the future husband at the table, but rather in his appearance later in the dreams of those girls who were able to stay silent through the entire meal.[58] I thought this was the end of my journey, but I later found British references to the "Dumb Cake," a ritual similar to the earliest references to the Dumb Supper, in that girls who could stay silent while eating it would dream of their future husbands that night. In one instance, actual visages of future husbands supposedly would chase after the girls, while those who were to die unmarried would have terrible dreams of newly made graves.[59] The earliest example of the Dumb Cake ritual I could find dated to the script of a 1713 British comedy play called *The Wife of Bath*,[60] although the *Oxford Dictionary of Folklore* says that the practice was documented as early as 1680.[61] I was also able to find a 1909 reference that asserts that the Dumb Cake originated on the Isle of Man, where it was called the "Soddag valloo"—but again it appears as one of the many matrimonial divination rituals long associated with Halloween and the supernatural.[62]

After all this research, I became somewhat discouraged to find that my beloved Dumb Supper may not always have been a ritual of the dead, and, if it was, there seemed to be no evidence for it. But then I realized that if Halloween and our cherished Festival of the Dead are truly a syncretic blending of all those traditions that have gone before, then I'm not sure that it matters. As we have discovered, leaving food for the dead is an ancient custom. So is the silent repose of mourning. To combine them into a beautiful ceremony may in fact be a twentieth-century invention, but it's one that I will continue as long as doing so carries the dead through the doorways of spirit that we may commune with them once more. Whereas most rituals of the dead help us to raise the spirits with the power of our voices, the Dumb Supper helps us to find the mighty wisdom hidden within the silence.

Ritual: The Dumb Supper

I recommend that you perform a dumb supper of your own, for it is an inspiring way to reach the spirit world that really works. You can do it alone, with a coven of other Witches, or even with family and friends. It can be held on or near Halloween night, or on the birthday or death day of a particular person you want to honor. If your dinner is dedicated to a specific person on the Other Side, make the meal one of his favorite foods! Otherwise, try to have a balance of different foods that appeal to those you have lost.

To begin, take pictures, mementos, flowers, the skull, incense burner, and other items that you normally keep on your altar of the dead and place them across the center of your dining table, much as you would at your altar. The silverware and glassware should be set opposite how you normally place it. The meal itself should be served in reverse—dessert first; appetizer, salad, or soup last—based on how you normally do things. This helps to create the shift in consciousness necessary to allow you to experience the spirits.

At the beginning of the meal, burn some necromantic incense to set the mood (see appendix A). Shake your ritual bell or rattle over the first course to call the spirits, making sure not to speak. Set the rattle down on the table and begin the meal. Nobody should speak over the course of the dinner. If you would like, you can play music like we do in Salem, but it should be either music honoring the dead in general, or music once enjoyed by the person you are trying to invoke. Was grandma a Sinatra fan? Play him! This can help participants slip into the mood of the evening, though perfect silence can work great with smaller numbers of people. As you sit through the dinner, make mental note of the visions that come to your mind, the scents that come to your nose, and the whispers that speak into your ears. You will find that few can go through an entire Dumb Supper without experiencing something. After the dinner is complete and everyone is done eating, it's always fascinating to go into another room with coffee to discuss some of the visions people had!

• • •

Ritual: The Mourning Tea

This is a very unique event that Shawn Poirier and I created for Salem Witch Leanne Marrama as a way of sharing memories of the dead. Shawn, Leanne, and I wondered what it would be like to create a counterbalance to the Dumb Supper, an event that would function as a communal eulogy of sorts, where participants could share joyful and solemn stories of their beloved dead.

In keeping with the lush mourning traditions of the Victorian era, when widows wore black dresses for years and the hair of the dead was carried in cherished mourning lockets, we decided to hold the event as a three-course Victorian-style tea, held on the late Sunday morning before Halloween. A harpist was present to remind us of the mortuary rites of yesteryear. Guests brought photos and paper mementos of their loved ones, like they do at the Dumb Supper, but they were permanently placed into our "Book of the Dead," a growing, annual compendium of memories for which there will soon be multiple volumes filled with photographs, newspaper clippings, hair, and even suicide notes. Death is not always pretty, and the Book of the Dead is a reflection of the whole of life. Participants are able to share stories of the beloved souls who have touched their lives and have helped make them who they are today.

If you would like to create your own Mourning Tea, we strongly recommend it. You can hold it in your dining room with friends, finger foods, small desserts, and, of course, tea! Your book of the dead can, like ours in Salem, be a simple scrapbook from a craft store that you add to over the years.

The most important ingredients of the Mourning Tea are you and your friends, whose stories will keep your departed loved ones alive in your hearts, and strengthen your connection to the spirits.

• • •

Ritual: Halloween Night

Every Halloween night, many of the Salem Witches gather on Salem Common, the large park area that has been a central hub of Salem for centuries. There, we educate tourists about the importance of honoring our dead. If you would like to honor this holiday, we present this ritual as a way of tapping into the energies of this sacred night, when the veils part and the spirits of the otherworld return.

To Prepare

The larger part of your ritual will take place either at your altar of the dead, or, if you're doing this ritual in a larger space, a temporary altar table in the western area of the room. The altar should be adorned with the skull, bronze dagger, yew wand, chalice of libation, pentacle of protection, offering cauldron, spirit powder, jar of honey, keys, spirit incense and burner, anointing oil, black candle, white candle, bowl filled with offerings for the dead, bowl of dry black beans (one bean for each participant), and any mementos and photos of the dead you wish to remember—especially items that remind you of those who have died over the past year. Participants should each bring a divination tool of some kind, such as the bronze bowl of water or scrying mirror discussed in chapter 6, a candle for flame-scrying, a Ouija board, or simply a pen and paper for automatic writing. Halloween is the best time for divination!

Stand a large, full-length mirror—or a mirror placed on a table so that you can see your face in it while standing—just outside the room where the altar is placed. If the ritual is outside, then the mirror should stand about three feet away from the outer edge of the ritual space. A solitary black candle should light the mirror. Beginning at the mirror, create a path of eighteen jack-o-lanterns, nine on each side of the path (according to numerology, 1+8=9, the number of the moon), extending through at least one other room or, if outside, about thirty feet. The jack-o-lanterns should be lit just before the ritual takes place.

The Ritual

Have each participant in the ritual stand silently in line at the beginning of the path of jack-o-lanterns, beginning with you, as the leader of the rite. Each person should be breathing deeply and entering into a visionary state in preparation for the magic to come.

As the first person in line, you should slowly and solemnly walk the lantern-lit path, thinking thoughts of the dead, especially of those who have passed in the last year. As you come to the mirror, gaze deeply into it, allowing your visionary state to deepen. Look into your reflection and contemplate your own mortality. Spirits may or may not appear in the mirror during this time. Do not be alarmed if they do, for this is the nature of the evening. When you have finished gazing into the mirror, turn and silently beckon the next person in line to walk the path of jack-o-lanterns, while you proceed into the circle.

Go over to the altar, pick up the skull, and bring it over to the circle's edge before the next person enters. As each participant comes to the circle, hold the skull up before her face, eye to eye, and say, *Do you dare confront your own mortality on this night? Do you dare become like the dead?!* If the participant says no, she must be turned from the circle. If she says yes, usher her into the space, motioning her to take her place at the edge of the circle. As you repeat this with each participant, they should together form a circle with the altar within in the western quadrant. If the altar is against a wall, participants should use the altar itself to complete the circle. Once everyone is present within the circle, hold the skull above your head and call out, *On this sacred Hallows night, Let now the dead attend our rite! For each of us shall die one day. And they shall guide us on our way!*

Place the skull back on the altar and take up the bronze dagger with your right hand. Beginning in the west, the place of the dead, draw a circle three times counterclockwise around the participants and the altar, visualizing a stream of pure white energy emanating from the dagger. As you cast the circle, say, aloud, *Here I draw the circle round. Let within this space be found, only Spirits pure of heart, while darker shades must now depart!*

Place the dagger back upon the altar and take up the anointing oil. Anoint the skull first; then, going to each participant counterclockwise, anoint each forehead in an "X" with the oil, saying, *You are blessed by the spirits, for you are a creature of spirit yourself.*

Take this time to call on particular deities of importance to you and your group (see appendix B for a list of deities of the dead and their offerings). You can also use this time to talk about the meaning of the holiday. I purposely leave this period of the ritual for inspired words from the heart, because it is important to have the spark of spontaneity in ritual. This can also be a time for participants to share their own feelings about the year that has passed and the year that is coming, for this is a time of prophecy.

When everyone has finished, go to the altar and raise the bowl of offerings above your head, and say, *This we offer to the dead. Let it be your holy bread!*

Place the bowl back down and pick up the other bowl of dry beans. Again, going counterclockwise, hand a bean to each participant and say, *Let this spark of life fuel your visions and dreams with magic!* Return the bowl to the altar that the dead continue to draw from their energy.

Each participant should now go up to the altar and cast a spell for the coming year by placing his right hand upon the skull and speaking what he wishes to come to pass. This can be done silently or aloud, depending on the level of comfort within the group. (I do not tend to perform blood magic in group settings for health reasons.) Once everyone has done this, go to the altar and take up the yew wand with your right hand. Stand before the altar and raise the wand high, saying, *Let every spirit present here; Now make our magics come to be; With wings of haste and will of might; On this, our sacred hallows night!*

Now is the time when you must honor your dead, especially those who have died during the past year. There are two ways to do this. If each coven member is comfortable speaking (and I hope they are!), then you should begin by calling out the name of someone you have lost into the direction of the west. Then, the coven as a group should speak names in their turn so that the energy of the beloved dead is drawn into the circle. If participants are less comfortable speaking alone, or if you have a very large group of people, then you could all call out the names loudly on the count of three. The latter is how I do this at my annual Witches' Ball.

Place the wand back on the altar and take up the bronze dagger with your right hand. Now, moving clockwise, draw the circle once around the participants, saying, *Spirits of the mighty dead; Sated now with holy bread; Go forth and let our will be done; As rising moon and setting sun!*

Now that the formal ritual is over, time should be taken for repose, reflection, and divination. Each participant should sit, if possible, and use his divination tool of choice, or simply meditate on the spirits, awaiting the voices of the dead to come through.

• • •

Afterword . . . and Beyond

To journey to the realms of the dead is to undergo one of the very same great labors that Hercules himself endured. The spirits will not suffer fools and you will be challenged if you travel on the roads of the dead. Since I began seriously writing this book, I have faced incredible adversity that seemed to indicate that, were I to continue, the spirits would throw all that they had at me. I can almost hear the voices of the dead whispering, "So you think you're going to teach people how to truly commune with us? Let's see if you can withstand the arduous trials that accompany any expedition beyond the veil."

This book tested my strength to the core. When I first decided to write it, I began to suffer the deaths of my closest confidants, including my best friend and even my own mother. Death was now more than just a spiritual concept to be pondered and explored; it had become hard, unforgiving, and accompanied by somber speeches from physicians recommending that life support machines be turned off. Later, when I announced an actual deadline for the book, old enemies began to surface in hopes of tearing me down and preventing its release. Close friends and family members came upon hard times and needed my help. I even suffered physically debilitating injuries. It seemed as though a force was set against this book ever reaching the hands of its readers.

Finally, on the very day before my deadline, my dear cousin Becci passed away from heart failure. We were raised together as children. Our mothers were best friends who considered one another sisters and so we considered one another cousins—the kind of family made by the bonds of love. It is no accident that the finality of this book was tied to the finality of Becci's life. She was a powerful Witch who traveled the paths of the dead and knew that someday she, too, would pass into the sweeter realms.

So, I see no better way to honor our forty-one years of cherished memories, love, and the deepest loyalty than to end this book in memory of her and how she has indelibly touched my heart and soul.

With death comes loss, but it is also a gift. The creation process of this book is now dead, and I must let it go and be transformed into something that will be the property of all who read it—interpreting and reinterpreting it to further their own journeys. Becci's journey to the next world reminds me that she, too, will become transformed, as each of us will when death comes for us in our turn. We who are left behind must move forward and be strong. Those of you who have lost someone to death's clutches must come back from the pits of grief, embrace the desire to search for meaning and connection with those you have lost, and face the challenge of finding new ways to continue the relationship. As you find ways of reaching out to those in the spirit world, know that once you have passed into the other realms, those you leave behind may someday be reaching out to you.

We will all meet death at the end of our journey. It comes for us whether we fight it or embrace its touch. It is the one thing that remains beyond our control. Science and magic might delay it, but nothing can stop it. Death reminds us of the importance of life, the importance to share more, to forgive more, and to love more. Death is not the end. Like magic, death is transformation, for every ending is but a beginning. May Becci's journey into the next world be as wondrous an adventure as anything we can imagine life's greatest voyage to be. And may your own journey into the worlds of the dead help you to embrace death's transformative power.

Appendixes

Appendix A: Recipes

On the following pages I share some of the recipes I've talked about through-out the book. Some are recipes I created myself, drawing from a variety of sources. Others were given to me by my mentor, Sicilian hereditary Strega Lori Bruno. I encourage you to experiment with ingredients and elements. Perhaps the dirt from only a particular cemetery will work for you, or maybe you only get results from local honey. You may even want to research herbalism, incense making, or oil blending further so that you can create your own. Magic is a very personal art, and it is a very powerful thing to make a recipe your own.

∏ECROMA∏CY I∏CE∏8E

This blend was created with the help of Salem alchemist and perfumer John Viens. It is drawn from a variety of traditions to create the best cross-cultural balance of energies and scents to appeal to the spirits of the dead. All you will need besides the ingredients are a good mortar and pestle, a large plate or tray, a few small plates for each ingredient, and a mixing bowl, preferably one you have designated for incense and not for food.

I∏GREƏIE∏†8

9 parts yellow sandalwood chips (crushed, not powdered)

9 parts myrrh tears (crushed, not powdered)

9 parts copal resin tears (crushed, not powdered)

9 parts plain honey (preferably local to draw on the energy of place)

3 parts wormwood (cut and sifted)

3 parts whole star anise (crushed, not powdered)

1 part vervain (cut and sifted)

1 part dittany of crete (cut and sifted)

1 part lavender buds

1 part graveyard dirt (from the grave of someone you love or respect)

3 drops of wine

3 drops of your own blood, taken from a sterile medical lancet
(available at any drug store)

Preparation

To prepare the ingredients that require crushing, process each resin or herb separately in a mortar and pestle, driving down the pestle in a counterclockwise motion (the direction of the dead). As you crush the ingredient, visualize the spirits of those you honor and respect. Feel the spirit power going into each ingredient in its turn. When each ingredient is crushed to a coarse grain (do not powder), place it on its own small plate.

Spoon the correct parts of all but the honey and liquids back into the mortar and pestle and blend, counterclockwise, until blended, being sure to visualize the love of the spirits going into every turn and being careful not to powder the mixture.

Pour this into the mixing bowl and add the 9 parts honey. Blend the mixture with your fingers, and feel your own energy pouring into the mixture. Using an eye dropper, place three drops of wine into the mixture.

With the sterile medical lancet, prick your finger so that you can squeeze three drops of blood into the mixture, saying, *By this sacrifice of my own blood, I ask that the spirits recognize the life force I have blended within!*

Continue to work the mixture with your fingers until fully blended. Say, *So this spirit incense is complete. Each time I use it, may the beloved dead heed my call and answer my request!*

Spread the incense mixture out onto a tray or large plate and allow it to cure for three days. Then, put in a bottle or other container and use whenever you have need of the spirits of the dead!

Spirit Powder

I created this recipe as a means of creating sacred and protective space. Circles of chalk, cornmeal, salt, and other powders have been used for centuries. Since salt should never be used when working with the dead, I set about to blend a recipe that I felt would not only protect from the harmful dead, but also welcome in benevolent spirits who wish to help.

Ingredients

33 parts graveyard dirt (from the grave of someone you love or respect)

9 parts powdered myrrh

9 parts powdered copal resin

9 parts powdered wormwood

9 parts powdered whole star anise

9 parts powdered vervain

9 parts dittany of crete

9 parts lavender buds

3 drops of your own blood, taken from a sterile medical lancet (available at any drug store)

Preparation

To prepare the ingredients that require powdering, process each resin or herb separately in a mortar and pestle, driving down the pestle in a counterclockwise motion (the direction of the dead). As you powder the ingredient, visualize the spirits of those you honor and respect. Feel the spirit power going into each ingredient in its turn. When each ingredient is entirely powdered, place it on its own small plate.

Now, gather all of the ingredients together and place into a bowl. With the sterile medical lancet, prick your finger so that you can squeeze three drops of blood into the mixture and say, *By this sacrifice of my own blood, I ask that the spirits recognize the life force I have blended within!*

Stir the mixture with a wooden spoon until fully blended and say, *So this spirit powder is complete. Each time I use it, may it create a wall of protection against all harmful spirits or energies. And may those beloved dead whose intentions are pure be welcomed within!*

Anointing Oil

This old recipe was passed down to Strega Lori Bruno by her family, a long line of Witches who can trace their lineage back to a necromantic dream priestess who lived on the slopes of Mount Etna in Sicily.

Ingredients

1 cup extra-virgin olive oil

3 tablespoons of warm honey

1 teaspoon pure pomegranate juice

9 fava beans

1 black bean

1 bead of barley

Preparation

Strain the extra-virgin olive oil through cheesecloth into a bowl. Point the finger of your right hand at the oil in the bowl and trace an equilateral cross above it. Say, **This oil is made sacred.**

Stir in the honey, stirring counterclockwise to invoke the dead until it is completely blended. Then, trace the equilateral cross over the mixture a second time and say, **This honey is sacred sweetness to those of the beloved dead.**

Stir in the pomegranate juice, stirring counterclockwise. Trace the equilateral cross over the mixture a third time, and say, **In the name** of Persephone, I add the sacred elixir of the pomegranate and it is done.

Raise the bowl above your head to the heavens and say, *Sacred, holy oil, bless me as I partake in its use to bring about all that I will to do. Make this oil be a link between those of the world of the dead and me! And from all evil we will be free!*

Pour the oil mixture into an amber-colored bottle (for the energy of the Sun).

Hold the fava beans in your left hand and say, three times, *This is the food of the dead,* tracing the equilateral cross over the beans with your right index finger each time you say it. Place each bean into the bottle of oil individually, and say, *Be of love between me and thee,* each time you place one into the bottle.

Do the same with the black bean, saying, *This is the food of the dead* three times and tracing the equilateral cross each time you say it, then placing the bean into the bottle, saying, again, *Be of love between me and thee.*

Now, do the same again, with the bead of barley.

Finally, place the bottle on the altar of the dead, and say, *On the altar of the dead I place this oil, that it is blessed and that it be a link between thee and me, the living and the dead.*

Food for the Dead

Throughout the book, I suggest making offerings to the dead based on what specific spirits enjoyed when they were alive. But if you wish to honor *all* the dead on your altar with offerings, this is a good universal recipe imparted to me by Lori Bruno from her own family recipes.

Ingredients

3 cups of pure extra-virgin olive oil

3 cups of pure honey (Grade A)

3 gallons of spring water

1-pound bag of dried fava beans

1-pound bag of dried black beans

1-pound bag of dried barley grain

½ cup pomegranate juice

Utensils Needed

3 new 40-quart stockpots with boil basket inserts

8 large glass bowls

1 large glass pitcher

3 sheets of parchment

Preparation

Start your preparation on Sunday at 8 AM by cleansing your kitchen. Wash all of the new utensils that you purchased with kosher salt and water. The utensils that you use to make the Food for the Dead are *never* to be used for any other purpose.

Take the three large stock pots and insert the boil baskets. Add a gallon of water to each stock pot and set each one on your stovetop with the burners turned off. Place the three sheets of parchment on your counter top and open the fava beans, black beans, and barley; place the contents of each bag on the separate parchment sheets. Search through the two types of beans and the barley to remove any foreign matter. After removing any foreign matter, take the fava beans, black beans, and barley and place each in its own separate stockpot, within the boil baskets. Allow the beans and barley to soak for four hours in the cold spring water to soften. After four hours have passed, turn on the burners under the pots and bring the spring water and contents to a boil. When the contents have completely softened, remove the boil baskets to strain the beans and barley. **Do not discard the water.** Allow the fava beans, black beans, and barley to dry out separately after straining. Place each into three separate glass bowls, and envision your beloved dead arriving at your home for dinner. Make the sign of the equilateral cross over the barley using your index finger, saying as you do so, *Food for our Beloved ones, you who dwell in the land of the Shadows, bring us blessing for this food that we have made.* Repeat for the two remaining bowls of beans.

Take the 3 cups of honey, 3 cups of pure extra-virgin olive oil, and the 1/2 cup of pomegranate juice, and place in three separate glass bowls. With your index finger, draw an equilateral cross over each bowl and say, *Food for our Beloved ones, you who dwell in the land of the Shadows, bring us blessings for this food that we have made.*

In a large glass bowl, mix the beans and barley together, stirring counterclockwise. After fully incorporating the beans and barley ingredients together, start adding in the honey, olive oil, and pomegranate juice, in that order. Stirring the beans, barley, honey, olive oil, and pomegranate together counterclockwise, say, *Holy oil I do add with joy and nothing sad, honey sweet as love I do add with joy and nothing sad, with the sacred fluid of the pomegranate I do blend for it is the beginning and not the end.* Continue stirring counterclockwise and chant nine times: *For this is the beginning and not the end.* As you finish blending the food together, say, *Sacred is this blend, for it is the beginning and not the end.*

Take the water that was left after straining the beans and barley and pour it into the large glass pitcher. To the water add 3 tablespoons of extra-virgin olive oil, 3 tablespoons of honey, and 3 tablespoons of pomegranate juice.

Take the bowl of the Food for the Dead and the pitcher of the blessed water to your ancestral altar, cemetery, or crossroads, and envision your Beloved ones sitting down to dinner. Serve your Beloved Dead. If you are at an ancestral altar, place the Food for the Dead in front of each picture on the altar. Dip your index finger in the blessed water and put it upon the lips of the Beloved Dead in the pictures. If there is any food or water left, place it outside of your front and back door for three nights to draw the dead to your home.

Appendix B: Deities of the Dead

The shadowy deities of the underworld, often referred to as chthonic deities, inspired so much fear in ancient times that they were often not even referred to by their names—since it was believed that merely naming a thing could summon it. Witches know that this is still true today, so if you're going to call something up by name, you'd better know how to handle it. Originally, many of these deities were ancestral spirits; as I mentioned in chapter 1, we often deify those souls who have truly achieved spiritual greatness. Such gods of the gloomy realms ruled over the fate of the souls of the dead, and were worshiped with propitiation and sacrifice.

In addition to the primary deities who reign over the underworld, there are many deities who have chthonic aspects to them. These include fertility gods and goddesses, for all things that live eventually die; and deities associated with the sun, for when the sun sets in the west it descends into the realm of the dead. Some deities of the night, magic, sorcery, Witchcraft, and the moon also have strong chthonic associations.

The following are some of the chthonic deities you might call upon in your work with the dead. You may want to investigate your favorites in more detail. You will feel affinities for certain ones at different times, depending on your magical needs. You may want to give those you work with the most a special place upon your altar of the dead.

Suggestions for some of the offerings favored by each deity are included as well. The ancients often sacrificed animals, a practice still done in certain traditions. As a substitution, you can offer figurines or other images of animals and birds.

Ankou

One of my favorite deities from Brittany (now France), Ankou is a skeletal figure enshrouded in a tattered cloak who travels the land in a creaking old cart in search of the souls of the sick and dying. He comes to collect the spirits of the dead for transport to the edges of the underworld, where the ferryman will usher them across to their shadowy destination. Some say that Ankou was an annual office, held by the last person to die on New Year's Eve. Other legends say that he was once a wealthy and cruel man who was punished by a mysterious and dark figure for having hunted a sacred white stag. Still others say that he personifies death itself. Ankou is considered to be a psychopomp, which is a deity or demigod who guides the souls of the dead to their final destination. You must never look Ankou in the face if you encounter him, for you shall die instantly. Although Ankou is usually thought to be male, some versions identify "him" as female. Call on Ankou to aid your loved ones in their transition to the next realms or appease him with offerings that he may pass by your house for the next.

Offerings to Ankou: Bread; spring water.

Anubis

Jackal-headed Egyptian god of the dead, Anubis is one of the oldest of the Egyptian gods and preceded Osiris as the ruler of the departed. Once Osiris assumed that role, Anubis, now said to be a son of Osiris, became a guide, escorting the souls of the dead to the underworld, the Duat. This was a role similar to that of the Greek Hermes. Anubis's totem animal, the jackal, comes from the jackal's habit of hunting around necropolises and cemeteries. Anubis tests newly departed souls for their knowledge of the gods and their faith, and places their heart on the Scales of Justice during the Judging of the Heart. If the heart of the deceased is heavier than the feather of Truth that belongs to the goddess Ma'at, this means that the soul is wicked and unjust. Anubis then feeds the souls of the damned to the monster Ammit, who devours them into oblivion. Anubis also presides over the process of mummification. Call on Anubis to help you usher the shades of the dead back across the divide between their world and ours.

Offerings to Anubis: Images of the jackal, representations of mummies, bread, beer, geese feathers, skeleton keys, obsidian.

Arawn

Welsh Celtic god whose name means "He of the Sown Field," Arawn rules the otherworld, also known as Annwfn (pronounced "ann-noon"), a labyrinthine realm where faeries and the spirits of the dead dwell and where magnificent treasures abound. Originally a deity of the tilled land, Arawn later became Lord of the Celtic otherworld—a place that remains ever fertile—and is the leader of the Wild Hunt, a time when the denizens of the underworld, including faeries, spirits, and other mythical beings, maraud the land of the living. In the first branch of the Welsh Myth cycle known as *The Mabinogion*, Pwyll, a noble of men, mistakenly sets his hounds upon a stag that is also being hunted by Arawn. To atone for this grievous insult, Pwyll exchanges places with Arawn for a year and a day, facing many tests and defeating Hafgan, who sought to usurp the rule of Annwfn from Arawn. Because Pwyll respected not only Arawn's kingdom, but Arawn's wife as well, he never defiled her though he had had a year to do so. This respect resulted in not only a bond of friendship between Pwyll and the king of the otherworld, but also a bond between this world and theirs. In the tale "The Spoils of Annwfn" from *The Book of Taliesin*, King Arthur passes living through the veil with his entire party into the otherworld to steal a magical cauldron from Arawn. Some suggest that these stories later evolved into the tales of the Holy Grail. Call on Arawn when you wish to pass beyond the veil and return again to tell the tale!

Offerings to Arawn: Ale, whiskey, offerings tied to trees.

Azrael

The enigmatic Necromancer Leilah Wendell, in her books *Encounters with Death, My Name Is Melancholy*, and *The Necromantic Ritual Book*, beckons us into the the shadowy realms of Azrael, the mighty Angel of Death. It is he who is appointed the task of heralding death and collecting souls for their radiant ascent into heaven or their fiery descent into hell. Azrael is truly terrible to behold, but has many guises as he seeks the souls of the living whose time has come—which, according to Islamic legend, even he is not aware of until Allah (God) drops a leaf to him with the name of that person to be collected. He is our most ardent lover, a final companion on the journey of life who clutches us tenderly in his cold, bony grip. He often takes the form that we can best relate to, whether it is as a winged angel, a grim reaper, or even hordes of black birds. In Islamic teachings, the righteous are carried to heaven on the winds of sweet-smelling incense while the wicked and hateful are pulled into hell by the many arms of the hellish minions that accompany Azrael when the truly evil justify the need. In his most transcendent and divine form, Azrael represents the very substance and flow of the Death Current itself, so you should call on him at early dawn or late dusk to embrace the energies of his vast powers.

Offerings to Azrael: Sincere understanding and an open heart filled with love and free of fear; burnt offerings of either sweet jasmine, bay laurel leaves, or both; amethyst crystals; and, as Leilah recently shared with me, "The best thing to give Him is an open hand . . . and let Him lead you home."

Astarte

The Phoenician great goddess of fertility, motherhood, war, and ruler of the dead, Astarte is the counterpart to the Babylonian goddess Ishtar; her cult dates to the Neolithic and Bronze ages. Tammuz, her son and consort, dies, and Astarte descends to the underworld to rescue him. The Phoenicians portrayed Astarte with cow horns, representing fertility. The Assyrians and Babylonians portrayed her caressing a child. She is associated with the moon and called the Mother of the Universe, the giver of all life on Earth. She rules all spirits of the dead who dwell in the heavens as bodies of light—visible on Earth below as stars. Her counterparts in other lands are Isis and Hathor of Egypt, Kali of India, and Aphrodite and Demeter of Greece. Call on Astarte to bless both the lands and the wombs of hopeful mothers with fertility.

Offerings to Astarte: Goddess cakes; clothing stained with menstrual blood; milk and honey.

Baron Samedi

Among the gods—or Loa—of Voodoo, the dead are ruled by the powerful spirits of Guédé. Chief among them is Baron Samedi, whose name means Baron Saturday. He rules alongside his wife Mama Brijit, Queen of the Dead; Baron Cimetière; and Baron La Croix. Some believe he is the spiritual father of the Guédé, while others consider him a chief member of the extended Guédé family. Baron Samedi is typically seen in his white, skull-like face, top hat, black tailcoat, and dark glasses that are usually missing one lens, symbolizing the Baron's ability to see into the worlds of both the living and the dead. Baron Samedi's dance is the provocative "Banda," for he is both a Loa of sex and death. Though he is famous for his association with phallic symbols, debauchery, and obscene language, this lewd behavior manifests in a very comical and at times sarcastic way. He is fond of cigars, tobacco, rum, and spicy foods, and he loves to cause mischief, especially of a sexual nature. It is usually preferable that the Guédé arrive last in rituals of Voodoo because of this mischief, but they are known to pop in uninvited at any time. It's thought to be better that all of this bawdy behavior be saved until after the main Loa have been served. He is also a very serious Loa of resurrection and healing, though his outward mannerisms may seem otherwise. You call on the Baron for fertility, to protect children, physical healing, burial, and to call on the spirits of the dead.

Offerings for Baron Samedi: A black rooster, peanuts, black coffee, spicy foods, cigars, bread, coins, spicy rum and other liquors.

Circe

A sorceress who is also considered a goddess in Greek Myth, Circe is renowned for her enchantments; in Homer's *Odyssey*, she turns Odysseus's men into swine. Fair-haired, she was sometimes said to be the daughter of Hecate, the patron goddess of Witchcraft and magic. She is also a goddess of the moon and of degrading love. She controls fate and the forces of creation and destruction with knots and braids in her hair.

When Odysseus found her, Circe was living in exile on the island of Aeaea ("Wailing") as punishment for murdering her husband, the king of Sarmatians, by poisoning. There she built herself a palace and taught herself the arts of magic. She cast a spell over the entire island so that anyone who came there would be turned into an animal. When Odysseus's men were turned into swine, Odysseus himself escaped, having been forewarned and forearmed by Hermes, who gave him a magical herb, "moly," for protection. Odysseus forced Circe to restore his men to their human form. He was so taken with her that he spent a year with her, and she advised him how to travel west to the underworld, and how to conjure the shades of the dead for prophecy. Circe eventually was slain by Telemachus, who married her daughter, Cassiphone. Now in spirit, you can call on Circe to aid you in speaking with the dead, the brewing of potions, and communing with animals.

Offerings to Circe: Feathers, wolf hair, or lion hair, all shed naturally from a live animal; baneful herbs of aconite or deadly nightshade; potions; figurines or images of pigs, birds, lions, or wolves; alder wood, willow, mandrake, or tamarisk. Adopting an animal from a shelter would please Circe greatly.

Ereshkigal

Ereshkigal is the dark Sumerian Queen of the Underworld and sister of Inanna, whom she despises. One legend tells that Ereshkigal was a sky goddess who was kidnapped by a dragon, Kur, and taken to the underworld, called by the same name (as Kurnugi, it is the gloomy Land of No Return). A violent and harsh goddess, she rules with her consort Nergal, whom she forced to stay in the underworld. Nergal was sent to her from heaven one day with an offering of food. They fell in love with each other. When Nergal left, Ereskigal was so distressed that she threatened the great god Anu that she would revive all the dead, who outnumbered the living, and send them back to Earth. Anu relented, and Nergal was sent back to her to be her consort forever.

Sometimes appearing with the head of a lion, Ereshkigal sits naked on a throne of lapis lazuli. Her palace is surrounded by seven walls, each of which has a gate that the dead must pass through to get to the underworld. They lose something at every gate, until they are left naked and powerless. In ancient times, Ereshkigal took the funerary offerings to the dead. Call on Ereshkigal in all of your funerary rites and in any forms of necromancy.

Offerings to Ereshkigal: Lapis lazuli; snakeskin shed from a live snake; figurines or images of lions and snakes.

Erinyes (Furies)

The Erinyes, or Furies, were three fearsome goddesses of vengeance and justice in Greco-Roman mythology who relentlessly punish wrongdoers to death, sometimes by driving them to suicide. "Erinyes" means "roused to anger"; the Romans called them Furies, meaning the same thing. Their Greek names are Tisiphone, Megaera, and Alecto. In Hades, they torment the souls of sinners, playing their lyres to cause souls to wither, and driving the souls of murderers to insanity. In appearance, the Erinyes are ugly and winged, with deadly serpents entwined in their hair and around their arms and waists. The Erinyes can be summoned for justifiable vengeance, but if you call upon them unjustly, they will torment you unto the end of your days . . . and beyond.

Offerings to the Erinyes: Things that are sweet enough to appease them and keep them from harming you or those you love, including honey and sweet meats; for vengeance, offer honey (for the sting of the bee) or your own blood, but remember: you *must* be justified!

Hades

The mightiest and most feared god of the classical Greek underworld is Hades, the King of the Dead. His underworld, which also bears the name Hades, was conceived as a gloomy realm where shades—the souls of the dead—roamed in listless longing for the pleasures of the material world. Hades is dispassionate but not evil; nor is he synonymous with the Devil of Christianity. He seldom leaves his kingdom, but prefers to remain in his huge, cold palace. He possesses a cap that makes the wearer invisible. The Romans associated him with the minerals of the Earth and called him Pluto, the god of wealth. Call on Hades that he may encourage the dead to more easily accept you, to show you the way to hidden treasures, or to grant you the powers of invisibility.

Offerings to Hades: Dates, figs, barley, honey, fava beans, black beans, or olive oil; cypress wood; figurines or images of pigs; your own blood or hair.

Hecate

Hecate is the Queen of all Witcheries, a powerful goddess who is the matron of magic and sorcery, guide to the dead, and a lantern to spirits seeking their way. Hecate has many facets, but has come to be known for three primary aspects: she is goddess of transitions; goddess of the moon; and queen of the night, ghosts, and shades. Hecate possesses vast chthonic power, and roams the Earth at night with a pack of red-eyed hell hounds and an entourage of departed souls. Hecate is heralded by the howl of dogs, which usually signify that the Goddess is about. In her aspect of Antea, she is the bringer of dreaded nightmares that can lead to insanity, and is so terrifying that many ancients referred to her only as "The Nameless One." She is the goddess of the dark of the moon, a keeper of the keys to the gates between life and death, able to usher souls between the worlds.

Hecate is the goddess of crossroads, always looking in three directions at the same time. Whether it is a place where three roads meet, or several, she shines her light upon the crossroads so that the spirits of the dead may choose their path, and guides and protects those souls who have made that choice. In ancient times, Witches and necromancers gathered at crossroads on the 30th of each month to pay homage to Hecate and to aid in releasing the earthbound dead; while on the 13th of each month, honey cakes were left in gratitude for her help. Three-headed statues of Hecate were set up at crossroads while secret rites surrounded by torches were performed there to appease her. Statues of Hecate carrying torches were erected in front of homes to keep evil spirits at bay. Call on Hecate for protection and mediation whenever you make contact with the dead and to ask her to help guide the souls of the recently departed.

Offerings to Hecate: Hecatean priestess and owner of Good Mojo Tattoo Parlor Mulysa Mayhem shared these offerings with me: fish, garlic, millet, honey cakes; waste products and garbage (left at the crossroads); menstrual blood; spring water.

Hel

The Christian "Hell" was named for both this Norse goddess and the gloomy underworld where she dwells, gathering all spirits of the dead who do not die in battle or at sea in her desolate domain. Some have said that Hel was the daughter borne of the union between the trickster god Loki and a giant-ess Witch. Odin himself, father of the Norse gods, fearing a prophecy of the destruction Hel might cause, cast her into the deepest darkest regions of the world that she may become Queen of the Dead.

Hel's demeanor is sullen and downcast. One half of her body is alive, while the other is entirely dead and decaying. The underworld where the goddess resides is also known as Hel, or Helheim, and is a multifaceted realm that spans the spectrum between repose and torment. Those who died in battle or at sea went instead to the hall of heroes known as Asgard. When the Norse god, Baldr, died, the gods of Asgard pleaded with Hel to release him, but Hel made it clear that every being must cry in sorrow for the god; all did but for a single giantess, and so Baldr was consigned to the underworld until the last battle at the end of time, known as the Ragnarök, when even the dead throughout Hel may arise.

Offerings to Hel: Figurines and images of black mare and hounds; mead; ashes of the dead; burnt offerings of personal sacrifices.

Hermes

The quicksilver messenger god of the Greeks, Hermes ("Mercury" to the Romans) is a psychopomp who escorts the souls of the dead to the underworld. Swift and cunning, Hermes is portrayed with winged feet and a winged helmet. He carries the caduceus, a serpent-entwined staff or magic wand, which symbolizes spiritual illumination and the power to manifest and to cast spells. Hermes is a patron god of magic and travelers, and like Hecate, his image was also once erected at crossroads. He is a trickster, shrewd and prone to malicious pranks. He can also be helpful; in Homer's *Odyssey*, he saves Odysseus from the magical spells of Circe. Hermes appears in Greek mythology more often than any other deity. The Greeks identified him closely with Thoth, the Egyptian god of wisdom and magic, and the teacher of the mysteries and secrets of the universe. Like Anubis and Hecate, Hermes can be called on to usher the souls of the dead back and forth between the veil of death, and to help guide the souls of the recently departed.

Offerings to Hermes: Silver coins; figurines or images of dogs, an animal sacred to Hermes for its intelligence and devotion; honey cakes or honey; wine, water, and incense. Adopting a shelter dog will give Hermes great pleasure.

Hypnos

God of sleep, the "little death," Hypnos is the twin brother of Thanatos, the god of death. Hypnos lives in a dark, sunless cave through which flows the river Lethe ("forgetfulness"), one of the rivers that bound Hades. At the entrance of the cave grow poppies and plants that induce sleep. He is often portrayed as a young naked man, sometimes bearded and sometimes with wings attached to his head. He sleeps on a bed of feathers surrounded by black curtains. Call on Hypnos when you are seeking to dream of the dead.

Offerings to Hypnos: Poppies or poppy seeds; sleep-inducing herbs such as mugwort and Saint John's wort; feathers; warm milk.

Inanna

Sumerian mother goddess, the Queen of Heaven, and the ruler of the cycle of life, death and fertility, Inanna (also called Nina) sacrificed her son-husband, Dumuzi, a shepherd, to the underworld, which parallels other myths that explain the seasons. Inanna descended to the Land of No Return, another name for the underworld, ruled by her sister, Ereshkigal. She passed through its seven gates, and had to surrender something at each gate—such as her crown and jewelry—so that by the time she reached the underworld, she was naked and powerless. Ereshkigal had her taken captive by her demonic attendants, the Galli, and ordered her to be killed and her corpse to be hung up. Inanna's death plunged the world into mourning and winter. Enki, the god of wisdom, animated clay poppets who went to the underworld and begged for mercy. Ereshkigal relented, and had Inanna's corpse fed the Water of Life and the Bread of Life. Inanna revived. But according to the law of the underworld, no one could ever return from death. Inanna was released on the condition that she send another life in exchange.

When she returned to her temple, Inanna was shocked to find Dumuzi dressed in royal robes and sitting on her throne, happy to have taken over in her stead. She gave him the Eye of Death, and the Galli came and dragged him off to the underworld. Inanna immediately repented and revived his corpse, but she had to agree to a compromise with Ereshkigal: Dumuzi would spend six months among the living and six months among the dead each year. Call on Inanna to aid you in your journeys to the underworld and to help show the spirits the personal sacrifices you are willing to make to show that you are worthy of their aid.

Offerings for Inanna: Jewelry for her power; salt for the salty tears she wept over Dumuzi; sweet cakes, wine, and fine beer.

Isis

The Egyptian Mother Goddess, the name of Isis is actually Greek for the Egyptian hieroglyphic representing "throne." Isis commands such powerful magic—she can raise the dead—that even Anubis bows to her whims. In ancient times, people prayed to her on behalf of the sick and dying. She also is goddess of fertility and childbirth. Isis was born a mortal, the sister of Osiris. Through magic, she acquired immortality by tricking the sun god, Ra, into revealing his secret name. She did this by obtaining his spit, from which she made a snake and left it in his path. Ra was bitten. She offered to relieve his agony if he would tell her his secret name, and he relented.

Isis married Osiris. When Osiris's treacherous brother, Set, murdered and dismembered him, Isis collected his body parts. She used magic to put them together and breathe life into the body so that she and Osiris could be together one last time before he left to rule the underworld. A son, Horus, was born from this union. Set once again cut up the body of Osiris, and Isis again collected the parts, but buried them in order to fertilize the land.

Isis is the prototype of the faithful wife and fertile, protective mother. She is associated with Sirius, the Dog Star, the rising of which signals the vernal equinox. Her symbol is the moon. She is often shown crowned with a lunar orb nestled between the horns of a bull or ram. In ancient times, she was worshipped at the full moon.

The Greeks considered her to be the goddess of wisdom, truth, and power, who had 10,000 names. Statues of her were decorated with stars, the moon, and the sun. Her priests controlled the elements and the forces of nature, as well as the unseen occult forces. Isis collaborated with Hermes to invent writing, and to teach law and the mysteries. They caused men to love women, invented sailing, ended cannibalism, made justice more powerful than gold or silver, and caused Truth to be considered beautiful.

Isis has a sister named Nephthys, who is also chthonic and stands at the gateway between the living and the dead.

The Isis of the mysteries is completely veiled by a scarlet cloth, which she lifts for those who learn her mysteries. Many of her symbols were later conferred upon the Virgin Mary. Call upon Isis to bring healing to those who are near death or for healing in general.

Offerings to Isis: Red scarves and cloth; images of bulls and rams; images of the moon; milk, honey, roses, and lilies.

Kali

Kali is the Hindu goddess of death, destruction, fear and terror, and the wife-consort of Siva, the destroyer. Since the eighteenth century, she has also been recognized as a mother goddess. Kali embodies powerful energy.

In her aspect of Kali Ma (the "black mother"), she is a bloodthirsty and powerful warrior, and a drinker of blood. Her appearance is fearsome: she is dark-skinned or black, with long and disheveled hair, four arms, and hands with claw-like nails. Her tongue hangs out and she has long, sharp fangs. She wears a necklace of skulls and earrings of corpses. She is spattered with blood, and gets drunk by drinking the blood of her victims. In art she is often shown naked or wearing only her grisly jewelry and a girdle, standing on the body of Siva with one foot on his leg and one on his chest. Two of her hands hold a sword and the severed head of a giant, and the other two beckon to her worshippers. Kali is a central figure in Tantrism, a practice that employs control of sexual and life forces to gain longevity and immortality. She personifies death. Call on Kali to help you to understand the importance of the balance of death and life.

Offerings to Kali: Red hibiscus flowers; raw sugar; cooked meat dishes; your own blood; fire.

Ma'at

Egyptian goddess of order, harmony, truth, morality, justice and law, and also the stars and seasons, Ma'at is often shown with wings and an ostrich feather in her headdress, holding a scepter and ankh. She has chthonic associations for her role with Anubis in judging new souls in the underworld, the Duat. The hearts of the newly dead were weighed against her ostrich feather in the Hall of Two Truths. The heart was regarded as the seat of the soul, and if it was heavier than her feather, it meant that the dead person had been wicked in life. The wicked were fed to Ammit, the Devourer or Bone-Crusher, and died a second death, thus being denied the bliss of the afterlife. Call on Ma'at when justice must prevail!

Offerings to Ma'at: Ostrich feathers, though any feather will do in a pinch; symbols of justice. Joining justice advocacy groups or those that help crime victims can be a powerful gift to Ma'at.

Oneiroi

In Greek mythology, the Oneiroi are minor deities who personify dreams, and are important mediums for contacting the dead. The offspring of Hypnos, the god of sleep, the Oneiroi live in a dark cave in Erebos, the land of eternal darkness beyond the rising sun. They fly out at night like bats, led by Morpheus, their leader. Morpheus appears as a young man in the dreams of kings, bringing prophecies and important messages from the gods. The ancients believed that the Oneiroi delivered good and true dreams when they passed through a gate of horn, and false dreams when they passed through a gate of ivory. Black dreams are nightmares. Oneiros can be addressed as a personification of dreams in general. Call on them when you seek to dream of the dead.

Offerings to the Oneiroi: An animal horn for true dreams; black cloth.

Osiris

An Egyptian deity best known as god of the dead, "Osiris" is a Greek name for "Ousir." Originally, Osiris was a nature spirit, embodied in the crops that die in harvest and are reborn again each spring. According to the legend of his transformation as god of death, Osiris was a handsome king of Egypt who married his sister, Isis. In a treacherous plot, his brother, Set, murdered him and hacked his body to pieces. Using magic, Isis reassembled the body and breathed life back into him. They had sex and created a child, Horus. Set murdered Osiris again, and he descended into the underworld, the Duat, preferring to remain there. He is king and judge of the dead. The Egyptian *Book of the Dead,* a guidebook for navigating successfully to the underworld after death, has about 100 litanies to him. In the Egyptian mysteries of Osiris, his passion, death, and resurrection are reenacted in a fertility drama. His symbol is the sun. Call on Osiris to resurrect the spirits of those who have passed.

Offerings to Osiris: Incense of frankincense and myrrh; lotus flowers; ale or wine; pine cones; vases of water; meats.

Persephone

Hades rules the underworld with his queen, Persephone. According to myth, Persephone (also Kore) was a lovely maiden of spring, the daughter of Demeter, goddess of corn and the harvest. Hades desired her, and Zeus, his brother, promised her to him without telling Demeter. One day Hades rose up out of a chasm in the Earth in his chariot drawn by black horses, and kidnapped Persephone, bringing her to the underworld. In her grief, Demeter caused all things on Earth to wither and die. Other gods entreated her to relent, but she refused in anger. Finally, Zeus intervened and ordered Hades to return Persephone to Earth. Hades acquiesced, but first made Persephone eat a pomegranate seed, which bound her to him forever. As a compromise, Persephone returns to Earth each spring, bringing a flowering of the Earth, and goes back to Hades each fall, bringing the death of winter. Her transits are marked by the equinoxes.

Offerings to Persephone: Pomegranates; spring flowers and roses; first fruits; honey.

Santisima Muerte

An increasingly popular folk deity who originated in Mexico and is weaving her way through other parts of the world, Santisima Muerte (Saint Death) has become a powerful aid in the magic and prayers of all who call on her. She is a skeletal figure, similar to the Grim Reaper, cloaked in a hooded robe of varying colors (depending on the intent she is called on for). Her cult has simmered beneath the surface of Mexican culture since the 1900s, but probably has ties to Aztec worship. She is prayed to by Catholics, while Mexican Witches (brujos and brujas) invoke her for their spells. Call on Santisima Muerte for love (yes, she has long been known to return a wandering lover), luck, healing, power, protection, and wealth. Whatever your cause, Santisima Muerte will aid you!

Offerings to Santisima Muerte: Flowers, apples and other fruits; candles; money; Tequila or other liquors; uncooked rice or beans; chili peppers; cigarettes.

Thanatos

Greek god of nonviolent death, Thanatos brings an easy death on feathery wings and, much like his twin brother, Hypnos, brushes people with his wings to induce sleep. Together, they gently carry off the dead. Thanatos is usually depicted as a bearded older man. The Romans portrayed him as a young man holding a down-turned torch, or a wreath and butterfly, the symbol of the soul. Like Hypnos, he lives in a sunless cave. He is pitiless and has a heart like cold iron: whomever he grasps dies. Call on Thanatos when trying to bring a gentle death to the dying.

Offerings to Thanatos: Poppies; figurines or images of butterflies.

Thoth

Thoth is the Egyptian god who created the universe and all mystical wisdom, magic, learning, writing, arithmetic, and astrology. Called "The Lord of the Divine Books" and "Scribe of the Company of Gods," Thoth usually is portrayed as an ibis-headed man with a pen and ink holder, or as a baboon-headed man holding a crescent moon. Thoth is a healer and magician. He restored the eye of Horus, which was torn to pieces when Horus battled his evil uncle, Set, to avenge the death of his father, Osiris. The eye of Horus, also known as the *udjat* eye, became a funerary amulet and magical, all-seeing eye. Because of this magical act, Thoth became the patron god of oculists in ancient Egypt.

Thoth is an important guide to the souls of the dead. He is petitioned in many of the spells in the Egyptian *Book of the Dead*, such as the opening-of-the-mouth spell to reanimate a corpse, which was spoken over a mummy by the high priest.

The Greeks associated Hermes so closely with Thoth that the two blended together, and became identified with the mythical figure of Hermes Trismegistus, patron of magicians and alleged author of the Hermetic books of occult philosophy and wisdom. The *Book of Thoth*, or the "Key to Immortality," kept in a secret location, is said to reveal the secret processes for the regeneration of humanity, and for the expansion of consciousness that will enable mortals to behold the gods. The book is said to be contained within the Tarot.

Offerings to Thoth: Quill pen and ink holder; the Magician card of the Tarot; images of eyes; images of the Eye of Horus; representations of mummies.

Appendix C: Resources

To perform the rituals and spells presented in this book, you will need to have access to special tools and resources. Whether the need is as simple and mundane as shopping for virgin olive oil and honey, or as mysterious as aquiring dittany of crete or a human skull, the following resources will put you on the right path for purchasing the proper tools that are vital to the practice of magic. I have included information for my own three shops, HEX and OMEN in Salem, MA, and HEX in New Orleans, and I am happy to provide reliable guidance and advice for whatever tools you seek.

Magical and Spiritual Supplies

HEX (Christian Day, proprietor)
246 Essex Street, Salem, MA 01970
(978) 666-0765
www.HexWitch.com

HEX (Christian Day, proprietor)
1219 Decatur Street, New Orleans, LA 70116
(504) 613-0558
www.HexWitch.com

OMEN (Christian Day, proprietor)
184 Essex Street, Salem, MA 01970
(978) 666-0763
www.OmenSalem.com

Angelica of the Angels
7 Central Street, Salem, MA 01970
(978) 745-9355
www.AngelicaOfTheAngels.com

Crow Haven Corner
125 Essex Street, Salem, MA 01970
(978) 745-8763
www.CrowHavenCorner.net

The Magic Parlor
213 Essex Street, Salem, MA 01970
(978) 740-3866
www.MagicParlor.com

Nu Aeon
88 Wharf Street, Pickering Wharf, Salem, MA 01970
(978) 744-0202
www.NuAeon.com

Necromantic Tools (skulls, bones, etc.)

The Bone Room: A Natural History Store
1569 Solano Avenue, Berkeley, CA 94707
(510) 526-5252
www.BoneRoom.com

Westgate Necromantic
www.WestGateNecromantic.com

Necromance
7220 Melrose Avenue, Los Angeles, CA 90046
(323) 934-8684
www.Necromance.com

Events for the Dead

Festival of the Dead
www.FestivalOfTheDead.com

Day of the Dead
www.DayOfTheDead.com

Ghost Tours

Bloody Mary's Tours
New Orleans, LA
www.BloodyMarysTours.com

The Salem Night Tour
www.SalemGhostTours.com

NOTES

1 Outlet Book Company Staff, *Children's Classics: Cinderella and Other Classic Italian Fairy Tales* (Outlet Book Company, Inc., 1993).

2 Éva Pócs, *Between the Living and the Dead* (Hungary: Central European University Press, 1999).

3 J.M. Robertson, *Pagan Christs: Studies in Comparative Hierology* (London: Watts & Co., 1903), 353.

4 Thomas Kelly Cheyne, *Bible Problems and the New Material for Their Solution* (London: Williams & Norgate, 1904), 217–225.

5 Laurence Austine Waddell, *Makers of Civilization in Race and History* (London: Luzak, 1929), 24.

6 Harold Bayley, *Archaic England, An Essay in Deciphering Prehistory from Megalithic Monuments, Earthworks, Customs, Coins, Place-Names, and Faerie Superstitions* (Philadelphia: J.B. Lippincott Company, 1920), 111.

7 Robert Murch, "The Ouija Board," *www.williamfuld.com/ouija1.html*.

8 Carlo Ginzburg, *Benandanti: de Goda Häxmästarna* (Benandanti: The Good Sorcerers) (Stehag: B. Östlings bokförlag Symposion, 1991. (In Swedish.)

9 *www.rheinische-geschichte.lvr.de/persoenlichkeiten/C/Seiten/HelenaCurtens.aspx* (In German.)

10 Éva Pócs, *Between the Living and the Dead* (Hungary: Central European University Press, 1999), 122.

11 Daniel Ogden, *Greek and Roman Necromancy* (Princeton, NJ: Princeton University Press, 2001), 17.

12 Daniel Ogden, *Magic, Witchcraft, and Ghosts in the Greek and Roman Worlds: A Sourcebook* (New York: Oxford University Press, 2002), 189.

13 Daniel Ogden, *Greek and Roman Necromancy* (Princeton, NJ: Princeton University Press, 2001), 44.

14 Daniel Ogden, *Magic, Witchcraft, and Ghosts in the Greek and Roman Worlds: A Sourcebook* (New York: Oxford University Press, 2002), 188.

15 Daniel Ogden, *Greek and Roman Necromancy* (Princeton, NJ: Princeton University Press, 2001), 44.

16 Ibid., 181.

17 Daniel Ogden, *Magic, Witchcraft, and Ghosts in the Greek and Roman Worlds: A Sourcebook* (New York: Oxford University Press, 2002), 34.

18 Daniel Ogden, *Greek and Roman Necromancy* (Princeton, NJ: Princeton University Press, 2001), 6.

19 Pierre Bonnechere, "Divination," in *A Companion to Greek Religion*, Daniel Ogden, ed. (West Sussex, UK: Wiley-Blackwell, 2010), 158.

20 Lucan, *Pharsalia of Lucan*, trans. Edward Ridley (New York: Longmans, Green, and Co.), 169.

21 Ibid., 172.

22 Daniel Ogden, *Magic, Witchcraft, and Ghosts in the Greek and Roman Worlds: A Sourcebook* (New York: Oxford University Press, 2002), 195.

23 Ibid., 187.

24 Georg Luck, *Arcana Mundi: Magic and the Occult in the Greek and Roman Worlds* (Baltimore, MD: John Hopkins University Press, 1985), 73.

25 Daniel Ogden, *Magic, Witchcraft, and Ghosts in the Greek and Roman Worlds: A Sourcebook* (New York: Oxford University Press, 2002), 43.

26 Peter Levenda, *Unholy Alliance: a History of Nazi Involvement with the Occult* (New York: The Continuum International Publishing Group, Inc., 2002).

27 Daniel Ogden, *Magic, Witchcraft, and Ghosts in the Greek and Roman Worlds: A Sourcebook* (New York: Oxford University Press, 2002), 64.

28 Craig Conley, *Magic Words: A Dictionary* (San Francisco: Red Wheel/Weiser, 2008), 111.

29 Daniel Ogden, *Greek and Roman Necromancy* (Princeton, NJ: Princeton University Press, 2001), 229.

30 Morton Kelsey traces the decline of dreams in Christianity in *God, Dreams and Revelation: A Christian Interpretation of Dreams* (Minneapolis: Augsburg Publishing, 1991).

31 David Shulman and Guy G. Stroumsa, eds., *Dream Cultures: Explorations in the Comparative History of Dreaming* (New York: Oxford US, 1999), 228.

32 Tzvi Abusch, *Mesopotamian Witchcraft: Toward a History and Understanding of Babylonian Witchcraft Beliefs and Literature* (Leiden: Brill Styx, 2002), 65, 280.

33 Laurence Austine Waddell, *Makers of Civilization in Race and History* (London: Luzak, 1929), 24.

34 Carlo Ginzburg, "Ecstasies: Deciphering the Witches' Sabbath," trans. Raymond Rosenthal (Chicago: The University of Chicago Press, 1991), 155.

35 Elaine G. Breslaw, *Tituba, Reluctant Witch of Salem: Devilish Indians and Puritan Fantasies* (New York: New York University Press, 1996), 193.

36 Peter Kingsley, *Ancient Philosophy, Mystery, and Magic* (New York: Oxford University Press Inc., 1995), 281–282.

37 Anthony Shafton, *Dream-Singers: The African American Way with Dreams* (New York: Wiley, 2002), 18.

38 Barbara Tedlock, "5 Sharing and Interpreting Dreams in Amerindian Nations," in *Dream Cultures: Explorations in the Comparative History of Dreaming,* ed. David Shulman and Guy G. Stroumsa (New York: Oxford US, 1999), 87–88.

39 Ibid., 87, 96.

40 Sigmund Freud, *The Interpretation of Dreams,* ed. James Strachey (New York: Basic Books, 1955), 431.

41 Rosemary Ellen Guiley, *Dreamspeak: Understanding the Language of Dreams* (New York: Berkley Books, 2001), p. xx.

42 John H. Taylor, *Death and the Afterlife in Ancient Egypt* (Chicago: University of Chicago Press, 2001), 178.

43 E. O. James, *Seasonal Feasts and Festivals* (New York: Barnes & Noble, 1963), 175.

44 Erwin Rohde, *Psyche: The Cult of Souls and Belief in Immortality among the Greeks* (London: Kegan Paul, Trench, Trubner, 1925), 168.

45 Michiko Iwasaka and Barre Toelken, *Ghosts and the Japanese: Cultural Experience in Japanese Death Legends* (Logan, UT: Utah State University Press, 1994), 26–28.

46 Edward Lawrence Davis, *Encyclopedia of Contemporary Chinese Culture* (New York: Routledge, 2005), 313.

47 Ronald Hutton, *Stations of the Sun: A History of the Ritual Year in Britain* (Oxford: Oxford University Press, 1996), 364–365.

48 Lesley Pratt Bannatyne, *Halloween: An American Holiday, an American History* (Gretna, LA: Pelican Publishing Company, 1998).

49 Stanley Brandes, *Skulls to the Living, Bread to the Dead* (Malden, MA: Blackwell Publishing, 2006).

50 James MacKillop, *Dictionary of Celtic Mythology* (Oxford: Oxford University Press, 1998), 333–334.

51   Lesley Pratt Bannatyne, *Halloween: An American Holiday, an American History.* (Gretna, LA: Pelican Publishing Company, 1998).

52   Charles Vallancey, *Collectanea De Rebus Hibernicis X* (Dublin: W. Spotswood, 1782), 444.

53   Ronald Hutton, *Stations of the Sun: A History of the Ritual Year in Britain* (Oxford: Oxford University Press, 1996), 365.

54   Raven Grimassi, *Witchcraft: A Mystery Tradition* (St. Paul, MN: Llewellyn Publications, 2004).

55   Vance Randolph, *Ozark Magic and Folklore* (New York: Columbia University Press, 1947), 178–181.

56   Ben Lucien Burman, *Heaven on Earth* (New York: Cosmopolitan Book Corporation, 1929), 117–122.

57   Daniel Lindsay Thomas and Lucy Blaney Thomas, *Kentucky Superstitions* (Princeton, NJ: Princeton University Press, 1920), 286.

58   Sadie F. Price, "Kentucky Folk-Lore" in *Journal of American Folklore* (Cambridge, MA: The Riverside Press, 1901), 35.

59   William S. Walsh, *Curiosities of Popular Customs* (Philadelphia: J.B. Lippincott, 1898), 350–352.

60   John Gay and Geoffrey Chaucer, *The Wife of Bath* (London: Bernard Lintott, 1713), 8.

61   Jacqueline Simpson and Steve Roud, *A Dictionary of English Folklore* (Oxford: Oxford University Press, 2000), 100.

62   A.W. Moore, *Manx Quarterly 6*, 1909, *http://www.isle-of-man.com/manxnotebook/ mquart/mq06537.htm*

Bibliography

Abusch, Tzvi. *Mesopotamian Witchcraft: Toward a History and Understanding of Babylonian Witchcraft Beliefs and Literature.* Leiden, Netherlands: Brill Styx, 2002.

Bannatyne, Lesley Pratt. *Halloween: An American Holiday, an American History.* Gretna, LA: Pelican Publishing Company, 1990.

Bayley, Harold. *Archaic England: An Essay in Deciphering Prehistory from Megalithic Monuments, Earthworks, Customs, Coins, Place-Names, and Faerie Superstitions.* Philadelphia: J.B. Lippincott Company, 1920.

Belanger, Jeff. *Communicating with the Dead: Reach Beyond the Grave.* Pompton Plains, NJ: Career Press, 2005.

Bonnechere, Pierre. "Divination." In *A Companion to Greek Religion.* Daniel Ogden, ed. West-Sussex, UK: Wiley-Blackwell, 2010.

Brandes, Stanley. *Skulls to the Living, Bread to the Dead: The Day of the Dead in Mexico and Beyond.* Malden, MA: Blackwell Publishing, 2007.

Brown, Rosemary. *Immortals by My Side.* New York: Henry Regnery, 1974.

Lucien Burman, Ben. *Heaven on Earth.* New York: Cosmopolitan Book Corporation, 1929.

Buckland, Raymond. *Buckland's Complete Book of Witchcraft.* St. Paul, MN: Llewellyn Publications, 2002.

_____. *Buckland's Book of Spirit Communications.* St. Paul, MN: Llewellyn Publications, 2004.

Cheyne, Thomas Kelly. *Bible Problems and the New Material for Their Solution.* London: Williams & Norgate, 1904.

Conley, Craig. *Magic Words: A Dictionary*. San Francisco: Red Wheel/Weiser, 2008.

Dash, Michael. *Culture and Customs of Haiti*. Westport, CT: Greenwood Press, 2001.

Davis, Edward Lawrence. *Encyclopedia of Contemporary Chinese Culture*. New York: Routledge, 2005.

Digitalis, Raven. *Shadow Magick Compendium: Exploring Darker Aspects of Magickal Spirituality*. St. Paul, MN: Llewellyn Publications, 2008.

Dugan, Ellen. *Practical Protection Magick: Guarding & Reclaiming Your Power*. St. Paul, MN: Llewellyn Publications, 2011.

Erman, Adolf. *Life in Ancient Egypt*. Vol. 2. London: Macmillan, 1894.

Flint, Valerie I.J. *The Rise of Magic in Early Medieval Europe*. Princeton, NJ: Princeton University Press, 1991.

Flint, Valerie, and R. Gordon, G. Luck, and D. Ogden. *Witchcraft and Magic in Europe*. Vol. 2, *Ancient Greece and Rome*. London: The Athlone Press, 1999.

Fortune, Dion. *Psychic Self-Defense*. San Francisco: Red Wheel/Weiser, 2001.

_____. *Dion Fortune's Book of the Dead*. San Francisco: Red Wheel/Weiser, 2005.

Foxwood, Orion. *The Tree of Enchantment: Ancient Wisdom and Magic Practices of the Faery Tradition*. San Francisco: Red Wheel/Weiser, 2008.

Freud, Sigmund. *The Interpretation of Dreams*. James Strachey, ed. 1st ed. New York: Basic Books, 1955.

Gay, John, and G. Chaucer. *The Wife of Bath*. London: Bernard Lintott, 1713.

Ginzburg, Carlo. *Benandanti: DeGoda Häxmästarna* (Benandanti: The good sorcerers). Stehag, Sweden: B. Östlings bokförlag Symposion, 1991. (In Swedish.)

_____, and R. Rosenthal, trans. *Ecstasies: Deciphering the Witches' Sabbath*. Chicago: The University of Chicago Press, 1991.

Grimal, Pierre. *The Dictionary of Classical Mythology*. Malden, MA: Blackwell Publishing, 1986.

Grimassi, Raven. *Witchcraft: A Mystery Tradition*. St. Paul, MN: Llewellyn Publications, 2004.

_____. *The Witches' Craft: The Roots of Witchcraft & Magical Transformation.* St. Paul, MN: Llewellyn Publications, 2002.

_____. *The Cauldron of Memory: Retrieving Ancestral Knowledge & Wisdom.* St. Paul, MN: Llewellyn Publications, 2009.

Guiley, Rosemary Ellen. *Dreamspeak: Understanding the Language of Dreams.* New York: Berkley Books, 2001.

Guiley, Rosemary Ellen, and T. Taylor. *The Encyclopedia of Ghosts and Spirits.* New York: Checkmark Books, 2007.

Gupta, Sanjukta. "Chapter 3: Carana-Tīrtha Kālīghāt, the Mahāpīt.Ha of Kālī," in *Encountering Kali: In the Margins, at the Center, in the West.* Rachel Fell McDermott and Jeffrey J. Kripal, eds. Berkeley, CA: University of California Press, 2003.

Huson, Paul. *Mastering Witchcraft: A Practical Guide for Witches, Warlocks, and Covens.* Bloomington, IN: iUniverse, Inc., 2006.

Hutton, Ronald. *Stations of the Sun: A History of the Ritual Year in Britain.* Oxford, UK: Oxford University Press, 1996.

Illes, Judika. *Encyclopedia of Spirits: The Ultimate Guide to the Magic of Fairies, Genies, Demons, Ghosts, Gods & Goddesses.* New York: HarperCollins, 2009.

Iwasaka, Michiko, and B. Toelken. *Ghosts and the Japanese: Cultural Experience in Japanese Death Legends.* Logan, UT: Utah State University Press, 1994.

James, E. O. *Seasonal Feasts and Festivals.* New York: Barnes & Noble, 1963.

Janowitz, Naomi. *Magic in the Roman World.* London: Routledge, 2001.

Johnston, Sarah Iles. *Restless Dead: Encounters between the Living and the Dead in Ancient Greece.* Berkeley, CA: University of California Press, 1999.

Jung, Carl G. *Memories, Dreams, Reflections.* New York: Vintage Books, 1965.

Kelsey, Morton. *God, Dreams and Revelation: A Christian Interpretation of Dreams.* Minneapolis: Augsburg Publishing, 1991.

Kieckhefer, Richard. *Forbidden Rites: A Necromancer's Manual of the Fifteenth Century.* Stroud, UK: Sutton Publishing, 1997.

Kingsley, Peter. *Ancient Philosophy, Mystery, and Magic.* New York: Oxford University Press Inc., 1995.

Klaniczay, Gábor and É. Pócs, eds. *Communicating with the Spirits*. Budapest: Central European University Press, 2005.

Lecouteaux, Claude. *The Return of the Dead: Ghosts, Ancestors, and the Transparency Veil of the Pagan Mind*. Rochester, VT: Inner Traditions, 2009.

Leland, Charles Godfrey. *Aradia or the Gospel of the Witches*. Blaine, WA: Phoenix Publishing, 1998.

Levenda, Peter. *Unholy Alliance: A History of Nazi Involvement with the Occult*. New York: The Continuum International Publishing Group, Inc., 2002.

Lucan, Edward Ridley, trans. *Pharsalia of Lucan*. New York: Longmans, Green, and Co.

Luck, Georg. *Arcana Mundi: Magic and the Occult in the Greek and Roman Worlds*. Baltimore, MD: Johns Hopkins University Press, 1985.

MacKillop, James. *Dictionary of Celtic Mythology*. Oxford, UK: Oxford University Press, 1998.

Martello, Leo Louis. *Witchcraft: The Old Religion*. Secaucus, NJ: Carol Publishing Group, 1987.

Meyer, Marvin and P. Mirecki, eds. *Ancient Magic and Ritual Power*. Boston: Brill, 2001.

Mitchell, Stephen A. *Witchcraft and Magic in the Nordic Middle Ages*. Philadelphia: University of Philadelphia Press, 2011.

Moody, Raymond. *Reunions*. With Paul Perry. New York: Villard, 1993.

Moore, A.W. "The November-May Year in Man." *Manx Quarterly* 6, 1909.

Morrison, Dorothy. *Utterly Wicked: Curses, Hexes & Other Unsavory Notions*. St. Louis, MO: WillowTree Press, 2007.

Murch, Robert. "The Ouija Board." *www.williamfuld.com/ouija1.html*. Accessed February 1, 2010.

Ogden, Daniel. *Greek and Roman Necromancy*. Princeton, NJ: Princeton University Press, 2001.

————. *Magic, Witchcraft, and Ghosts in the Greek and Roman Worlds: A Sourcebook*. New York: Oxford University Press, 2002.

_____. *Night's Black Agents: Witches, Wizards and the Dead in the Ancient World*. New York: Hambledon Continuum, 2008.

_____, ed. *A Companion to Greek Religion*. Oxford, UK: Wiley-Blackwell, 2010.

Olmos, Margarite Fernández, and L. Paravisini-Gebert. *Creole Religions of the Caribbean*. New York: NYU Press, 2003.

Penczak, Christopher. *Spirit Allies: Meet Your Team from the Other Side*. San Francisco: Red Wheel/Weiser, 2002.

Pócs, Éva. *Between the Living and the Dead*. Hungary: Central European University Press, 1999.

Price, Sadie F. "Kentucky Folk-Lore." In *Journal of American Folklore*. Cambridge, MA: The Riverside Press, 1901.

Randolph, Vance. *Ozark Magic and Folklore*. New York: Columbia University Press, 1947.

Robertson, J.M. *Pagan Christs: Studies in Comparative Hierology*. London: Watts & Co., 1903.

Rohde, Erwin. *Psyche: The Cult of Souls and Belief in Immortality among the Greeks*. London: Kegan Paul, Trench, Trubner, 1925.

Schmidt, Brian B. "The 'Witch' of En-dor, Samuel 28, and Ancient Near East Necromancy." In *Ancient Magic and Ritual Power*. Marvin Meyer and Paul Mirecki, eds. Boston: Brill, 2001.

Scott, Janet Lee. *For Gods, Ghosts and Ancestors: The Chinese Tradition of Paper Offerings*. Hong Kong: Hong Kong University Press, 2007.

Shafton, Anthony. *Dream-Singers: The African American Way with Dreams*. New York: Wiley, 2002.

Shulman, David, and G. Stroumsa, eds. *Dream Cultures: Explorations in the Comparative History of Dreaming*. New York: Oxford US, 1999.

Simpson, Jacqueline, and S. Roud. *A Dictionary of English Folklore*. Oxford, UK: Oxford University Press, 2000.

Striewski, Jennifer. "Helena Curtens (1722–1738), Hexenprozessopfer." In *Landschaftsverband Rheinland* (news site). Undated. (German).

Taylor, John H. *Death and the Afterlife in Ancient Egypt*. Chicago: University of Chicago Press, 2001.

Tedlock, Barbara. "5 Sharing and Interpreting Dreams in Amerindian Nations." In *Dream Cultures: Explorations in the Comparative History of Dreaming*. David Shulman and Guy G. Stroumsa, eds. New York: Oxford US, 1999.

Thomas, Daniel Lindsay, and L.B. Thomas. *Kentucky Superstitions*. Princeton, NJ: Princeton University Press, 1920.

Thompson, John. "Santisima Muerte: On the Origin and Development of a Mexican Occult Image," *Journal of the Southwest 40*(4), 1998.

Vallancey, Charles. *Collectanea De Rebus Hibernicis X*. Dublin: W. Spotswood, 1782.

Van Scott, Miriam. *The Encyclopedia of Hell*. New York: St. Martin's Press, 1998.

Waddell, Laurence A. *Makers of Civilization in Race and History*. London: Luzak, 1929.

Walsh, William S. *Curiosities of Popular Customs*. Philadelphia: J.B. Lippincott, 1898.

Wendell, Leilah. *Encounters with Death: A Compendium of Anthropomorphic Personifications of Death from Historical to Present Day Phenomenon*. New Orleans: Westgate Press, 1996.

_____. *The Necromantic Ritual Book*. New Orleans: Westgate Press, 1996.

_____. *Our Name Is Melancholy: The Complete Books of Azrael*. New Orleans: Westgate Press, 1996.

INDEX

Clytemnestra, 145

corpse reanimation, 100, 102–104

Corwin, Jonathan, 50–51

crossroads, 137–139, 186

Cryptique®, 70–71

crystal balls, 74

crystals, 53

Curran, Pearl, 69

curses, 101, 131

Curtens, Helena, 84–85

cymbals, 55

D

daemons, 3

Dagda, 193

daggers, 40, 58, 59, 119, 134, 156

Danvers State Mental Hospital, 50

Darius, King, 99–100

Day of the Dead, 187–189

Dead Famous (television program),
    50–51, 159

death celebrations

in ancient history, 183–186

of Christianity, 186–188, 189

dumb suppers, 195–199

in Mexico, 188–189

modern, 189–194

mourning teas, 200–201

overview and purpose, 183, 194

in Salem, 10, 181–182, 183, 194–
    195

Death Current, 16, 18–19, 65, 116,
    120, 136

Dee, John, 75

deities, 4, 8, 31–32, 221–238. *See also*
    specific names of deities

Demeter, 93, 236

Devil, 4, 146, 228

Día de los Muertos, 188–189

dolmens, 183–184

doorway metaphors, 11, 44, 77

dragons, 40

dream journals, 155, 157

dreams

characteristics of, 152–154

deities for, 231, 235

in history, 144–151

libations promoting, 42

magic rituals using, 139–141

modern perception of, 151–151

spirit messages as, 122

summoning the dead rituals,
    154–158

drums, 42

Duat, 234

Dumb Cake rituals, 197

Dumb Supper, 184, 195–199

Dumuzi, 231–232

Duncan, Helen, 86–88

E

Earth (element), 41

earthbound souls, 163

Easter, 186

ectoplasm, 82

Egyptians, ancient, 74, 129, 184

Elysium, 28, 93

necromancy compared to, 112–113

styles of, 81–83

Megaera, 93–94, 228

Melissa, 97

Merrill, James, 69

Mesopotamia, 148

"Messages from the Spirit World" (séance), 80–81

Mexican festivals, 188–189

Michael, Saint, 56–60, 148

Mikalu, 57

Miok, 57

mirrors, 74, 75–76, 121–122

Mithra, 57

Montgomery, Ruth, 69–70

moon phases, 54

Mount Etna, 150

Mukhla, 57, 148

Murch, Robert, 70–71

Π

Native Americans, 151

nature of spirits, 30–31. *See also* unwanted (bad) spirits

Nazism, 107

necromancy. *See also* necromantic magic; oracular necromancy

in ancient Greece, 92–101

in ancient Rome, 101–107

benefits, 17

early Christians and, 107–109

graveyard rituals, 124–126

literary references to, 6–7

mediumship compared to, 83, 112–113

preparation, 12–17

protection methods for, 43–44

word origins and definitions, 91–92

Necromancy Incense, 212–213

necromantic magic

crossroad rituals for, 137–139

dream rituals for, 139–141

ethics and, 130–131

graveyard rituals for, 136–137

preparation, 129–130

skulls used for, 127–128, 131–135

spirit relationship building, 131

Necromantic Ritual Book, The (Wendell), 224

nekuomanteions, 83, 94–95, 147

Nephthys, 233

Nergal, 227

Nero, 106

nigromancy, 92

nonconformity, 14

Norris, Deborah, 70

Nostradamus, 75

O

objects, spirit-attached, 50–51, 54

Obon, 185, 191

Oboth, 33

Odilo of Cluny, Saint, 187

Odysseus Acanthoplex (Sophocles), 98

Odyssey (Homer), 6–7, 92–93, 97, 98–99, 226, 230–231

visions and visitations, 42, 43, 101. *See also* dreams

voices, 171–176

Voodoo, 42, 44, 136, 138, 225–226

W

Wall Street Journal, 56

wands, yew, 41

Warlock (term usage), 7

Warren, Ed, 67

Water (element), 42, 43

water, spring, 29, 74

water divination, 74

Wendell, Leilah, 224

west (direction), 28

White, Betty, 69

White, Stewart Edward, 69

Wicca, 5, 8–9

Wife of Bath, The (play), 197

will, 129

Witch (term origin), 5

Witchcraft (Grimassi), 193

witchcraft, overview. *See also related topics*
   altered states of consciousness for, 17–20

components of, 14–16

cosmic force of, 16

dangers of, 16–17

in history, 2–5

modern, 8–10

pact-making rituals, 20–23

preparation, 12–14

Witchcraft Act (1735), 87, 193

Witchcraft Today (Gardner), 193–194

Witches' New Year, 189–196

Witches' Sabbath, 149

Witch of Endor, 6

writing, automatic, 63–66

X

Xavante, 151

Y

Yama, 33, 34

yew trees, 41

About the Author

Photo by Scott Lanes, www.scottlanes.com

CHRISTIAN DAY is a modern day Warlock living in the "Witch City" of
Salem, Massachusetts. He is a practitioner of the ancient arts of Witchcraft—
a spiritual path devoted to old world folk magic, healing, and veneration
of the dead. Christian owns two occult shops in Salem: HEX: Old World
Witchery, dedicated to the practices of Witchcraft, Hoodoo, and Conjure;
and OMEN, a psychic parlor and Witchcraft emporium which features a
staff of gifted psychic readers. Every October, Christian hosts Salem's annual
Festival of the Dead, an event series that includes popular events such as
the Official Salem Witches' Halloween Ball, an Annual Psychic Fair and
Witchcraft Expo, and an authentic séance. Among his many media appearances, Christian has been featured on the Travel Channel, Showtime, TLC,

MSNBC, Biography, and Dish Network and in *The Chicago Tribune, The Wall Street Journal, The Boston Globe, The Boston Herald, CNN.com, USAToday.com* and, of course, *The Salem News.*

Christian calls himself a Warlock rather than a Witch. After much research into the term—used for centuries to describe male practitioners of Witchcraft, necromancers, and those who challenge the authority of the Church, he adopted the word in 2010 as a means of celebrating the divine masculine and as a vow to protect and empower his family, tribe, and, of course, his city.

Visit him online at:

www.christianday.com
www.festivalofthedead.com
www.salemhex.com
www.omensalem.com
www.salemtarot.com
www.psychicsforhire.com

To Our Readers